# *Your Indoor Garden*

# Your Indoor Garden

The comprehensive guide to living with plants

**George Seddon**

**Consultant**
Kenneth A. Beckett

**Photographer**
Roger Phillips

**Editor**
Rachel Grenfell

**Art Editors**
Peter Wrigley
Linda Francis

**Assistant Editors**
Michael Janson
Gail Howell-Jones
Gillian Abrahams
Marsha Lloyd

**Designers**
John Ridgeway
Allison Blythe

**Picture Research Editor**
Sue Pinkus

**Editorial Assistant**
Margaret Little

**Production**
Barry Baker

**Publisher**
Bruce Marshall

**Art Director**
John Bigg

**Executive Editor**
Glorya Hale

**Your Indoor Garden**
This edition published in 1982 by
AH, Artists House, 14–15 Manette Street,
London, W1V 5LB

ISBN 0 86134 042 6

© Mitchell Beazley Publishers Limited, 1976
All rights reserved

Filmset by Servis Filmsetting Limited, Manchester
Reproduction by Gilchrist Bros. Ltd., Leeds
Printed and bound in Hong Kong by
Mandarin Publishers Limited

**Plants supplied by**
The House of Rochford
Stuart Low & Company (Enfield) Limited
Selwyn Davidson, Florist

# Contents

# Introduction

We cannot live without plants. They provide the oxygen we breathe and the food we need to stay alive. We could exist without their beauty, but the quality of life would be immeasurably diminished. The biblical account of Creation recognized this: The Garden of Eden was not only "good for food" but "pleasant to the sight".

Long before the Christian era, around the Mediterranean and in the Far East, plants were cultivated outdoors for their beauty, and by the time the Ancient Greek and the Roman civilizations were at their height plants were being grown in pots in courtyards and in rooms. It was after the Old World had been opened up again, towards the end of the Middle Ages, and after the New World was discovered that indoor gardening in Europe really began, based on the flora of the East and the Americas. By the beginning of the seventeenth century it was firmly established.

Until the nineteenth century, however, indulging a taste for new and rare plants was costly and out of the reach of most people. Then the Victorian middle classes became as enthusiastic about indoor plants as the upper classes continued to be, and the lower orders were encouraged to follow suit, if only to keep them at home and away from low company in public houses.

For much of the twentieth century indoor plants were out of favour, but today no exhortations to grow them are needed; the more remote from Nature modern life becomes the more we feel the need for the reassurance of living plants around us.

And now the world on a window sill is within the reach of every house-plant enthusiast. China could contribute an Azalea, Japan a *Hydrangea*, Australia a *Callistemon*, India a *Begonia rex*, the Mediterranean a *Cyclamen* and South America a *Tradescantia*. Or you can make a choice from hundreds of other plants from all parts of the globe.

The choice has never been wider, but that creates problems. For a start, how do you find your way through the jungle of Latin names? And even if you choose the right plant too often you have an uneasy feeling that you are not looking after it correctly. Such problems are now easily solved, for *Your Indoor Garden* is aimed at helping you to look after your plants confidently and with the fullest enjoyment and to make them an important part of your life.

# The history of indoor plants

The hunting of plants is a long saga of extraordinary human endeavour. On the walls of the temple of the Egyptian Thutmose III at Karnak there are carvings of almost three hundred plants, the booty of a military campaign in Syria that took place nearly one thousand five hundred years before the Christian era. Such early records are sparse, but it is known that in the first place it was plants for food and other useful purposes that were most sought after. In the last five hundred years plants have been hunted by botanists and horticulturists in the interests of science and for the sake of gardeners. Their appetite has been insatiable and catholic.

Early in the seventeenth century the two John Tradescants, gardeners to King Charles I, between them were responsible for introducing many plants into England. The father brought them from Russia and the son from Virginia. They included soft fruits, flowers, such as Phlox, Lupins, the Passion Flower, and trees, notably the Larch and the Tulip Tree. Later explorers, who went farther afield to tropical lands, brought back plants which had to be grown in hothouses. It is from these that many of today's house plants have been developed.

Bartering of new plants was quite common, so that once discovered a plant would eventually go into cultivation in several countries. *Mimosa pudica*, for example, was a plant which the younger Tradescant brought to Europe from Barbados in 1638. Some hundred years later Pierre d'Incarville, a French Jesuit missionary in Peking, hoping to persuade the Chinese Emperor Ch'ien Lung to trade Chinese plants for those growing in Europe, bribed him with two *Mimosa*. The Emperor thought the way in which the plant recoiled when touched was highly amusing and gave d'Incarville the run of the Imperial gardens.

Missionaries, diplomats, the staff of trading companies (especially their surgeons) and captains of ships in all parts of the world were among a motley crowd of part-time plant collectors. Some did magnificent work. Jean Delavey, for example, another Jesuit priest, who was stationed near Canton, sent two hundred thousand specimens to the Natural History Museum in Paris. But the main work of plant collecting was done by full-time botanists, naturalists, horticulturists or mere gardeners (as they were snobbishly regarded). Some were wealthy amateurs who had the enthusiasm, time and money to spend exhausting years abroad. The majority had their patrons—botanical or horticultural gardens and societies, commercial nurseries, royalty and the aristocracy, among whom the cultivation of the rarest plants was another sign of rank.

In Russia the Empresses Anne, Elizabeth and Catherine the Great were patrons of the most lavish scientific explorations, which included natural history, but, because of the

lack of Russian scientists, many of those taking part were Germans. England's George III, who with his mother was responsible for the creation of the Royal Botanic Gardens at Kew, had a hand in sending the first resident professional plant collector to China. The king's profligate illegitimate son, who went by the name of George Rex, also made his contribution to the house-plant scene. On his estate in South Africa, where he had been

sent for propriety's sake, a gardener from Kew discovered *Streptocarpus rexii* and *Clivia nobilis*.

When George III was on the throne his friend and gardening adviser Sir Joseph Banks was the uncrowned king of British horticulture and the patron saint of plant hunters, although not all of them saw him as saintly. He was autocratic, understandably so with an education at Harrow, Eton and

Early in the century the craze was for cacti. These were expensive at first, but when prices dropped everyone, regardless of class, began to grow them. Charles Dickens pointed out that one of the failings of Paul Dombey's nurse, Mrs Pipchin, was a fondness for cacti: "In the window of her parlour were half a dozen specimens writhing round bits of lath like hairy serpents."

Then there was a craze for ferns. In 1848 the cultivation of ferns was judged "a fashionable pursuit". By 1856, according to the *Gardener's Chronicle*, "Ferns have become universal favourites". Towards the end of the century the fashionable craze was for orchids.

Then the great enthusiasm for house plants petered out. It was not until two world wars had been fought and a world depression had been sandwiched between them that house plants soared back into favour.

China and Japan have made large contributions to our window sills, even though for long periods of time foreigners were virtually barred from entering these countries; beginning early in the seventeenth century Japan was out of bounds for more than two hundred years. Because of their long traditions of horticulture many of the "discoveries" in both countries were of cultivated varieties. China's contributions include the *Aspidistra*, the *Gardenia* and a host of Lilies. The *Hydrangea* and many *Chrysanthemum* come from Japan.

North America has provided more plants for the garden than for indoors. Sixteenth-century colonists brought plants to Europe from the Eastern Seaboard, but it was not until the beginning of the nineteenth century that botanists followed Lewis and Clark westwards, braving the hostility of Indians and mosquitoes.

From Central and South America and the Caribbean have come innumerable exotic plants, among them *Fuchsia*, *Philodendron*, *Monstera*, *Calathea*, *Rhoeo*, *Dieffenbachia* and bromeliads.

For a long time plant collectors tended to shy away from northern Africa because of the risk of being taken as slaves. In equatorial Africa there was every prospect of their dying from malaria, but among the rewards were *Impatiens wallerana*, *Dracaena* and *Sansevieria*. At the tip of South Africa there was a brilliant harvest, including *Erica*, *Gladiolus*, *Chlorophytum*, *Pelargonium* and *Saintpaulia*.

The East Indies attracted the later plant collectors who were scouring the world for orchids, and from Polynesia came such still popular house plants as *Pandanus veitchii*, *Codiaeum* and more *Dracaena*.

Early plant collectors found collecting arduous in Australia and even more dangerous in New Zealand, for while they botanized they were in danger of being cannibalized. Moreover, many of their plants do not take kindly to the northern hemisphere. However, we have *Cissus antarctica*, *Eucalyptus*, *Hoya carnosa* and *Callistemon*.

Christ Church, Oxford, and an inherited fortune behind him. He had influential friends and a finger in every pie.

Banks himself was a botanical explorer, first to Labrador and Newfoundland and then to Australia with Captain Cook from 1768 to 1771. When he became royal adviser to the gardens at Kew he despatched plant collectors in all directions, to South Africa, Australia, the Pacific islands, India and North America. Vast numbers of seeds and plants poured into Kew, although far more died on the way there or were lost at sea.

In the nineteenth century exotic plants became big business as more and more people began to bring plants into their homes. China, Japan and South America were overrun with nursery firms' collectors, who were searching for tropical plants to meet the demand of the public.

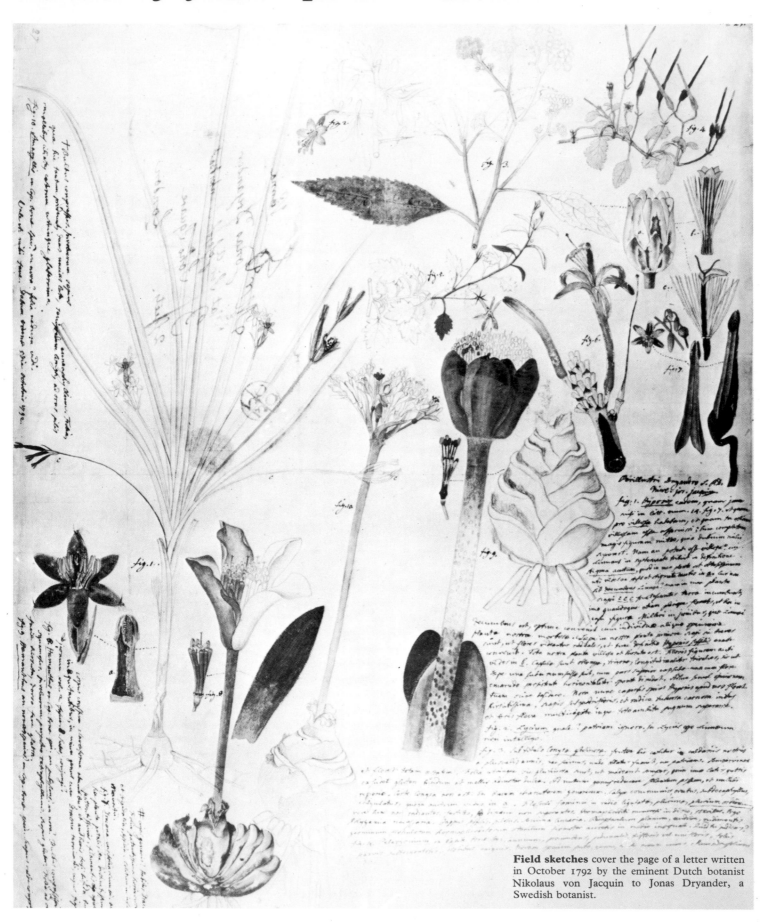

**Field sketches** cover the page of a letter written in October 1792 by the eminent Dutch botanist Nikolaus von Jacquin to Jonas Dryander, a Swedish botanist.

Plant collectors, to judge from the accounts of their expeditions, seemed unusually prone to being shipwrecked, attacked by armed brigands or pirates or robbed and imprisoned. They fell down mountains, risked being killed and eaten and were often devoured by mosquitoes. They committed suicide, were drowned, died from tuberculosis, cholera and malaria and one even fell to his death while sleepwalking. Some took refuge in drink or opium or women; others became eccentrics or recluses. It is remarkable that they managed to bring back any plants at all.

They were a mixed lot, but what they had in common was an obsessive love for plants, far more than the excitement of the chase—although that came into it as well. The famous collector who was dubbed "Chinese Wilson" thought that all the hardships counted for nothing "since I have lived in Nature's boundless halls and have drunk deeply of her pleasures".

In spite of the hazards they faced, there was never any shortage of plant collectors. Hundreds went from Europe, and later from America, to most parts of the world in search of the unknown. There were no typical collectors; the only division was between those who made a big name for themselves and those who did not, often unjustly.

One such "failure" was the eighteenth-century gardener Anton Hove. A Pole by birth, he was sent to India by the formidable Sir Joseph Banks of the Royal Botanic Gardens at Kew to discover good varieties of cotton and other useful plants, as well as new exotics. He had not been long at work before he was twice robbed and his camp twice attacked and looted by tribesmen. But he pushed on. For a time he had a young cavalry officer as a travelling companion, but Hove brought him no luck either; one night as they slept the captain's hair, smothered in pomatum, was eaten by rats.

Returning to Bombay, Hove with difficulty managed to raise a loan, and set off again. His liver was troubling him and he was in no mood to enjoy the girls and the hashish with which a friendly rajah regaled him. One of the two native boats taking his plants to Bombay disappeared in a gale, along with all his personal possessions. The captain of the East Indiaman, aboard which he was due to sail for England, refused to have the cases with the remaining plants on deck, and Hove was forced to take a Danish ship. Gales delayed them, water ran short, the plants were dying. When finally they reached Kew, Banks was not at all pleased with the collection, and even less with Hove's (quite reasonable) expenses. And no record exists of what plants he did manage to bring back.

One of the most successful collectors was Robert Fortune, a Scottish gardener who, around the middle of the nineteenth century, spent nineteen years looking for plants in the Far East. He encountered as many hazards

as Hove, but an invincible belief in the superiority of the British helped him to surmount them. He arrived in China in 1843 with a list of instructions from his employers, the Horticultural Society in London. He was urged, for example, to "try to get some of the 2 lb peaches that grow in the Emperor's garden in Peking, and blue peonies and yellow camellias, if they exist".

As well as much advice, the Society reluctantly provided him with a double-barrelled fowling piece and pistols. They had at first insisted that a stick would be adequate, but Fortune pointed out that "a stick would scarcely frighten an armed Chinaman". The fowling piece not only frightened but killed many Chinese when Fortune, single-handed, beat off several attacks by pirate junks. He was delayed by

**A seventeenth-century** German copper engraving of a Passion Flower, from an encyclopedia on horticulture and housekeeping for noblemen.

storms at sea, robbed several times on land, recurrently went down with fever and narrowly escaped falling into a wild boar trap. At times, for safety's sake, he wore Chinese clothes and a pigtail.

His later visits to China were in search of tea plants, either for the East India Company or the American Government. In 1860 he reached Japan, which had lived in isolation for two centuries. His prize finds there were a number of *Chrysanthemum* and *Primula japonica*. They were hardly "discoveries", for with travel still restricted the source of many of Fortune's plants were nurseries—*Primula japonica*, in fact, was delivered to his door. Nevertheless, we owe many plants to him, in part because he was unusually skilful in getting them home alive and healthy.

E. H. Wilson is among the greatest of plant collectors, his expeditions spanning the first quarter of the twentieth century. He is credited with more than one thousand five hundred introductions, among them many Lilies and the Karume Azaleas. He made four trips to China, two for James Veitch and Sons, the British nurserymen, and two for the Arnold Arboretum of Harvard University, of which he eventually became director. He also visited Japan, Korea and Formosa.

Wilson was able to travel to more remote and more mountainous country than Fortune was allowed to, and he did so in considerable style. He travelled by houseboat and sedan chair, with several dozen coolies and attendants, a large box camera and tripod, a bed, his dog and insect powder. He had many escapes from death, none more hair-raising than when, returning from lily gathering, he leaped out of his sedan chair as it was carried away by an avalanche. But his leg was broken and as he lay on the narrow path unable to move (his leg in splints made from his tripod) more than forty mules coming in file from the other direction had to step over his body. Ironically he died in the United States when his car skidded on a wet road.

If it was hazardous collecting the plants, it was a gamble getting them home—one in hundreds survived the long sea journey, especially in the days of sail. The plants were housed on deck in large wooden cases, solid or slatted, which were opened in fine weather. Both captains and crews hated the plants because they got in the way, and they were the first things to be thrown overboard if the ships ran into bad weather. (Fortune was in luck again when he found a captain who let him put his plants in one of the two life-boats.) Salt from the waves that swept the deck was the great killer, and many consignments were also lost when fresh water supplies ran dangerously low and could not be spared for the plants.

It was a London surgeon, Nathaniel Bagshaw Ward, who saved the lives of hundreds of thousands of plants by developing glazed cases for transporting them. The idea came to him after he had placed a chrysalis in damp soil in a sealed jar to observe its turning into a moth. What happened to the chrysalis is not known, but grass and a fern sprouted in the jar and for four years, until the top rusted, the plants grew without being watered or given fresh air. Ward during this time experimented with glass cases. In 1832 he sent plants to Australia in glazed cases and they survived the eight-month voyage.

Fortune took eighteen of the cases on his first trip to China and, as a result, lost few of the plants he brought home. By the middle of the century Wardian cases were transporting plants all over the world. Filled with ferns, they also invaded Victorian parlours and in a different guise are the fashionable bottle gardens of today.

# The history of indoor plants/Nurserymen

The plant collectors brought the plants home; the nurserymen thereupon set about changing them. To meet their customers' appetite for new plants many nurseries helped to finance expeditions or sent out their own collectors, but their most important role has been in "improving" the plant hunters' discoveries. This usually meant breeding for bigger and more brilliant flowers and for more striking leaves. As a result, many of today's house (as well as garden) plants are scarcely recognizable as the offspring of their wild ancestors. Even plants which had long been under cultivation—notably in China or Japan—before being introduced to the West have undergone further change. This has been achieved in two ways, both far removed from Darwin's theory of natural selection.

One method, and this was the earliest, was to choose the most attractive seedlings raised from seed of the original plant and to raise seed from them. This was followed by further selection. The second method was to create a hybrid plant, which for practical purposes means interbreeding different species of the same genus. But it was not until 1717 that Thomas Fairchild, a botanist and a London nurseryman, deliberately produced the first hybrid, a cross between a Carnation and a Sweet William. His success worried him, for, being a pious man, he feared that he was competing with the Creator.

In the following years further experiments with hybridization were carried out with vegetables, fruits and some flowering plants, notably *Pelargonium*. But it was not until the nineteenth century that the raising of hybrids became widespread, almost a craze. There was plenty of material to work on—the flood of new exotic plants had continued and the nursery trade was booming.

As a recognizable trade, the nursery business goes back at least to the middle of the sixteenth century. By the end of the century there were about fifteen nurseries of some size in London and two or three more in the provinces; little more than fifty years later there were about a hundred throughout the country. By the nineteenth century the number had grown to two hundred and fifty.

Many of these nurseries were minnows, but there were big fish—none more famous than the English nursery run by five generations of the Veitch family, one branch operating from Chelsea and the other from Exeter. John Veitch, a gardener from Scotland, founded the business in 1808, but his great grandson, John Gould Veitch, is the most notable member of the family. In 1860 he was the first plant hunter to arrive in Japan after the opening of the country to foreigners. In the best tradition of plant collectors he was shipwrecked off the coast of Ceylon and lost all his possessions. When finally he reached Nagasaki he was not allowed to explore the countryside, but could only visit nurseries around the city. He was a member of one of the first parties of Europeans to ascend the sacred mountain of Fujiyama, an event they celebrated by drinking champagne at the temple on the summit and singing *God Save the Queen*. His next expedition, to Australia and the South Sea islands, was for stove plants, which were then in vogue. The finds he brought home in his Wardian cases included *Pandanus veitchii*, *Dizygotheca veitchii*, *Codiaeum*, *Cordyline* and *Dracaena*. Soon afterwards he developed tuberculosis and died when he was only thirty-one. His cousin Peter (an Exeter Veitch) trailed all around the world and brought back ferns, orchids and the carnivorous Pitcher Plants. And his elder son, James, spent two years looking for plants in the Far East.

Collectors working for the Veitches included Thomas Lobb, who flitted around the Far East for orchids and found *Vanda tricolor*; Charles Maries, who brought *Primula obconica* and *Hydrangea macrophylla* from Japan and China; and E. H. Wilson, who went out to China for them when he was only twenty-two years old. It was a Veitch gardener, Richard Pearce, who brought back from South America three of Veitch's five *Begonia* discoveries. From these, plus one other, Veitch developed the tuberous *Begonias* of today—an outstanding achievement in hybridization of which any nursery could be justifiably proud.

Rochford is the name which now dominates British house plants. The line was founded by Michael, who arrived in London from Ireland fifty years after Veitch arrived from Scotland. He built a nursery at Tottenham. Although his passion was grapes, he also grew *Dracaena*, *Ficus*, ferns and *Solanum* for the Christmas market. When he died in 1883 two sons, Tom I and Joseph, already had flourishing nurseries of their own in the Lea Valley, Joseph concentrating on tomatoes and Tom on pot plants. Before long Tom had a hundred greenhouses filled with palms, grew hundreds of thousands of ferns and had more than four hundred people working for him. His great loves were orchids and lilies, and when he died in 1900, at the age of only fifty-two, his workmen made a nine-foot-high cross of orchids as a tribute.

For a time after his death the firm continued to expand, but the First World War, the death of Tom II, the Depression of the Thirties and the Second World War brought it down to rock bottom. Tom Rochford III came back from the war, saved the firm and turned it into the vast organization it is today, all on a foundation of house plants.

**Rochford's nursery** packed an ill-fated cargo of palms for shipment in the *Titanic* to the United States. The palms went down with the ship when she sank on her maiden voyage in April 1912.

This nineteenth-century engraving shows
Londoners taking their plants to be judged at a
window-gardening flower show in Westminster.

# The history of indoor plants/Hothouses

The lure of exotic plants first gripped the aristocracy of northern Europe in the sixteenth century. So that these precious imports should not die from unaccustomed cold their owner would build a "winter home" for them —a rather grand description of a shed containing a stove. The plants were then more likely to be killed by fumes from the stove than by the weather.

In the seventeenth century growing orange trees was the rage and winter protection had to be provided for them. At first this was likely to be a wooden building erected each autumn and dismantled in the spring; in 1620, for example, one was built for the Elector Palatine in Heidelberg to accommodate four hundred and thirty trees. It was not long before the temporary orangeries were replaced by permanent, and often beautiful, buildings in stone. Some included banqueting halls.

The eighteenth century saw the development of proper glass houses, by botanical gardens and wealthy private collectors, to house the tropical exotics which began to arrive from the East, from Africa and from the Americas. Not all the private collectors were aristocrats; in the latter half of the eighteenth century a garden in East Ham, in London, with the reputation of possessing more rare plants than any other garden in Europe, had been created by a Quaker doctor from Yorkshire, Dr John Fothergill. From his house you could walk into his two-hundred-and-sixty-foot-long greenhouse.

The early greenhouses hardly deserved the exotic plants that increasingly filled them. They were too dark and were not properly heated. Although glass was being used for the roof instead of, as at first, for only the south wall, much light was lost because the glass was tinted, distorted and manufactured only in comparatively small panes.

Advances in heating were slow. The original stoves, or open fires, were gradually replaced by a system of flues through which the smoke and hot air passed from a furnace outside. It was not until the 1820s that hot-water systems began to be taken seriously, even though the flue system was still in use forty years later.

The more reliable methods of heating, plus the production of sheet glass, coincided with the exotic plant craze of the mid-nineteenth century. The delicate plants from the tropics needed better greenhouses, and these in turn boosted the demand for more species of plants. Never had hothouse plants been so popular. The Victorians bought conservatories in their thousands.

Around the middle of the nineteenth century more than three-quarters of the plants being introduced into Britain needed heat to grow them. But at the turn of the century reaction was setting in; it was once more the turn of the outdoor garden, and the collectors were turning to hardy plants. Palms and ferns still sold well, but the bottom fell out of the orchid market.

Since then the change has been radical; most pot plants have come into the house. New varieties of the old exotics have been bred that need far less of the pampering they once received. At the same time, houses have become lighter, cleaner and warmer.

Since the middle of the twentieth century imaginative architects, realizing that living with plants is the way in which people like to live, have designed rooms that need plants as much as the occupants do.

Such rooms recall the English banqueting rooms—orangeries of the seventeenth century, or the room imagined by Sir Hugh Platt (1552–1611) in his book *The Garden of Eden*. "I hold it for a most pleasing and delicate thing," he wrote, "to have a fair Gallery, great Chamber or other lodging, that openeth fully upon the East or West Sun, to be inwardly garnished with Sweet Hearbs." In every window there would be frames filled with flowers, rosemary would grow up the transoms, and vines cover the ceiling. He could then be describing one of the plant rooms or winter rooms especially dear to the Scandinavians, who have been most successful in designing them. Their architects have managed to harmonize the needs of plants and people so that both live happily together, and in far greater luxury than Sir Hugh could ever have dreamed of.

**A hothouse** filled with exotic plants at the Jardin des Plantes, Paris, is shown in this old print. The wild animals which shared the gardens were slaughtered for food during the siege of Paris.

**This nineteenth-century conservatory**, right, filled with cool, green plants and classical statues, provided a haven of contemplative quiet in the middle of Paris.

**In the seventeenth century** European noblemen discovered the delights of the winter garden, where, with their families, they could stroll between avenues of trees while remaining indoors.

**The Swedish garden room**, below, is an excellent example of the way twentieth-century architects have adapted the concept of the winter garden to fit in with modern styles of architecture.

# The history of indoor plants/Containers

**Ornate versions of Dr Ward's plant case** were used to display plants in Victorian drawing-rooms.

**Bamboo jardinières,** such as this one illustrated in *The Queen* in 1876, were the height of fashion in the late nineteenth century.

Collectors found the plants and with luck brought them safely home. Nurserymen hybridized them. The plants were then at the mercy of the house-plant enthusiast, who filled his conservatory or adorned his home with them. Unfortunately the history of indoor gardening, especially in the last two centuries, shows that affection for house plants and loving care in looking after them are not necessarily accompanied by appreciation of how to display them.

The hapless house plant has been a prisoner of changing fashions in taste, just as much as outdoor garden plants have been. The same plants have been grown in pots and displayed on stands designed to harmonize with the background of a room, regardless of whether the owner's taste was Tiffany extravagance, Bauhaus simplicity, chinoiserie, Gothic Revival, Victoriana, revived Victoriana (either nostalgic or camp), Art Nouveau or just bad.

The traditional container for a plant is an earthenware pot, and there are no more graceful shapes than those of Minoan storage pots of four thousand years ago or the old olive oil jars of Provence or Italian orange pots, all of which have influenced the best-designed plant pots for centuries. But the craze for exotic plants coincided in the nineteenth century with a taste for unbridled decoration in house furnishings, including plant display.

The Victorian English were not the only culprits; the disease was widespread. In 1801 there was an outrageous French design for a jardinière, which served also as an aviary and an aquarium and was supported by sphinxes (winged half-woman, half-beast) with plant pots on their heads and embellished with nude human figures. All this was for the delectation of a Swedish Count. "Fancy

jardinières in fancy clay, finished in assorted tints and gold" were advertised in the United States. They were "really exquisite and must be seen to be appreciated", or indeed believed.

For much of the nineteenth century the English produced ornate jardinières, some incorporating goldfish bowls or bird cages. But the item of plant furniture they took to their hearts in the second half of the century

**Grecian-style containers** were displayed at the 1853 Exhibition of Art and Industry in Dublin.

was the fern case. It was the offspring of the Wardian case, which, since the 1830s, had greatly reduced the gamble of transporting plants by sea. But the sturdy wood and glass containers lashed to storm-swept decks were a far cry from the elegant versions that ornamented, or cluttered, middle-class Victorian drawing-rooms. Inside the miniature greenhouses, supported on curvaceous legs or hefty pedestals, the ferns flourished, out of harm's way from gaslight and coal-fire fumes. (Because the air was so pure inside the case, Dr Ward experimented by using one as a vivarium, and kept a robin alive in it for six months.)

The cases also invaded middle-class American homes, ousting in popularity the ubiquitous hanging baskets. One reason for this, it has been cynically suggested, was that hanging baskets were cheap enough for almost everyone to buy, whereas Wardian cases were out of the reach of the poor.

Plant windows also came into use—*hortus fenestralis* they were called by Shirley Hibberd, one of the most pontifical of Victorian writers on gardening. This, like the Wardian case, was a miniature greenhouse formed by having a double window. The second window could be situated inside the room or it could be built out from the wall. Either way the plants between the glass were protected from the fumes in the room.

Today the Wardian case has reappeared as a terrarium, with the bottle garden as an alternative version. In general, the coal and gas fumes have gone, and the one role of these enclosed cases now is to protect the plants from the excessive dryness of warm rooms in modern houses.

Jardinières are back, after a period of neglect; a doubtful gain since the worst of them provide endless scope for the perpetrators of ornamental plastic. Plant windows, as well as plant walls and plant rooms, are a common feature in Scandinavia and the United States, but in Britain they have not regained their Victorian popularity.

And the greatest change on the window sill is that it is plastic pots that now stand on saucers, whereas once they were all of nostalgia-inducing red clay.

**Victorian extravagance** is epitomized by this magnificent jardinière, which incorporates a birdcage and a fish pond.

**Elaborately designed** hanging baskets and plant stands were often part of the décor of middle-class homes at the end of the nineteenth century.

**Outrageously fussy**, this "flower stand for indoor plants" was illustrated in *Cassell's Family Magazine* of 1882.

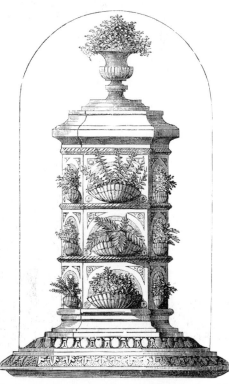

**A terracotta fern case**, advertised in an 1862 catalogue as "a graceful object for the conservatory or the drawing-room".

# Living with plants

Times have changed for house plants. In fewer than a hundred years their environment has altered almost as much as when they were uprooted from their native lands. The heavy, plush curtains saturated with cigar smoke that blocked out light from the *Aspidistra* on the table by the window have gone. So has the maid who raised a cloud of dust when she cleared the ashes in the morning before lighting the fire that would belch out fumes all day. So has the poison gas that lit the rooms, as far as it could in competition with sombre wallpaper and gravy-brown paint.

The successors of the few potted plants that survived such treatment are likely to find themselves in a totally different world of light, airy and warm rooms. These rooms may be too warm for many plants in winter and uncomfortably dry all year, but nevertheless we can now choose what to grow in them from among scores of plants.

As the environment of plants has changed so have our attitudes towards them. Not only has a major industry been built up on growing exotic plants, they have become the stock-in-trade of the interior decorator. Today, too, there has been a proliferation of plant-hire firms for the home as well as for offices. But most of us want to choose, display and tend our plants ourselves. We can, however, learn many lessons from the ways in which professional interior decorators use plants—their disasters as well as their successes—but bear in mind that they are concerned with instant effect. Certainly they are not concerned if a plant dies because conditions are not suitable; it can be replaced. But for many of us the death of a plant means failure, and we cannot afford plant displays that involve perpetual replacement.

Although today much emphasis is put on the decorative value of plants in the home, in recent years there has been an increasing recognition of their therapeutic effect in offices (especially in open-plan offices) and in forbiddingly vast public buildings. Indeed, indoor plants soften the hard edges of impersonal city life.

At the same time, the traditional appeal of indoor gardening as a hobby has not been usurped. In fact, thanks to the nurserymen's unceasing introduction of new varieties, it has become more pleasurable. And indoor gardening is an ideal occupation for the housebound, the elderly and the handicapped.

In more ways than one, long live the house plant.

# The focal point

Growing a plant indoors may have become easier than it was only twenty years ago, but certainly it has become far harder to choose which plant to grow. The choice is bewildering. Novices can easily get lost among the names, let alone the plants themselves. Even the knowledgeable can go wrong and will sometimes buy plants that are not in harmony with the rest of their plant collection or with their home.

Your choice of plant should always be influenced, and will also be made more simple, by the kind of environment that you can offer it. This may mean that you have to forego a favourite plant, but better that than watch it staggering to its death. Quite often, too, there will be an acceptable alternative that will thrive in the room that would be too dark, too cold or too hot for the other.

To choose from the many available and suitable plants, those which will be objects of breathtaking beauty in your home, demands the eye of an artist as well as the fingers of a gardener. Like an artist, you are working with form and colour, but as a gardener you are dealing with living, growing things. There are few hard rules to guide you, only fashionable clichés that are best ignored.

The first step when choosing the right plant for your home is to study the form of the plant, and the shape and texture of the foliage, because the appeal of the most easily manageable house plants is in the leaves rather than in the fleeting brilliance of the flowers. Awareness of the structural qualities of the plant will show how it can be used—either as a single plant or in a group—to have the

**Only a mature, healthy plant,** such as a handsome *Schefflera actinophylla*, should be used as the focal point of a room.

**Massed flowering plants** create a transient but exciting blaze of colour—an inexpensive way to create a bright accent in your living-room.

greatest impact and to give the greatest sensual pleasure.

The most straightforward dramatic effect is achieved with a striking individual plant, so sited in a room that attention is drawn to it and it becomes a focal point. This is often called an accent plant. Since there is no point in drawing attention to a miserable weed of a plant, only a mature, healthy specimen should be bought for this purpose. This may be expensive, but will give the greatest impact-for-money value.

The most effective accent plants are usually evergreen foliage plants, because they remain attractive all year round. In general, flowering plants are more effectively used in a group, where they stand out while they are doing their star turn. They can then retire into the background when flowering finishes.

A plant may merit being put in the limelight for a number of reasons—if it has delicate foliage, for example, or bold variegation. The position of the plant in the room, however, is more than a question of décor; you must also take into consideration the levels of light and warmth that the plant needs. It should also be kept out of draughts. After that comes the test of your own artistic skill in placing the plant in just the right place. Remember that the more striking the plant is the more it will call attention to that part of the room in which it is situated. The plant must also be positioned so that it does not compete with other dominating features of the room which it is in. Decorating with

plants involves a very special kind of artistry.

Some of the most popular, and most successful, accent plants have large, glossy green leaves, will grow to a substantial size and need shade. Two will thrive in cool rooms—the fast-growing *Fatsia japonica* (False Castor Oil Plant) and its even faster-growing hybrid offspring × *Fatshedera lizei* (Fat-headed Lizzie). A more unusual pair of plants, which need rather more warmth although they are not difficult to grow, are *Coffea arabica* (Coffee Plant) and *Schefflera actinophylla* (Queensland Umbrella Tree), the long stems of which give it a grace lacking in most of the broad-leaved plants.

Warm rooms are needed for the ubiquitous *Ficus*, *Monstera* and *Philodendron* as well as for two other plants on a large scale, *Philodendron selloum* (Lacy Tree Philodendron), with glossy dark green leaves up to three feet (90 cm) long, and the related *Monstera deliciosa* (Swiss Cheese Plant), with leaves which may reach four feet (120 cm) in length. *Philodendron andreanum* (Velour Philodendron) is a smaller-leaved climber, but if given support and allowed to grow about four feet (120 cm) high it makes an extraordinarily handsome accent plant. It differs from other *Philodendron* in that its leaves are velvety, dark green on top and pale purple underneath.

Flowers are transient, but variegated leaves give more permanent colour. Variegation, however, can fade or even disappear if the plant is not given adequate light. Plants with variegated leaves will therefore need more light than the corresponding green varieties. Moreover, many of the most beautiful variegated plants are difficult to keep healthy in a living-room environment and need the very moist atmosphere of a conservatory or an enclosed plant case.

One of the most striking of variegated plants, *Rhoeo spathacea* (Boat Lily), gives little trouble. Its spear-shaped leaves are variegated in green and yellow stripes on top and purplish-red below. Other variegated plants are less co-operative. The *Dieffenbachia* have showy leaves in many shades of green marbled with cream, but in living-rooms, infuriatingly, they tend to lose their lower leaves. The leaves of *Dracaena deremensis* (Dragon Plant), which are dark green with well-defined, silvery-white stripes, may curl up if the plant is kept indoors all the time. The markings on *Cordyline terminalis* (Cabbage Palm) are more varied in colour, and include brilliant reds, which may fade if the plant is not kept in a good light.

The *Maranta* (Prayer Plant), the most excitingly marked of all, is another plant that is difficult to cultivate, but some of the cultivated varieties are less demanding. The undoubted favourite is *Maranta leuconeura* 'Kerchoveana' (Prayer Plant); blotches of brown make a regular pattern of leaf shapes on the plant's brilliant green leaves.

Other plants with remarkable variegations

include *Codiaeum variegatum pictum* (Croton), *Calathea insignis* (Rattlesnake Plant), *Caladium* and *Aglaonema commutatum* (Chinese Evergreen), but they really demand—and deserve—to be cosseted in a plant case or plant window. The most flamboyantly coloured variegations are provided by *Begonia rex* and *Coleus blumei* (Flame Nettle), but they are probably best used to enliven a group of plants, rather than alone.

An accent plant with delicate leaves has a different and often more lasting appeal than any other plant. If the quality you are looking for is grace it can be found in plants with long thin stems, or arching stems and branches, and narrow leaves. It is the form of the plant as a whole that draws the eye; colour has little part in it.

One of the easiest plants to grow is undoubtedly the graceful *Cyperus alternifolius* (Umbrella Grass). Its long stems and sword-shaped leaves give it a palm-like quality, but in fact it is a bog plant and looks at its best and thrives well when grown in a pot surrounded by pebbles and standing in water or in a glass aquarium-type container. It has been slightingly described as a plant with no vices and no virtues; in a plant nothing is so virtuous as beauty. *Araucaria heterophylla* (Norfolk Island Pine) is also easy to cultivate, as long as you can keep it cool in winter. If you do not the lower leaves drop off and will never grow again.

For elegance, there is no plant to approach a young, flourishing *Dizygotheca elegantissima* (False Aralia). But in a living-room even the most loving care and adoration may not save a mature plant from losing its lower leaves, so that in the end it looks like a chimney sweep's balding brush. The small-leaved *Ficus benjamina* (Weeping Fig) has little difficulty in reaching six feet (180 cm) and its arching or pendulous branches grow in grace as they grow in size.

Palms have come back in favour and they, too, do not lose their air of grace when large, even though the leaves grow more coarse. The least demanding is *Chamaedorea elegans* (Dwarf Mountain Palm), but the larger *Howea forsteriana* (Kentia Palm) is equally easy, being tolerant of both shade and the light music of hotel lounges. *Microcoelum martianum*, the feathery Dwarf Coconut Palm, is more elegant, but it is also likely to die unless it can be kept cool in winter. The variegated *Pandanus veitchii* (Screw Pine) has a palm-like grace—although it is not a palm—and when large makes a striking accent plant. It needs, however, a lot of warmth in winter.

Ferns which could be chosen for their delicate foliage include: *Asplenium bulbiferum* (Hen and Chicken Fern), *Pteris cretica* (Ribbon Fern) and *Nephrolepis exaltata* (Sword Fern). And the hardy, epiphytic *Platycerium bifurcatum* (Stag's-horn Fern) is hard to beat as a hanging accent plant.

Plants grown for their flowers can be used as arresting short-term accent plants. They include *Rhododendron simsii* (Indian Azalea), tuberous *Begonia, Chrysanthemum, Fuchsia, Hydrangea, Clivia miniata* (Kaffir Lily) and such bulbs as *Amaryllis belladonna* (Belladonna Lily), *Hippeastrum, Lilium longiflorum* (Easter Lily) and *Vallota speciosa* (Scarborough Lily).

**The stark simplicity** of a single, large plant with beautiful leaves enhances a sparsely furnished living-room.

# The focal point

Even the most well-chosen plants imaginatively placed in a room will look commonplace if the containers they are in are not as well chosen. Many house-plant owners fail to realize this. Unlike the Japanese, who give unstinting attention to the harmony between the living plant and the inanimate container, many indoor gardeners tend to be unthinkingly slipshod. Much can be learned, too, from the Scandinavians, whose indoor gardening reflects their traditional love of house plants and the functional brilliance of their contemporary design.

A plant is usually sold in a clay or a plastic pot. In your home this pot may be placed within another large container and the space between filled with peat that is constantly kept moist. The advantages of adopting this system of growing a plant in a pot within a container are both practical and aesthetic.

Plants surrounded by damp peat need less frequent watering, which is pleasant for you, and the moist air rising from the peat is balm to the plants. (Sodden roots and dry air spell death.) And although the pots have drainage holes, the outer containers do not, so there is no need to worry about escaping water. Such containers as cane baskets can be lined with polythene to make them watertight. Consequently, all those chipped saucers and cracked dinner plates that clutter the house-plant scene are made redundant.

The aesthetic advantage of this method is that you are free to choose the containers you like. Lest freedom should go to your head, remember that containers should harmonize with both the plant and the room. Clean shapes and restrained colours are best.

Terracotta is effective with green and green-and-cream variegated plants. Muted brown, glazed pottery containers suit many plants, but the stale milk-chocolate brown of plastic is disastrous. Utterly plain cuboid and cylindrical plastic containers can be effective, in white or black, both for accent plants and for grouped plants. In a large container of clear or slightly tinted green glass, pebbles can be substituted for the peat. They serve the same practical purpose of holding moisture, and look pretty, too.

Only you can decide whether or not to include such objects as shells, china gnomes, rocks or *objets d'art* among plant displays. It is treacherous ground and many people cannot keep themselves away from it, even though they fall flat on their faces every time. Others manage to enhance both plants and objects by using them in conjunction in simple or sophisticated and witty ways.

Ideas in books and magazines for displaying plants should never be followed slavishly. The most successful and effective arrangements are those which reflect your own personality. When treating house plants as an aspect of interior decoration let joy be unconfined but exuberance somewhat restrained.

**Always choose containers that harmonize** with both the plant and décor. Large plants such as *Ficus* are particularly suited to those made of copper or glazed earthenware.

# Plants in groups

The dramatic effect of an accent plant would be lost if you tried to repeat it in every room of the house. The alternative is to arrange plants in groups, and the ways of doing this are legion.

The group may be of the same plant, a common method in outdoor gardening. Plants such as *Pelargonium* (Geranium) or *Coleus*, with brilliantly coloured flowers or foliage, are usually chosen. A considerable number of plants is often necessary to achieve an eye-catching effect.

Another approach is to group plants with a common characteristic, such as variegation of leaves. The appeal here is more subtle—even with highly coloured variegations—and lies in both the similarity of the plants and the differences between them. The best groupings are those which juxtapose plants in order to contrast colours and shapes and yet produce an overall harmony. Achieving harmony is the difficult part. It will certainly not be done merely by choosing your favourite plants and placing them next to each other in one container. Nor, in general, is it wise to imitate the groupings of nurserymen, whose skill in growing is not necessarily matched by a sensitive eye; horticultural shows offer irrefutable evidence of that. Interior decorators, on the other hand, may have an eye for design, but are often blind to the requirements of the individual plants.

The starting point of any grouping is that the plants included should have similar requirements in light, warmth and water. If they are compatible they will be happier in a group, for the moisture that each gives off will create a slightly more humid microclimate for them all. The choice of plants from among those which can be grown together depends upon the owner's taste.

Not only are plant groupings aesthetically satisfying, they also have a practical advantage; large accent plants are expensive, whereas smaller plants, which are effective when grouped, are far cheaper.

House plants can be grouped charmingly in indoor window boxes. A box in a well-lit dining-room or kitchen could appropriately be filled with herbs. The most suitable are thyme, sage, chives, marjoram and basil (which in Britain is easier to grow indoors in a window box than outdoors). Mint, which can swamp other herbs, should be contained in a pot within the window box. In a kitchen window box dwarf tomatoes or salad plants could also be grown.

Other indoor window boxes might start the year with spring-flowering bulbs, followed by flowering annuals. Parsley decoratively curling over the edges of window boxes provides an unusual (and useful) frame to boxes full of flowers. For a long period of bloom at a sunny window a varied collection of *Pelargonium* (Geranium) is still unrivalled.

Plants which need a fair amount of light may be grouped in a plant window. This can be divided from the room by glass to give an enclosed space as hot or as humid as you wish to provide for tropical plants which would otherwise require a heated conservatory. Flowering plants are an obvious choice for a plant window, but plants with bracts of brilliant reds and yellows make a longer-lasting but no less showy window. *Euphorbia pulcherrima* (Poinsettia) is obviously the most popular. Other suitable plants include the bromeliads, with their distinctive leaves and drinking habits (many grow equipped with their own cup). Those which in the wild grow on trees could be displayed on a branch above the earthbound. Beautiful bracts are borne by *Aechmea fulgens* (Coral Berry), *Aphelandra squarrosa* (Zebra Plant), *Nidularium innocentii* (Bird's Nest), *Rhoeo spathacea* (Boat Lily), *Tillandsia lindeniana* (Blue-flowered Torch) and *Vriesea splendens* (Flaming Sword).

A line of tall, fairly bushy plants can be used to create a room divider. × *Fatshedera lizei* (Fat-headed Lizzie) and *Schefflera actinophylla* (Queensland Umbrella Tree) are excellent for cool and temperate rooms respectively, while *Ficus benjamina* (Weeping Fig), *Philodendron oxycardium* (Parlour Ivy) and *Syngonium podophyllum* (African Ever-

A **flamboyant arrangement** of brilliantly coloured *Coleus* will effectively accent an indoor window sill or a well-lit corner.

green) are recommended for warmer rooms.

An interesting room divider can be made from a bamboo screen to which are secured a few pots, each holding a different plant that is allowed to trail. *Cissus striata* (Miniature Grape Ivy), *Tradescantia fluminensis* (Speedy Jenny) and *Zebrina pendula* (Wandering Jew) are good choices for a temperate room. *Philodendron oxycardium* (Parlour Ivy) and *Scindapsus aureus* (Devil's Ivy) can be used in a room where the temperature is higher.

It is sad that so many fireplaces were bricked up when central heating took over their job, for they make an ideal display area for groups of plants. Of course, the choice is usually limited to plants which tolerate shade, since most fireplaces were built a fair distance from the window.

Ferns are an obvious choice, providing subtle contrasts of greens and bold contrasts of shape between the sword-like and the feathery ferns. A fern with undivided leaves is *Asplenium nidus*, the beautiful pale green Bird's-nest Fern. *Asplenium bulbiferum* (Hen and Chicken Fern) on the other hand is as feathery as you could wish and could be used with *Nephrolepis exaltata* (Sword Fern).

Instead of grouping the ferns at floor level the pots can be buried in a bank of peat

A **graceful screen** of tall plants such as *Ficus benjamina*, the Weeping Fig, creates a delightful green room divider.

**A number of plants** with variegated leaves can be grouped together to display subtle variations of colour, pattern and shape.

Unless you decide you want a mass effect with only one kind of plant in a single container, the effective grouping of plants in large containers is far from simple. It is often best to use separate containers for each large plant. The plants can then be moved easily for cleaning.

Even after deciding on the general approach —bold contrast or more subtle variety, or an element of both—the choice of plants and their arrangement will be affected by the siting of the containers. If they are on the floor you will be looking down into them, but will see them at different angles when standing or sitting. If they are on a table or desk you will look down into them when standing, but they will be at about eye level when you are sitting. Most house plants look at their best when seen from above: the undersides of some leaves may be more brilliantly coloured than the tops, but the texture is usually less appealing.

The choice and certainly the arrangement of the plants will be affected by the shape of the containers—whether they are circular or square or oblong. Equally it will be affected by whether the plants are to be seen from all sides, or from the front and sides only, as when the container is placed against a wall.

formed by peat blocks and loose peat. By keeping the peat moist you provide the humid atmosphere in which the ferns flourish. *Pellaea rotundifolia* (Button Fern) may be planted at the front of the bank of ferns to spill over on to the hearth, where (unusually for a fern) it will enjoy the drier conditions. If the fireplace is cavernous you could hang in it a fern such as *Nephrolepis exaltata* (Sword Fern) or *Platycerium bifurcatum*, the Stag's-horn Fern.

Bottle gardens and plant cases, or terrariums, are used for grouping plants which need a thoroughly humid atmosphere. In a bottle a plant is given the warmth and moisture in which it is most likely to flourish, but not the room to do so, and if it does spread itself it has to be banished. In a large plant case—heated, artificially lit, humidified and altogether automated—conditions are luxurious, and in house-plant terms more "natural". Not all plant cases need be elaborate nor need they be totally enclosed. Growing *Saintpaulia ionantha* (African Violet) in a simple glass or clear plastic container, illuminated from above by fluorescent lights, is the most likely way of having them in bloom almost all year round.

**Aesthetically satisfying**, a group of many different ferns looks pleasantly at home in the shade of an unused fireplace.

# Special places for special plants

In 1849 *The Cottage Gardener*, a magazine published in England, introduced a weekly feature on hothouse gardening. The writer, Robert Fish, reasonably expecting some lowly readers to suggest that such a feature was inappropriate for a magazine of that name, rebuked them in advance: "If you have no hothouse of your own, yet in that of your neighbour you may see much to admire, much to stir to emulation, nothing for mean jealous envy, but many things practised, which will act as hints and lessons."

Nevertheless a conservatory is a justifiable cause for envy, which need not necessarily be mean or jealous. Possessing a conservatory adds a new dimension to indoor gardening, for it makes indoor gardening possible in a way that does not exist in any other room of the house. It is a place in which you can potter endlessly during the day, if you have a mind to, as well as sit admiringly in the evening having drinks with your friends.

Mr Fish was perfectly aware of the distinction between the spectator and participator pleasures of gardening. "What is beautiful in plants should be admired for its beauty alone. The pleasure arising from producing and tending that beauty is a different thing." Every gardener knows just how deep that pleasure can be.

A conservatory not only gives a gardener more to do, it adds to the variety of plants he or she can grow. The range will of course depend on the level of warmth in winter. A conservatory warm enough to grow difficult tropical plants is for the real enthusiast—and one who can afford the heating costs. It will also be too warm and too moist to serve as a room for relaxing or entertaining. A temperate conservatory will give you the widest range of plants and the greatest personal comfort. But even a conservatory that has little more heating than is needed to keep it frost free can be used for the growing of alpines or cacti.

The Victorians were great builders of conservatories, but in Britain the fashion went out early in the twentieth century. The modern version of the conservatory is the winter garden, garden room or plant room, as it is variously named. This is built to provide more satisfactory conditions for the plants—in particular better light—than there are in an ordinary living-room and more comfort for the humans than in a conservatory.

The Scandinavians, presumably to compensate for their grim winters, have developed the most beautiful "winter gardens", with lush foliage in perfect harmony with the tasteful furnishings. In more favoured climates—notably in parts of the United States and in Italy—garden rooms have been designed to abolish the barrier between indoors and outdoors. In Britain, where winters are not too bad and summers not too good, a strong distinction persists between what is indoors and what is outdoors.

# Hobby gardening

The owner of a conservatory is almost overwhelmed by the number of ways in which he can use it—like A. A. Milne's old sailor on a desert island who had so many things he could do that he never knew where to begin. The starting point is that a conservatory is a room for plants, not people, to live in. People may spend hours there pottering or sitting around, but they are not the residents, the plants are. If our gas-lit, coal-heated forebears wanted to grow beautiful plants they had to do it in a conservatory; the plants simply could not tolerate the conditions their owners lived in. And for the household the conservatory was somewhere light and airy to escape to. There, away from the claustrophobic living-rooms, where overbearing relatives laid down the law or snored after indulging in enormous meals, they could feast their eyes on the cool, green plants, refreshing their senses and renewing their patience and energy. But today garden rooms and many living-rooms are as green a haven as conservatories ever were, and much more comfortable. So what use does the conservatory serve now?

The conservatory can be turned into a garden room, landscaped, the roof shaded against the summer sun and adequately warmed in winter. It can be used as a room in which to grow and enjoy those foliage plants and, more especially, those flowering plants which are still tricky or impossible to grow indoors. (And that would mean having to provide the plants with considerable warmth.) Or it could be given over to specialized indoor gardening, an outlet for a desire to grow things which goes far beyond tending a few beautiful house plants.

This desire is most often directed to a particular group of plants. The already dedicated hobbyists will take their own specializations into their conservatories, but for the undecided there are two vast groups of plants to become involved with—cacti and other succulents and bulbs, which can provide a show of flowers all year round. Either group would be an economical choice in that they would need the minimum of heat. Cacti and other succulents can generate greatest interest if they are grown from seed. Bulbs need little attention once they have been planted and their delicate or flamboyant flowers give much pleasure. And even the most single-minded specialist should be willing, or forced, to give up some space for growing such food plants as tomatoes, sweet peppers and aubergines.

There are about two thousand cacti and four thousand other succulents—enough to keep anyone happy for a lifetime. For the hobby gardener cacti and other succulents are a good choice. As much or as little time as desired can be devoted to them because, unlike most house plants, they can be left to themselves if necessary.

The shapes of cacti are often weird or comic; that is part of their appeal. By contrast, their beauty when in flower is all the more staggering. Shapes include: globes, for example the hairy *Mammillaria bocasana* (Powder Puff) and the spiny *Echinocactus grusonii* (Golden Barrel); pillars, *Cephalocereus senilis* (Old Man Cactus), so hairy that it can be combed; and the "prickly pear" type of cactus, *Opuntia microdasys* (Bunny Ears). Among the most magnificent flowers are those of the epiphytic cacti that grow on tropical forest trees. They include *Epiphyllum × ackermannii* (Orchid Cactus), *Rhipsalidopsis gaertneri* (Easter Cactus) and *Schlumbergera truncata* (Christmas Cactus).

Succulents require somewhat different treatment, but both cacti and other succulents can be accommodated in the same conservatory. For pretty, odd or interesting shapes you can choose *Aloe variegata* (Partridge-breasted Aloe), *Echeveria gibbiflora* 'Carunculata', *Gasteria verrucosa*, *Haworthia margaritifera* (Pearl Plant) and *Lithops lesliei* (Living Stones), which makes a great success of imitating pebbles. *Euphorbia milii*, the well-named Crown of Thorns, can be forgiven its viciousness because of its

**Bulbs** can keep the hobby gardener occupied all year round. As well as the usual spring varieties there are the gorgeous, easy-to-grow, flowering bulbs for other seasons.

almost endless supply of red bracts that look very much like flowers.

Bulbs can keep an indoor gardener gently occupied all the year round. They are not for spring alone; indeed many of the most popular spring-flowering bulbs do not take kindly to being indoors. Those which are

**Cacti** and other succulents are an excellent choice for the busy hobby gardener because, unlike other house plants, they will thrive with little attention.

after year. They may be expensive to buy, but they freely reproduce by offsets and bulbils (small bulbs which appear on the stems). If you have room for them in a conservatory, you can build up a vast stock of flowering bulbs over the years.

A bulb-growing programme may be so planned that there are some bulbs in flower virtually the year round. The bulbs may be brought into the house when flowering is imminent and returned to the conservatory when they are past their prime, to be replaced by others—guest stars always at hand to add stunning colour to a group of foliage plants.

Many of the exotic bulbs are lilies, or look like lilies. When deciding which to buy, bear in mind that some grow tall; the climbing *Gloriosa rothschildiana* (Glory Lily) may reach a height of four feet (120 cm) and will then need support. Those which would be out of scale in a mixed group of plants can be used as short-term accent plants, and the showy *Hippeastrum* (Amaryllis), *Amaryllis*

*belladonna* (Belladonna Lily) and *Vallota speciosa* (Scarborough Lily) are not so much conversation pieces as conversation stoppers.

The peak periods for flowering bulbs are at the beginning of the year and around mid-summer. The following bulbs have been listed in their likely order of flowering, from December onwards:

*Narcissus, Hyacinthus orientalis, Crocus vernus, Tulipa, Hymenocallis calathina, Zantedeschia aethiopica, Hippeastrum, Sparaxis tricolor, Ornithogalum thyrsoides, Veltheimia viridifolia, Habranthus robustus, Zepyhranthes grandiflora, Gloriosa rothschildiana, Haemanthus multiflorus, Canna, Lilium longiflorum, Vallota speciosa, Amaryllis belladonna, Nerine flexuosa, Lachenalia aloides.*

These bulbs should provide some colour most of the year, except perhaps in November, although flowering times vary according to the temperature in which the bulbs are being grown. (For cultivating instructions see the Catalogue of Plants.)

forced indoors exhaust themselves and either have to be planted outdoors to recover or, more probably, have to be thrown away.

On the other hand, there is a wide range of exotic looking and reasonably untemperamental summer- and autumn-flowering bulbs which can be induced to flower indoors year

# Choosing your plant

However much you read about house plants, or talk to friends about theirs, or gaze at them in shop windows, the knowledge is academic until you actually go out and buy one. Those who have had no experience of house plants should start with inexpensive and easy-to-grow plants. Buy a few and see how successful you are with these.

Some easy-to-grow plants to choose from which have growing temperature requirements as low as 45° to 55°F (7° to 13°C) are *Araucaria heterophylla* (Norfolk Island Pine), *Chlorophytum elatum* 'Variegatum' (Spider Plant), *Fatsia japonica* (False Castor-oil Plant) or the more vigorous × *Fatshedera lizei* (Fat-headed Lizzie), *Hedera helix* (Common Ivy), the flowering plant *Pelargonium* × *hortorum* (Geranium) for a sunny well-lit position, or *Hydrangea macrophylla* for a shady corner.

Five plants for slightly higher temperatures are *Cyperus alternifolius* (Umbrella Grass), *Impatiens wallerana* 'Holstii' (Busy Lizzie), which blooms for a long period, *Rhoeo spathacea* (Boat Lily), *Sansevieria trifasciata* 'Laurentii' (Mother-in-law's Tongue) and *Tradescantia fluminensis* (Speedy Jenny).

As you gain confidence and experience add some of these plants for the cooler rooms: two contrasting ferns—*Adiantum capillus-veneris* (Maidenhair Fern) and *Pteris cretica* (Ribbon Fern), *Cissus antarctica* (Kangaroo Vine), a palm, *Phoenix roebelinii*, and a few colourful *Nertera depressa* (Bead Plant).

And for the warmer rooms there are *Asplenium nidus* (Bird's-nest Fern), *Begonia rex*, *Calathea insignis* (Rattlesnake Plant) or *Calathea makoyana* (Peacock Plant) and the delicate trailing *Cissus striata* (Miniature Grape Ivy).

No matter which plants you choose you will have equal success as long as you realize that if you cannot provide the minimum needs of the plant you buy it will surely die. Failure to accept what is possible, what is a gamble worth taking and what would be sheer folly could well mean that you finish up frustrated and out of pocket.

You can buy plants by mail from a specialist nursery, or in person from a specialist plant shop, florist, garden centre, supermarket or street market. For rarer house plants, nurseries are often the only available source.

Ultimately, of course, all house plants come from nurseries, but some growers deal only with wholesalers and retailers. Many others sell entirely by mail. You therefore have no chance of inspecting a plant before buying it. And catalogue photographs always show the perfect plant in perfect condition, never suffering from any of the defects or ailments that the plant you buy might have. Since you have to take so much on trust, it is essential to deal with a trustworthy nursery, for even among gardeners there is, sadly, the odd rogue. A flower show is a good hunting ground for reliable companies. If you have a nursery near your home where you can collect your plant and talk to an expert then you are lucky indeed.

House-plant shops, which are rapidly increasing in numbers, are the town shop windows for nurseries. If there is someone in charge who knows how to look after plants while they are in his or her temporary care, such shops are as good a place as any to buy a plant, particularly since there you can—and must—inspect the plant before you buy. Plant shops, however, can be a trap for impulse buyers, because, except in the larger shops, you are unlikely to get expert advice.

In florists, house plants are often merely a sideline and the range is more limited. It is also unlikely that a florist will be able to give you objective advice about a house plant.

Garden centres are less specialist than house-plant shops, but the plants are there for inspection, and except at weekends this can often be carried out leisurely and thoroughly.

Supermarkets are best avoided when it comes to buying plants. However reliable its source of supply, a supermarket is no place for a living plant to be hanging around in for any length of time. There is of course the other view that if a plant can survive that it can stand anything.

Bargains can be found on street-market stalls, especially those stalls which are owned by a local nursery. But constant travelling of unsold plants is bad for them, and exposure on cold days can harm them irrevocably.

The plant you buy will have been raised in a greenhouse in conditions which differ greatly from those in a house. Before being offered for sale the plant should have been hardened off, that is toughened up to prepare it for the change. It is often difficult to detect immediately from outward signs whether this has been done. This is one of the reasons why it is necessary to go to a reliable supplier. Hardening off is particularly important for plants bought in the autumn or winter, for a sudden change of temperature may make them drop their leaves. Less hardy plants are best bought in late spring or early summer to avoid the danger of shock from cold.

Wherever you finally go for a plant inspect both the plant and the pot it is in before you buy. If you take home an unhealthy or pest-ridden specimen you have merely bought a troublemaker.

There should be no insects on the plant, but look and make sure. Generally, plants in houses are not plagued with pests and diseases as much as plants are in the garden, but the warm, moist conditions of a nursery which the plants relish are also appreciated by pests. In looking for signs of pests do not forget that leaves have undersides—greenfly and scale insects never do.

Green scum on a clay pot points to overfeeding, and a slimy pot indicates overwatering. Plastic pots reveal little. If possible steal a look at the bottom of the pot (but don't turn it upside down or you will be unpopular). Plastic pots all too often have ridiculously small drainage holes, making waterlogging a probability. If roots are growing through drainage holes pass that plant by—it is already potbound.

Small plants bought in supermarkets and from stalls are often in flexible pots. Handle them gently; squeezing the pots may damage the roots. Such pots are quite unsuitable for house plants to pass their lives in and they should be repotted in late April and May. But if you buy an unsuitably potted plant in June don't wait a whole year to repot it.

Always ask what kind of compost the plant is growing in. If the salesman is competent enough to give you the answer, make a note of it. Then when the time comes to repot the plant you will know which type of compost to use. It is better not to mix types, such as loam-based or loamless.

When the plant has passed your inspection the problem is to get it home safely if the shop has no delivery service. Intense pride in owning a new plant should be tempered with acute apprehension of the disasters that may overtake it on the way home.

If the purchase has been planned and you intend to carry the plant home, take a lightweight plastic bag large enough to put over the top of the plant. This keeps it warm on cold days and helps to guard against minor mishaps, such as being caught by a sudden gust of wind as you turn a corner. If it is an impulse buy see that the wrapping envelops much of the plant and does not just cover the pot.

If you are collecting the plant in a car or taxi take a cardboard box and newspapers to pack around the pot so that it will stay upright even if the car swerves. Don't ever put a plant in the boot. If you have to take the plant home by bus or train avoid the rush hour.

Having got the treasured plant safely home admire it. Not only is this satisfying, but it provides another opportunity of finding any defects or pests that you might have missed in the shop. For a few days keep it cool and shaded. Then put it in the place you have chosen for it. Thereafter restrain yourself from shifting it around all the time.

While house plants are more than bits of interior decoration there is no need for them to become an obsession. As your confidence grows in dealing with them you learn which corners you can safely cut, and which you do at your peril or the plant's. It does, however, add to the interest of living with plants if you keep a simple record of them. The basic entries should be when and where bought, what compost, if known, and when repotted. But you can add as much as you like, including photographs. The more observant you are, the most expert you become, increasing your pleasure and the plant's well-being.

# Plants for your office

Plants in the home may go through difficult times, but life in the office is even more hazardous for them. They deserve to be chosen thoughtfully and looked after with care; the effort is worth while because house plants soften the impersonality of offices and public buildings.

Choosing the right plant for an office is even more fraught with complications than making the choice for your home. The office is likely to be warm, but draughty, for five days of the week and much colder at the weekend. The air will be dry and, possibly, filled with smoke. The light will probably be poor. On the other hand a plant at a window that cannot be shaded will be too hot. Moreover, a plant that has to stay in the same office all the year will not get that essential cooler period when it is dormant.

In spite of the difficulties, however, many plants will survive in offices. But do not be tempted to buy a vast array of huge plants, such as can often be seen on the premises of large companies. To enhance their image, these companies buy expensive plants and have them looked after by contract firms. The plants are always glowing with health because the sickly ones are whisked away and replaced—they are not allowed to die in public. This system is extravagant and unsatisfying, so forget your fantasy of buying impressive specimens of *Monstera* and *Ficus*, or even small ones that you dream will grow big, and settle for a few tough smaller plants that can be grouped to make an equally effective display. Growing together in a planter, their pots surrounded by damp peat, they will help to keep each other moist.

Not all the plants on the following list will relish office conditions, but they should be able to cope: *Sansevieria trifasciata* 'Laurentii' (Mother-in-law's Tongue), *Fatsia japonica* (False Castor Oil Plant) or × *Fatshedera lizei* (Fat-headed Lizzie); *Philodendron oxycardium* (Parlour Ivy); and *Rhoicissus rhomboidea* (Grape Ivy) could be added, if given support. Dangling over the side of the planter use *Tradescantia fluminensis* (Speedy Jenny), *Zebrina pendula* (Wandering Jew) and *Chlorophytum elatum* 'Variegatum' (Spider Plant), all of which are variegated. Another indestructible is *Cyperus alternifolius* (Umbrella Grass), which can be left standing in water, and therefore is in no danger of drying out over the weekend. It must be grown on its own, however, for the other toughs could not share that treatment and survive. Alternatively you could invest in a terrarium to provide a more suitable microclimate and choose from a far wider range of plants (see pages 182–3).

For a pretty little pot on your desk there is the long-flowering *Kalanchoe blossfeldiana* (Tom Thumb). Or, given trustworthy colleagues, you might have a small bottle garden on your desk in which, as in a terrarium, the plants will almost look after themselves.

**An array of plants** along an office window sill helps to soften the harsh reality of the brick and concrete world outside.

**Even a small office** where space is limited can be transformed by a single plant such as this beautiful *Hibiscus* with its brilliantly coloured flowers.

**In the reception area of an office** the un-restrained splendour of large full-grown palms is well worth the initial expense and the time required to care for them properly.

# The catalogue of plants

Plants are for pleasure. To enjoy them to the full it is necessary to know how to look after them, and where to site them. On the following pages you will find advice on how to care for more than three hundred and fifty plants. The photographs included in the catalogue show you how to use plants imaginatively in your home.

Most of the plants have been grouped according to whether they need cool, temperate or warm conditions in which to grow. Bulbs, cacti and other succulents, orchids, window-box plants, food plants and herbs and plants for fun have separate sections.

The temperature ranges are cool, 45° to 55°F (7° to 13°C); temperate, 55° to 65°F (13° to 18°C) (the range in which most house plants grow); and warm, 65° to 75°F (18° to 24°C). The lower temperatures in each range are the temperatures at which the plants will begin to grow. The higher temperatures are roughly the upper limit of beneficial warmth. The divisions are necessarily arbitrary, and in each group plants will survive some degrees below the lower figure and will continue to thrive when above the higher. Many plants have, and need, resting periods in which they cease to grow and must not be prevented from doing so by being kept too warm.

Within the temperature groupings plants are further divided into those that need direct light and the many more that need shade. Remember, however, that almost every plant will suffer in strong sunlight shining through glass and none can grow in deep gloom what we consider merely a shady room may be dark to a plant.

To feed your plant use a good-quality proprietary liquid fertilizer and follow the manufacturer's instructions unless the catalogue entry advises otherwise. When the instructions recommend a dilute fertilizer water it down until it is about half strength.

When spraying is recommended to increase humidity or to clean the plant use a fine mist spray. Never spray plants that are standing in direct sunlight, however, because the droplets of water act as small lenses which cause the rays of the sun to scorch the leaves.

When repotting is recommended, the term is used for repotting and potting on. And, although the terms compost and soil are used synonymously, always pot in a good-quality compost rather than in garden soil.

Every genus and species of plant and every individual plant varies in the amount of water needed. The general fault is overwatering, and in the catalogue "water liberally" does not mean that the compost should be kept sodden. Conversely "water sparingly" does not mean that the compost should be allowed to become bone dry. When watering do not give a little and often, but water thoroughly and do not water again until the compost is a little on the dry side.

No two plants respond in exactly the same way to the same treatment. Some plants will confound novices and experts alike by thriving in conditions that would seem to doom them to death; others will give up in despair when there is no obvious cause.

# Plants for cool rooms

Cool conditions suit some of the most popular house plants. A cool, light room, for example, could be colourfully furnished with such long-flowering plants as *Chrysanthemum*, the many varieties of *Pelargonium*, the less showy but equally free-flowering and beautiful *Campanula isophylla*, the pink and purple *Erica gracilis*, the perfumed *Heliotropium* and the ice blue *Plumbago*. There are some foliage plants that also like it light as well as cool; these include the graceful *Cupressus cashmeriana*, the aromatic *Myrtus communis* and *Chamaerops humilis*, Europe's only native palm. Some of the most indomitable and enduring plants, however, prefer partial shade—for example such old favourites as *Aspidistra*, *Hedera* and the glossy large-leaved *Fatsia* and, among the flowering plants, the outstanding and adaptable *Hydrangea* and the more tricky *Rhododendron* and *Cyclamen*.

## Direct light

## Acacia armata
KANGAROO THORN

A tall bush or tree in its native Australia, *A. armata* grows to a modest height—three to four feet (90 to 120 cm)—as a pot plant. In spring it produces a profusion of tiny, fluffy, yellow flowers which are splendidly backed by narrow, dark green, spine-tipped phyllodes.
**Good Care Guide**
Light and cool conditions are ideal for this plant. It will grow well on the sill of an east- or west-facing window. In winter the plant should rest at about 40°F (4°C) and be watered sparingly. Water more liberally in spring, but never overwater. Feed every two weeks during the growing period, from March to August. After flowering in May repot in any good proprietary potting compost. Propagate by cuttings in March.

## Agapanthus campanulatus
BLUE AFRICAN LILY

This lovely South African summer-flowering lily has long, strap-like leaves, which die back in winter, and round heads of blue, funnel-shaped flowers at the top of stout stems that may grow to a height of more than two feet (60 cm).
**Good Care Guide**
Water *A. campanulatus* moderately from May until October. From November until the end of April the plant should be kept completely dry and cool—35° to 40°F (2° to 4°C)—or there will be a disappointing show of flowers. Feed once a week from May to July and be on the lookout for greenfly. About every fourth year it is necessary to divide the roots and repot in separate pots in any good proprietary potting compost, preferably an all-peat mixture.

## Asclepias curassavica
BLOOD FLOWER

*A. curassavica*, from tropical America, has glossy, spear-shaped leaves and orange-red flowers, which account for this gentle shrub's dramatic common name. Growing to a height of two to three feet (60 to 90 cm), *A. curassavica* flowers from June until October.
**Good Care Guide**
Overwinter *A. curassavica* at a temperature of 45° to 50°F (7° to 10°C), watering it just enough to prevent the soil getting completely dry. Cut back hard in March and water more liberally; feed at fortnightly intervals until October. Repot in a peat-based compost. Propagate by seed during February or March in seed compost. Young shoots may also be used for propagation.

## Bougainvillea × buttiana 'Mrs Butt'
BOUGAINVILLEA

'Mrs Butt' has beautiful, bright, crimson-pink bracts which surround the plant's insignificant flowers and is a shrubby climber with thorny stems.
**Good Care Guide**
Water 'Mrs Butt' liberally in summer and sparingly in winter, when it should be kept at a temperature of 40° to 45°F (4° to 7°C). This plant likes a humid atmosphere and fresh air in warm weather. Feed once a week in summer. When the plant is young, repot every February in any good proprietary potting compost. An older plant may be repotted every other year. This can be a difficult plant to propagate, but a small percentage of stem cuttings, taken in spring or summer, will take root.

## Bougainvillea glabra 'Variegata'
BOUGAINVILLEA

A native of Brazil, *B. glabra* is a thorny, climbing plant which flowers from March to July. The cream-coloured flowers are enclosed by papery purple and red bracts. Although it grows very tall in its natural habitat, regular pruning will result in a smaller, bushier plant.

**Good Care Guide**
Train the plant around hoops or up canes or trellis in front of a south-facing window. In winter the temperature should not fall below 45°F (7°C). Water well from March to August, but keep the plant drier from September to February. Feed weekly from February to September. Repot in January in potting compost. Propagate by cuttings in spring.

## Bouvardia × domestica
TROMPETILLA

An evergreen shrub of garden origin derived from plants native to Central America, *B. × domestica* has clusters of white, pink or red tubular flowers which open from June to December.

**Good Care Guide**
Maintain a minimum temperature of about 45° to 50°F (7° to 10°C) throughout the year, keeping the plant in front of an east- or west-facing window. Water and spray liberally from spring until flowering stops, then keep the plant fairly dry until the following March. Feed weekly from April to September. Repot in spring in equal parts of peat and sand. Cut back main shoots hard in early February. Propagate by cuttings in spring. After the second year discard the plant.

## Browallia speciosa
BUSH VIOLET

*B. speciosa* is a bushy plant from South America. It grows to a height of about twenty inches (50 cm) and has deep violet, white-centred, tubular flowers which look superb against the plant's dark green leaves. *B. speciosa* flowers in summer if it is sown in spring, or in winter if sown in July or August.

**Good Care Guide**
Water *B. speciosa* moderately and be sure that the soil never dries out completely. Winter-flowering plants require a minimum winter temperature of 65°F (18°C). Feed every two weeks from the time the flower buds show until the plant is in full bloom. Pick off the flowers as they die to encourage the growth of new blooms. Discard the plant when it ceases flowering. Propagate by seed.

## Callistemon speciosus
ALBANY BOTTLEBRUSH

The flowers of *C. speciosus*, which look just like brilliant red bottle brushes, open from May to August. Native to Australia, the plant grows to two or three feet (60 or 90 cm) indoors.

**Good Care Guide**
*C. speciosus* will take direct sun, but light shade during the hottest days is advisable. In summer it will benefit from fresh air. In winter the temperature must not drop below 45°F (7°C). In early spring bring the plant into a warmer, bright room. From March until August feed fortnightly with a proprietary liquid fertilizer and water well, always using soft water. Keep it drier in winter. Repot in early March in lime-free compost. Propagate by stem cuttings in June.

## Celosia argentea Cristata
COCKSCOMB

*C. argentea* Cristata, an annual from tropical Asia, grows to a height of about twelve inches (30 cm). Its crimson, yellow or orange flowers give it a flamboyant appearance.

**Good Care Guide**
*C. argentea* Cristata likes plenty of fresh air when the weather is warm, but does not take kindly to too many hours of strong sunshine. It should be watered fairly frequently but should not be allowed to get water-logged. Discard the plant when the flowering period is over in autumn. Propagate by seed in spring, making sure the seed trays are kept at a minimum temperature of 65°F (18°C). When the seedlings are large enough to handle, prick them out and pot in a peat-based compost.

## Celosia argentea Pyramidalis
PLUME CELOSIA

This annual has feathery, plume-shaped, yellow or scarlet flowers. Like *C. argentea* Cristata, it enjoys warm, fresh air and protection from very strong sunshine.

**Good Care Guide**
Water moderately and discard the plant when it has finished flowering in October. Propagate by seed in spring, keeping the seed trays at a minimum temperature of 65°F (18°C). When the seedlings are large enough to handle without damaging them, prick them out and pot in a peat-based compost. Make a first potting in 3-inch (8-cm) pots, then into 5- or 6-inch (13- or 15-cm) pots for flowering. Feed weekly with liquid fertilizer when the young flower clusters just begin to show.

# A place by the window

*Pteris* ferns and a Dwarf Coconut Palm bask in the diffused light which filters through a rose window, left.

A hanging basket in a window lends a pleasant, garden-like aspect to a room. Black-eyed Susan grows prolifically and, if encouraged, will cover ceilings, windows and walls.

## *Celsia arcturus*
CRETAN BEAR'S TAIL

A native of Crete, *C. arcturus* has lobed basal leaves and twelve- to eighteen-inch-long (30- to 45-cm) spikes of pretty yellow flowers, with purple, bearded stamens, which open from July to September. This shrub is usually grown as an annual, but it can be kept and will eventually reach a height of two to three feet (60 to 90 cm).

**Good Care Guide**
*C. arcturus* likes plenty of fresh air when the weather is warm. Keep the soil moist at all times but never let it get waterlogged. Feed once a week from July to September. After flowering has finished, discard the plant. Propagate by seeds in March or April. The seedlings should be planted in any good-quality proprietary potting compost.

## *Chamaerops humilis* 'Elegans'
EUROPEAN FAN PALM

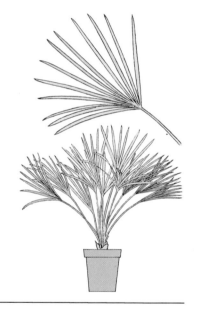

This is the only palm that grows wild in Europe. Found in Spain, Sicily and southern Italy, it has elegant, grey-green, fan-shaped leaves which are split into several narrow segments and grow at the top of two- to four-foot-long (60- to 120-cm) spiny stems. As a pot plant the stems rarely attain half this size.

**Good Care Guide**
Tolerant of the cold, this palm can survive a winter temperature as low as 40° to 45°F (4° to 7°C). Keep the soil moist throughout the year, and give a fortnightly feed from March to October. Repot every other March in a good-quality proprietary potting compost. Cut off any dead leaves. To propagate, in spring remove any suckers and plant separately.

## *Chrysanthemum*
CHRYSANTHEMUM

China and Japan are the countries of origin of this most popular of all flowering house plants. There are two hundred known species of *Chrysanthemum*, but it is the short-day treated types that are most commonly grown indoors.

**Good Care Guide**
Short-day *Chrysanthemum* need little attention; keep cool, water well and do not feed. When flowering ceases discard the plant. Other *Chrysanthemum* need to be kept cool, watered well, especially in hot weather, and fed weekly from April until flowering begins. Pinch out the tips of the main shoots in March to encourage bushiness. The following spring propagate by basal cuttings and discard the old plant.

## *Citrus mitis*
CALAMONDIN ORANGE

A slow-growing, dwarf orange from the Philippines, the Calamondin is an attractive, bushy plant. The small, scented, waxy flowers appear off and on throughout the year, frequently alongside the miniature orange-coloured fruit.

**Good Care Guide**
The Calamondin requires plenty of sunlight and fresh air. The ideal winter temperature for it is 55°F (13°C). Spray occasionally, when the buds open, to set the fruit. Water moderately the year round, but more liberally when the fruit begin to swell. Keep drier in June. Feed fortnightly from May to August. In May repot if necessary in a loam-based compost. Prune back in spring if the bush gets too leggy. Propagate by seeds or cuttings in spring.

## *Cupressus cashmeriana*
KASHMIR CYPRESS

Stand this graceful, pyramid-shaped tree in front of a street-facing bay window and you will not need curtains—its pendant, blue-green, frond-like branchlets will ensure your privacy. *C. cashmeriana*, which comes from Tibet, grows four to six feet (120 to 180 cm) tall indoors.

**Good Care Guide**
Provide a winter temperature of not less than 45°F (7°C). Water liberally in spring and summer. In winter keep the soil just moist. Feed once a month from March to September. Prune top shoots in February. Repot every other spring in any reliable potting compost. Propagate by cuttings, taken with a heel, from June to August, or by seed in spring.

## *Cyanotis kewensis*
TEDDY-BEAR VINE

The leaves and the stems of this trailing plant from India are thickly covered with rust-coloured fur. The rather fleshy, broadly elliptic leaves are green on top and purple underneath. Small, purplish-red flowers open in winter and spring. *C. kewensis* looks at its best in a hanging basket.

**Good Care Guide**
Although *C. kewensis* likes a cool position, the temperature should never drop below 45°F (7°C). Water liberally in spring and summer, but let the soil dry out between waterings. In winter water sparingly. Feed fortnightly from May to September. Repot every other April in any good-quality proprietary potting compost. Propagate by cuttings in spring or summer.

## *Erica gracilis*
CHRISTMAS HEATHER, ROSE HEATH

A native of southern Africa, *E. gracilis* is a small, bushy shrub with pale green leaves and tiny, bell-shaped, pink and purple flowers. As a pot plant it rarely grows taller than eighteen inches (45 cm) and flowers from October to January.

**Good Care Guide**

*E. gracilis* requires a well-lit position all year round. Overwinter at about 50°F (10°C). Throughout spring and summer spray the plant about once a week. Water and spray only with soft water, always keeping the soil moist. Feed fortnightly from May to July. In spring, after flowering has ceased, repot in a lime-free, soilless compost. In April pinch out the tips of the new shoots to encourage bushiness. Propagate by cuttings of young shoots in March.

## *Eucalyptus globulus*
BLUE GUM TREE

A native of Australia, *E. globulus* has a distinctive, astringent scent. The leaves of the young plant are blue-grey and oval, but after two to four years long, narrow, dark, adult leaves appear. The fluffy, white flowers seldom appear on the pot plant. The top shoots may be pinched out to prevent the tree from growing too tall; in its natural state it reaches a height of at least one hundred and fifty feet (45 m).

**Good Care Guide**

Water *E. globulus* well in spring and summer. In winter give it less water, but do not let the soil dry out completely, and keep it cool—40° to 45°F (4° to 7°C). Feed fortnightly from April until October. Repot young plants every spring in any good proprietary potting compost.

## *Fortunella margarita*
KUMQUAT

The Kumquat is a small tree growing to an average height of three feet (90 cm) in a pot. An easy plant to grow, it produces clusters of small, white, scented flowers in spring and summer and small, orange fruit which ripen in autumn and winter. The leaves are glossy green.

**Good Care Guide**

In winter the Kumquat should be kept at a temperature not below 50°F (10°C). In summer put it in front of an open window in the sun. The plant requires plenty of water, except in winter when it should be kept considerably drier but always moist. Feed it fortnightly from April to October. Repot in February using a loamless mixture. If it gets too tall prune back the growing shoots in spring. Propagate by cuttings.

## *Heliotropium* × *hybridum*
HELIOTROPE, CHERRY PIE

An evergreen shrub whose parents come from Peru, Heliotrope produces masses of small, delicately perfumed flowers from May to October. They range in colour from deep purple through lavender to white.

**Good Care Guide**

In winter keep your Heliotrope at a temperature between 40° and 45°F (4° and 7°C). This plant enjoys being in a bright window, but it must be shaded from scorching sun. Water it well, keeping it moist at all times, and spray occasionally in hot weather. From May to August feed the plant fortnightly. Repot in a loamless mixture every March and pinch out the top shoots to shape the plant and encourage flowering. Propagate by stem cuttings in late summer.

## *Myrtus communis* 'Microphylla'
SMALL-LEAVED MYRTLE

An aromatic evergreen bush with small oval leaves and white flowers, Small-leaved Myrtle, a form of the common Myrtle, is a native of the Mediterranean. In a pot it grows one to two feet (30 to 60 cm) tall.

**Good Care Guide**

An easy plant to grow, Small-leaved Myrtle dislikes too much direct sun. It rests best at a winter temperature of 40°F (4°C) in a light, well-ventilated room. Turn the plant regularly so that it grows straight. Always water with rain or lime-free water, liberally in summer and sparingly in winter. From March to July feed once a week using a lime-free fertilizer. Repot in spring in any good proprietary compost. Propagate by cuttings in summer.

## *Nerium oleander*
OLEANDER

This poisonous plant is a tall, evergreen shrub with narrow, grey-green leaves and delicately scented, white, pink, red or yellow flowers. There is also a cultivated variety with variegated leaves.

**Good Care Guide**

From early April to September water liberally with tepid water. Reduce the water in autumn and in winter water only enough to prevent the soil from drying out. Overwinter at 40°F (4°C) in a light position. Feed weekly from April to August. Repot in February in a loam-based potting compost with added bonemeal. In February or March cut back the previous season's young stems by half. Propagate by cuttings in May or September.

### *Campanula isophylla*
BELL FLOWER

Sometimes *C. isophylla* produces so many blue or white star-shaped flowers in late summer that the downy, grey-green leaves are almost hidden from view. This plant, from the mountains of northern Italy, can be trained up a small trellis or allowed to trail from a hanging basket, but the stems are very fragile and it should be treated gently.

**Good Care Guide**
Water *C. isophylla* well in summer and sparingly the rest of the year. Feed every week from April to August. Keep in a cool but frost-free room, about 40° to 45°F (4° to 7°C), during the winter months. Repot every February, preferably in any good-quality proprietary, loam-based compost. Propagate by cuttings in spring.

### *Punica granatum* 'Nana'
POMEGRANATE

'Nana' is a miniature Pomegranate especially suited to indoor gardening. It grows to two feet (60 cm) and may be cultivated as a standard. Its main attractions are the scarlet flowers and bright orange-red fruit.

**Good Care Guide**
From the middle of May until the end of summer the Pomegranate is happy in front of a sunny, open window. In winter the plant should be kept at a temperature of about 45°F (7°C). Water liberally and spray in summer; keep it drier in winter, but never let the soil dry out. Feed every two weeks from March until the end of August. Repot, if necessary, in February in a good proprietary potting compost. A fortnight after repotting cut back straggly stems. Propagate by cuttings.

### *Thunbergia alata*
BLACK-EYED SUSAN

This plant's bright yellow flowers have dark brown centres or "eyes" and deep purple throats. A climber from southeastern Africa, *T. alata*, which is usually grown as an annual, can reach the top of a ten-foot (3-m) trellis in one year.

**Good Care Guide**
Overwinter *T. alata* at a temperature between 45° and 50°F (7° and 10°C). Water well and never let the soil dry out completely. Feed every week in spring and summer. Spray in hot weather. To promote side stems and early flowering, pinch out the tips of young plants when they are about three inches (8 cm) tall. Propagate by seed in spring, using a moist, loam-less mixture.

# Simple elegance

The unconfined luxuriance of this mature *Bougainvillea*, left, dominates its setting and creates a pleasing contrast to the formality of the french windows and the view beyond.

A bright window ledge, top, makes an ideal home for a light-loving *Citrus mitis*, with its orange fruit and glossy, green leaves.

Massed groups of a single species can be very effective. A simple urn filled to overflowing with *Chrysanthemum*, above, delights the eye.

## Pelargonium crispum
SCENTED-LEAVED GERANIUM

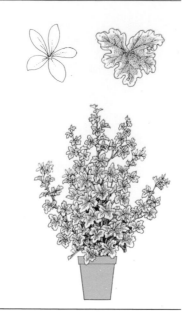

The leaves of all *Pelargonium* have a distinctive smell, but the lemon-scented, fan-shaped leaves of *P. crispum* are particularly pleasant. This erect South African shrub grows about two feet (60 cm) tall and has pink or pale violet flowers which open from May until October.

**Good Care Guide**
*P. crispum* likes lots of summer sunshine and fresh air. Water freely from March until August and feed once a week during the same period. Water sparingly in winter and keep at a minimum temperature of 40°F (4°C). Repot in February in a good proprietary potting compost. Prune and take cuttings from the plant in spring, but discard after flowering in the third year.

## Pelargonium × domesticum
REGAL PELARGONIUM

This *Pelargonium* has large, often frilled, pink, red or white flowers which are marked with a deeper colour and are open all through the summer. The leaves are downy and more pointed than those of the common *Pelargonium*. Recommended varieties are Aztec, Grand Slam and Kingston Beauty.

**Good Care Guide**
The Regal Pelargonium likes plenty of fresh air. Overwinter at 40°F (4°C). Keep the soil just moist at all times, and water even more sparingly from late autumn to late winter. Feed every week from April until August. Prune in August when flowering has ceased. Repot in February in any good proprietary potting compost. Propagate by cuttings in spring or late summer.

## Pelargonium × hortorum
GERANIUM

This most common *Pelargonium* has round, green leaves sometimes patterned with brown rings. The flowers, which are pink, red, mauve or white, single or double, open from April until October. Recommended cultivated varieties are Henry Cox, Mrs Pollock, Sprite, Red Black Vesuvius and Irene.

**Good Care Guide**
Water liberally from spring to autumn, but make sure the roots never get waterlogged. In winter keep the soil barely moist; the temperature need not exceed 40°F (4°C). From March until August feed once a week. Repot annually in late February, using any good proprietary potting compost. Prune in early spring. Stem-tip cuttings may be taken in spring or in late summer.

## Pelargonium peltatum
IVY-LEAVED GERANIUM

This Geranium is suitable for hanging baskets because the large, dark-centred, white, pink, red or purple flowers grow on trailing stems which can reach three feet (90 cm) in length. The leaves closely resemble those of the Ivy. Recommended varieties are L'Elegante, Sussex Lace and Madame Crousse.

**Good Care Guide**
*P. peltatum* likes plenty of sunshine and fresh air. Water regularly in summer. In winter keep fairly dry at a minimum temperature of 50°F (10°C). Feed once a week from April to September. Repot every spring in a loamless mixture to which some sand or gravel may be added. Cuttings may be taken and planted in the same type of loamless mixture at the end of summer after flowering.

## Pelargonium tomentosum
PEPPERMINT GERANIUM

This South African low climber has mint-scented, grey-green leaves and white flowers, which open from early summer until late autumn. It grows about two feet (60 cm) tall in a 5- to 6-inch (13- to 15-cm) pot and much larger if it is potted on.

**Good Care Guide**
Although this plant requires plenty of sunshine, it must be shaded from very hot sun. Water well in spring and summer and feed once a week. In winter keep the plant at about 45°F (7°C) and water less often; the soil should be just moist. Repot each February in any good proprietary potting compost. In spring prune back the stems by about half. Propagate by cuttings in spring or late summer.

## Plumbago capensis
BLUE CAPE PLUMBAGO
CAPE LEADWORT

A South African climber with pale green leaves and clusters of sky blue flowers, Plumbago is an attractive house plant. It has a long flowering season from late April to November.

**Good Care Guide**
In summer keep the plant in front of an open, south-facing window. In winter it will not tolerate temperatures below 45°F (7°C) and requires a well-lit position. Keeping the plant in a cool position until April will promote profuse flowering in May. Water well and feed weekly from March to November. After cutting back the long shoots in February repot in any good-quality potting compost, preferably an all-peat mixture. Propagate by lateral shoot cuttings in June or July.

# Plants for cool rooms

## Partial shade

## Acorus gramineus 'Variegatus'
MYRTLE GRASS

A tufted, moisture-loving plant, *A. gramineus* 'Variegatus' is a native of Japan and one of the hardiest of house plants. It is grown for its attractive variegated cream and green grass-like leaves, which can grow to ten inches (25 cm) in length, and not for its insignificant flowers.
**Good Care Guide**
*A. gramineus* 'Variegatus' likes plenty of light and some direct sun. In winter leave it in a cold but frost-free room. It is a thirsty plant and likes to be kept moist, so water liberally in summer but decrease the amount slightly in winter. Repot in a loam-based compost in March, when it can be propagated by division.

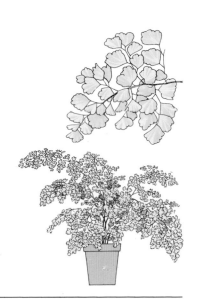

## Adiantum capillus-veneris
MAIDENHAIR FERN

This species of Maidenhair Fern grows wild in many parts of the world. The fronds are fragile-looking, pale green and triangular on black stems which grow to a height of eight to ten inches (20 to 25 cm) before the fronds curve over.
**Good Care Guide**
Direct sun and a dry atmosphere are fatal to this fern, which enjoys shade and moisture. Water well during the growing season from March to August. In winter water less, but never let the plant dry out completely. The minimum temperature it will tolerate during winter is 45°F (7°C). Feed every three weeks from March to August. Repot at the end of March, preferably in an all-peat compost. Propagate by dividing the plant in spring.

## Araucaria heterophylla (A. excelsa)
NORFOLK ISLAND PINE

A native of Norfolk Island, north-west of New Zealand, this evergreen conifer is usually kept indoors until it is about four feet (120 cm) tall, after which it loses its lower branches.
**Good Care Guide**
In winter *A. heterophylla* likes light and a temperature of not less than 40°F (4°C). It likes plenty of fresh air in summer. It will grow well in sun or shade, but screen it from the hottest sun. Water liberally with soft water and feed fortnightly from May to August. In winter water far less often. Pot on every alternate spring. Any proprietary compost is suitable. Old plants, which become leggy, can be cut back to about six inches (15 cm) and the resultant shoots used as cuttings.

## Aspidistra elatior
PARLOUR PALM, CAST IRON PLANT

Uprooted from its native China, this undemanding plant made itself thoroughly at home in Victorian parlours, apparently impervious to smoke, gas fumes, cold and blatant neglect. After a period out of favour, except as a music-hall joke, it has staged a comeback.
**Good Care Guide**
Water moderately in summer and less often in winter. It will not tolerate its roots standing in water, nor does it enjoy direct sun. Feed once a month during summer. Over-winter at about 50°F (10°C). Do not be too eager to transplant into a bigger pot, but when you do repot use an all-peat compost. Propagate by division in spring when repotting.

## Aucuba japonica
SPOTTED LAUREL

This bushy evergreen from Japan has insignificant brownish or green-ish-purple flowers which open in March and April, and glossy, dark green leaves which look better for being sponged regularly. Tolerant of deep shade and capable of growing to a height of six feet (180 cm) or more in a large pot or tub, the Spotted Laurel is a good plant for a hallway or for a landing.
**Good Care Guide**
*A. japonica* likes cold but frost-free conditions in winter. Water liberally in summer and sparingly in winter. Feed every fortnight from May to September. In spring prune lightly and repot in any good proprietary potting compost. Propagate by cuttings in late summer or autumn.

45

# Evergreens–cascading and climbing

*Hedera helix* and *Chlorophytum elatum* complement the upright formality of the *Aspidistra elatior* in the mixed group of plants, left. The Ivy helps to soften the edge of the wooden bowl.

Plants are not just for rooms; the *Rhoicissus rhomboidea*, below, has been trained to climb the whole height of the stairwell.

Both climbing and trailing plants are displayed to advantage in hanging baskets. *Hedera helix* and *Cyclamen persicum* have been combined, right, to make an attractive arrangement set in front of a circular window. The blind has been drawn to protect the plants from bright sunlight.

Trailing plants can be used with great effect. Asparagus Ferns cascade over shelves, below right, lending a delicate softness to a modern dressing-room.

## Carex morrowii 'Variegata'
JAPANESE SEDGE

This tufted, grass-like plant, which belongs to the same family as Papyrus, is a native of Japan and one of the very few sedges that are suitable as house plants. The slender arching leaves have a white central area and green margins and may grow to twelve inches (30 cm) in length.

**Good Care Guide**

The Japanese Sedge is fairly undemanding but fares best if kept at a cool temperature. This should not exceed 45°F (7°C) in winter. The soil must always be kept moist. Feed once a month from April to September. Repot every alternate year in any good proprietary potting compost. It is easily propagated by division.

## Chlorophytum elatum 'Variegatum'
SPIDER PLANT

This fast-growing, prolific plant comes from South Africa. It has long, arching, green-and-white-striped leaves and looks its best in a hanging basket. In spring and summer long wiry stems develop on which white starry flowers and small plantlets appear, giving the plant a spidery appearance and its common name.

**Good Care Guide**

From February to September water C. elatum liberally and feed once a week. Water sparingly from October until the end of January and keep at a temperature no lower than 45°F (7°C). Repot in spring, using any good proprietary potting compost. Propagate by division or by pegging down well-grown plantlets into pots.

## Cissus antarctica
KANGAROO VINE

An easy-to-grow climber from Australia, the Kangaroo Vine has leathery green leaves which, when the plant is young, have a metallic sheen. It can reach seven feet (210 cm) or more in a large pot but by pinching out growing tips and using a smaller pot it will grow to only half that size.

**Good Care Guide**

This vine requires a winter temperature of about 50° to 55°F (10° to 13°C). Water moderately in summer and sparingly in winter. Feed fortnightly from March to September. Repot every other year in February in any good proprietary potting compost. In spring pinch out main growing shoots to encourage bushiness. Propagate by cuttings from lateral shoots in April and May.

## Dionaea muscipula
VENUS' FLY TRAP

When an insect lands on this macabre plant the leaf promptly folds, trapping the prey. Special glands secrete a substance that digests the insect. This provides the plant with essential food materials not present in the acid, boggy soil of North and South Carolina, where D. muscipula grows wild. Spikes of pretty white flowers appear in summer.

**Good Care Guide**

In winter the temperature should not fall below 45°F (7°C). The plant should always stand in a shallow tray filled with water. Small, newly swatted flies may be dropped on the leaves occasionally. Repot every second or third spring in pans containing equal quantities of peat and sphagnum moss. Propagate by division when repotting.

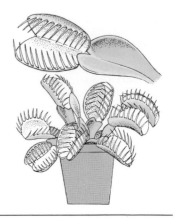

## Duchesnea indica (Fragaria indica)
INDIAN STRAWBERRY

Brought to Europe from India in the seventeenth century, this delightful creeping plant has wiry stems, green leaves and small, bright yellow flowers which open in succession from spring to autumn. The flowers are followed by glossy, red, strawberry-like fruit which are, unfortunately, quite tasteless. D. indica is an excellent plant for a hanging basket.

**Good Care Guide**

Overwinter in a frost-free, unheated room. In spring and summer water liberally. In winter keep the soil just moist. From April to September feed fortnightly. Repot in winter or early spring using a good-quality potting compost. Propagate by division when repotting, or by detaching plantlets in late summer.

## Euonymus japonicus
JAPANESE SPINDLE TREE

When cultivated indoors this plant, which resembles a small-leaved laurel, rarely grows to more than six feet (180 cm), although in its native Japan it can reach fifteen feet (4·5 m) or more.

**Good Care Guide**

E. japonicus requires a light and airy position, but will tolerate considerable shade. Water liberally in summer. Beginning in August reduce the amount of water, then keep the soil barely moist in winter, when the plant should be kept in an unheated but frost-free room. Feed fortnightly from April to August. Repot annually for the first two years and after that every second year in March. Pinch out the tips of the shoots in spring or summer. Propagate by cuttings in late summer.

## × *Fatshedera lizei*
FAT-HEADED LIZZIE, IVY TREE

Fat-headed Lizzie has glossy, dark green, five-lobed leaves and greenish flowers, which appear in October and November. A semi-climbing hybrid of Irish Ivy and Japanese Aralia, × *F. lizei* can grow with support to six feet (180 cm) or more in a large pot or tub. But it can be kept small and bushy by judicious pruning in spring.

**Good Care Guide**
In winter the plant should rest at a temperature no lower than 35°F (2°C) and should be watered sparingly. From April to August feed fortnightly and keep the soil moist but do not overwater. Pinch out top shoots to encourage bushiness. Repot in March in any good proprietary potting compost. Propagate by cuttings in late summer or autumn.

## *Fatsia japonica*
FALSE CASTOR-OIL PLANT
FIG-LEAF PALM

Popular for more than one hundred and fifty years, this quick-growing house plant from Japan and Taiwan has large, five- to nine-lobed leaves. The greenish-white, round flower heads appear in autumn only on large plants. In a pot it will grow to about three feet (90 cm).

**Good Care Guide**
*F. japonica* likes a winter temperature of 40° to 45°F (4° to 7°C) and will survive light frost. Give it plenty of fresh air and water and a fortnightly feed from April to August. In winter water sparingly. In February cut back the top shoots. Repot every March in any good proprietary potting compost. Propagate in April by seed, or remove sucker shoots and treat as cuttings.

## *Grevillea robusta*
SILK BARK OAK

In Western Australia the Silk Bark Oak grows to a height of one hundred and sixty feet (48 m). It can be cultivated indoors as a foliage plant for its evergreen fern-like leaves, but it will not produce its beautiful yellow, nectar-filled flowers. Within three or four years it will grow tall enough to reach the ceiling. It is then suitable for a conservatory.

**Good Care Guide**
Water moderately and regularly. Feed every two weeks during summer and always keep at an even temperature. Extremes of temperature, like extremes of moisture, can cause leaf-fall and may kill the plant. It should, ideally, be potted in an all-peat compost. Propagation is by seed or from lateral shoot cuttings in spring or late summer.

## *Hedera canariensis*
CANARY ISLAND IVY

*H. canariensis* has larger leaves and grows more slowly than the Common Ivy. It is a climber, so tie the stems to a trellis. The leaves of the most beautiful cultivated variety, 'Gloire de Marengo', have dark green centres paling through silver-grey to a white border.

**Good Care Guide**
From April to August keep the soil moist, but never overwater; give a fortnightly feed and spray in dry weather. From late October to early February keep in an unheated, frost-free place and water sparingly. Do not repot until the plant is three years old; then repot every other year, in spring, in any good potting compost. In March pinch out shoots to encourage bushiness. Propagate by cuttings in summer.

## *Hedera helix*
COMMON IVY, ENGLISH IVY

Of widespread origin, this adaptable evergreen attaches itself by aerial roots to whatever support is offered, or will trail decoratively from a hanging basket. Cultivated varieties of *H. helix* are numerous. The size and shape of the leaves vary and some are variegated.

**Good Care Guide**
You may not rejoice to find yourself living without heating, but *H. helix* actually thrives in cold but frost-free rooms. Always keep the soil moist and sponge the leaves regularly. Feed fortnightly from April to September. Repot every other February in any good proprietary potting compost and cut the plant back to half its size in March or April. Propagate by cuttings in autumn.

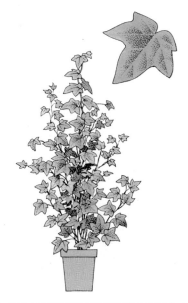

## *Hydrangea macrophylla*
HYDRANGEA

*Hydrangea* flowers are white, pink, red, purple or blue. Blue flowers occur when the soil is acid—this makes the aluminium in the soil available to the plant. The best blue flowers are produced from cultivated varieties of pink *Hydrangea*.

**Good Care Guide**
Feed weekly and water freely from February to August. In hot weather a well-rooted plant may need water twice a day. Beginning in August reduce the amount of water gradually. Water sparingly in winter, when the plant should be kept in an unheated but frost-free place. Cut back the flower stems when flowering is finished and repot in an all-peat mixture. Use a proprietary bluing compound for blue flowers. Propagate by cuttings in spring.

### Cyclamen persicum
CYCLAMEN

A native of the Middle East, Cyclamen is one of the most popular house plants. There are many cultivated varieties.

**Good Care Guide**

In winter keep the plant at a temperature of 55° to 60°F (13° to 16°C). When the plant is in full growth, from autumn until late winter, keep the compost just moist. After the growing season gradually water less and allow the plant to dry out. Carefully pull all dead and yellowing leaves and flowers from the corm. Keep dry from May until July, then gradually begin watering again. Repot every August in any good proprietary potting compost. Feed fortnightly when the flower buds begin to show. It is only possible to propagate from seed.

### Nertera depressa (granadensis)
BEAD PLANT

This low, hummock-forming, creeping perennial is native to New Zealand and South America. Tiny whitish flowers appear in late April to early May. By August these develop into glassy, orange, ornamental berries which last all winter.

**Good Care Guide**

This plant requires plenty of fresh air and shade from direct sunlight. In summer the soil must be kept quite moist, but in winter allow it to dry a little. It is advisable to spray regularly before and after flowering. Feed once a month from April to September with a weak liquid fertilizer. Repot in an all-peat compost. Propagate from seed in February and March or by division when the pot gets congested.

### Passiflora caerulea
COMMON OR BLUE PASSION FLOWER

This climbing plant from South America has long been associated with the story of the Passion of Christ. It flowers during July, August and September, but each of the white and blue flowers lasts for only a few days.

**Good Care Guide**

Feed every week from April to September and water well. Water less in winter, but never allow the soil to dry out. The winter temperature should be about 40°F (4°C). Repot in early spring using any good proprietary potting compost. Every spring cut back the flowering shoots of the previous year to the sixth or eighth bud, or six to nine inches (15 to 23 cm). Propagate by cuttings, layers or seeds when available.

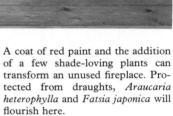

A coat of red paint and the addition of a few shade-loving plants can transform an unused fireplace. Protected from draughts, *Araucaria heterophylla* and *Fatsia japonica* will flourish here.

That paragon of Victorian stoicism, the *Aspidistra* is enjoying a well-deserved popular revival. An undemanding plant, it will grace a poorly lit corner for many years.

The use of mirrors is a traditional method of creating visual depth in a confined space. Here, they reflect the light from a small window and double the impact of the *Peperomia* and *Philodendron* on the shelf.

## Jasminum mesnyi
PRIMROSE JASMINE

The common name of this rambling evergreen from China is descriptive of the lovely yellow colour of its pretty, semi-double flowers, which have no fragrance and open from March to May. To enjoy the full beauty of this Jasmine train it to grow up a trellis or around a window embrasure.

**Good Care Guide**
This plant requires plenty of light, but be careful not to let it get scorched by direct sunlight. Over-winter in a cool but frost-free room. Water regularly throughout the year, decreasing the quantity slightly in winter. Spray in spring. Feed weekly from March to September. Repot in February in any good proprietary potting compost. Propagate by cuttings in late summer.

## Jasminum polyanthum
JASMINE

A native of China, *J. polyanthum* is a vigorous climber with rich green leaves and white, pink-flushed, fragrant flowers that bloom in spring. Usually a wire hoop is inserted into the pot around which the leading shoot is trained.

**Good Care Guide**
Overwinter in a cool, frost-free room. Put the plant in a warmer position in January. Water sparingly until the end of December. Increase the water slightly in January and again when the buds begin to swell, but be careful not to overwater. From February to July feed weekly. Treat the plant as an annual and discard it or repot it in March in a loamless mixture. Cut back in February and use the cuttings for propagation.

## Nandina domestica
CHINESE SACRED BAMBOO

An evergreen shrub native to China, *N. domestica* resembles Bamboo with its long stems and narrow leaflets, which, unlike those of Bamboo, turn red in the autumn. It grows to six feet (180 cm) and so it is the young plant that is most suitable for indoor cultivation. White flowers may appear in July.

**Good Care Guide**
*N. domestica* likes a light, well-ventilated position. In winter it rests best in a cold but frost-free room. Water liberally during summer. Keep the plant drier in winter. Feed fortnightly from April to August. Repot in late March in any good proprietary potting compost. Prune out dead wood after flowering has finished. Propagate by division in April or by stem cuttings in August.

## Ophiopogon jaburan
WHITE LILY TURF

*O. jaburan* is a Japanese evergreen plant with leathery but grass-like, two- to three-foot-long (60- to 90-cm), dark green leaves which grow in dense clumps. Drooping clusters of white or pale purple flowers are borne on stalks in July. The best cultivated variety for growing in a pot is the cream-striped *O. jaburan* 'Variegatus'.

**Good Care Guide**
This plant can overwinter in an un-heated but frost-free room. Keep the soil just moist at all times, being careful not to let the compost dry out. From May to August give the plant plenty of fresh air and a fortnightly feed. Repot every other March or April in any good proprietary potting compost. Propagate by division when repotting.

## Ophiopogon planiscapus
LILY TURF

Although the species plant is seldom seen today, a cultivated variety, 'Nigrescens', is widely available. It has intriguing purplish-black, arching leaves, which grow in small clumps, and clusters of tiny white or pale purple flowers, which are borne on short stems in June.

**Good Care Guide**
In winter this plant can be kept in an unheated but frost-free room. Water sparingly to keep the soil just moist all the year round, being careful not to let the soil ball dry out. Give a fortnightly feed from May to July, when it will also appreciate plenty of fresh air. Repot every March or April in any good-quality proprietary potting compost. When repotting propagate by division.

## Oxalis deppei
LUCKY CLOVER

Considered lucky because the leaves resemble a four-leafed clover, *O. deppei* is often given as a New Year's present in Europe. A pretty plant, the small, red flowers have yellow hearts and each of the four mid-green leaflets bears a red-brown, curved marking.

**Good Care Guide**
This is an easy plant to grow indoors. It likes cool conditions all year round and will do well on the sill of a west-facing window. Water well and feed fortnightly from March to August. In winter water sparingly. Repot in March in a loamless mixture. Propagate by separating side tubers from the plant when repotting.

## Rhododendron simsii
INDIAN AZALEA

This compact little bush comes from China. It has pointed evergreen leaves and clusters of single or double pink, white, crimson or red flowers which open in May. Many nurseries sell forced plants, which will flower in winter or early spring.
**Good Care Guide**
Indian Azalea intensely dislikes hard water, so water well with soft water, keeping the soil moist at all times, but make sure it is never water-logged; if it is ever allowed to dry out the leaves will fall. Feed every week from March to August. Repot after flowering in an all-peat mixture. It can be propagated by cuttings, but these are often slow and difficult to root without a propagating case with bottom heat.

## Saxifraga sarmentosa
MOTHER OF THOUSANDS
STRAWBERRY GERANIUM

This tufted plant from the Far East has dark green leaves with white veins on the top and red underneath. Its conspicuous feature is the long, red, slender, trailing runners which have small plantlets at their ends. Clusters of insignificant, crimson-spotted, white flowers appear in late spring and summer.
**Good Care Guide**
Overwinter S. sarmentosa at a temperature of not less than 40°F (4°C). Keep the compost just moist at all times. Feed once a fortnight from April to September. Repot in any good proprietary potting compost in early spring. Propagate by taking the plantlets from the runners and potting separately.

## Senecio cruentus (Cineraria)
CINERARIA

The original species of Cineraria is native to the Canary Islands, but since the eighteenth century it has been cultivated in Europe and many different strains are now available. They vary from dwarf, large-flowered, cultivated varieties to tall, smaller-flowered ones and colours range through the spectrum from red to blue. As a house plant Cineraria flowers from winter to early summer and will remain in flower for up to six weeks.
**Good Care Guide**
Water liberally, but feeding is unnecessary. Cineraria has a limited life and is never kept after it has ceased flowering.

## Solanum capsicastrum
WINTER CHERRY, CHRISTMAS CHERRY

A native of Brazil, S. capsicastrum has dark green, lance-like leaves and small, white, star-shaped flowers which bloom in May and are followed in late summer by round, dark green fruit which turn to yellow and then to orange-red.
**Good Care Guide**
Although S. capsicastrum likes a partially shaded position, a little direct sunlight in late autumn will help to ripen the fruit to a vivid colour. In winter keep the plant cool at a minimum temperature of 45°F (7°C) and water sparingly. In summer water liberally and feed fortnightly from April to August. Plants can be pruned back hard in late February and repotted in a loamless compost in March, but it is best to raise plants annually from seeds.

## Sparmannia africana
HOUSE LIME, AFRICAN HEMP

In South Africa S. africana reaches a height of twelve feet (3.5 m), but as a potted house plant it will grow only two or three feet (60 or 90 cm) tall. An evergreen shrub, it has broad, pale green, downy leaves. The white flowers, which appear in late winter and early spring, have conspicuous clusters of yellow stamens with dark red or purple tips.
**Good Care Guide**
Water well in summer, but less during the winter, when the temperature must not fall below 45°F (7°C). Feed once a week from March to September and ventilate well. If you want a very large plant pot on every February in a good proprietary potting compost. Otherwise replace the plant every year or two by cuttings in spring.

## Tolmiea menziesii
PICK-A-BACK PLANT
MOTHER OF THOUSANDS

This luxuriant North American plant with downy leaves acquires its common names from its way of producing a small plantlet at the base of each leaf blade where it joins the stalk. Mature leaves arch over and touch the soil, allowing the young plant to root. The green-brown flowers are inconspicuous.
**Good Care Guide**
T. menziesii can tolerate very shaded positions, such as stairways or corridors, and winter temperatures near freezing point. The soil should be kept moist at all times. From March to September feed once a week. Repot in spring using a loamless mixture. Propagate by taking the plantlets from the leaves or by division of older plants.

# *Working with plants*

This dentist's delightful waiting-room was once a conservatory. The original rockery has been maintained and planted with a great variety of indoor plants.

Plants make work more pleasant by relieving the austerity of an office atmosphere.

What could be more refreshing in a doctor's study than a bowl of beautiful *Cyclamen*. The pink and red of the flowers harmonize with the rich colour of the chairs.

# Plants for temperate rooms

Most indoor plants thrive best in the temperate conditions also favoured by most people. Among the light-loving plants in this category are many strikingly coloured foliage plants, but if the brilliance of the colouring is not to fade good light is essential. There are also two great favourites here—*Euphorbia pulcherrima* (Poinsettia) and the more modest *Impatiens wallerana* (Busy Lizzie). Partial shade is preferred by the large number of variegated plants in this group, but if they are kept in too deep shade they may revert to green. Luxuriating in shade are palms, ferns, climbing and trailing plants and such flowering plants as the beautiful *Saintpaulia*, *Begonia*, *Fuchsia*, *Clivia* and *Gardenia*.

## Direct light

## *Alternanthera amoena*
PARROT LEAF

This attractive plant from Brazil is grown for its broad, lance-shaped leaves, which are marked with orange and red blotches. Insignificant white flowers open in summer.
**Good Care Guide**
Although *A. amoena* is perennial, it is usually grown from cuttings annually. The old plant, if kept, may be overwintered at a temperature of not less than 60°F (16°C). During this period water sparingly. In spring and summer keep the soil moist and spray regularly. From June to October feed fortnightly. If the plant is being treated as a perennial, repot in spring in a good-quality potting compost. Otherwise, take cuttings and propagate in spring, preferably using a heated propagating case.

## *Callisia elegans* (*Setcreasea striata*)
STRIPED INCH PLANT

A native of North America, *C. elegans* has dense and very decorative foliage. The undersides of the neat, green-and-cream-striped leaves are purple. It also has small, white flowers, which open from May until October. The plant grows to a height of about twelve inches (30 cm).
**Good Care Guide**
Water the plant well in summer. During the winter months keep the soil just moist. Feed once a week from March until October. Repot in any good-quality proprietary potting compost every April. *C. elegans* may, however, be past its prime after a couple of years. Fortunately, it is a remarkably easy plant to propagate by cuttings, which should be planted in spring or summer.

## *Capsicum annuum*
ORNAMENTAL CHILLI PEPPER

*C. annuum* is a South American plant grown for its brightly coloured fruit. In spite of its name, it is a short-lived perennial but is always grown as an annual. After the fruit, which ripen in autumn and winter, have faded the plant is usually discarded. There are many cultivated varieties; the fruit of some is edible, while that of others is purely decorative.
**Good Care Guide**
*C. annuum* requires fresh air and light. When the flowers form, spray daily to set the fruit. From March to September water liberally. Decrease the water slightly in autumn and winter, but be careful not to let the soil dry out or the fruit and leaves may drop off. Propagate in spring from seed using any good proprietary potting compost.

## *Carissa grandiflora*
NATAL PLUM

*C. grandiflora* is a large—five to seven feet (150 to 210 cm)—shrub with tough, oval leaves and clusters of white, fragrant flowers which open in May and are sometimes followed in July by scarlet berries.
**Good Care Guide**
This plant likes plenty of fresh air and light so keep it in front of an airy, south-facing window. Give it protection from the sun on very hot days. Overwinter at about 55°F (13°C). Water the plant well in summer, but keep it drier in winter. Feed fortnightly from April to August. Repot in spring in any good proprietary potting compost and pinch out the tips of the young shoots. Propagate by seed in spring or by cuttings in summer.

## *Coleus blumei*
FLAME NETTLE

One of the prettiest of foliage plants, *C. blumei* is a native of Java. There are many cultivated varieties which grow to between one and two feet (30 and 60 cm) and produce leaves of different colours.

**Good Care Guide**
The Flame Nettle requires full sunlight for the leaves to maintain their bright colours. They will, however, lose some colour in winter. Using soft water, water moderately in summer and slightly less in winter, when the plant should be kept at a temperature of not less than 55°F (13°C). Spray regularly during hot weather. Feed fortnightly from March to September. Cut back in February and repot in lime-free compost. Propagated best by cuttings from spring to midsummer.

## *Cordyline terminalis*
CABBAGE PALM

The sword-shaped leaves of this tropical Asian shrub grow about eighteen inches (45 cm) long and, depending on the variety, are green flushed with red or with red and cream. In its natural state this plant will grow to about ten feet (3 m), but in a 5- to 6-inch (13- to 15-cm) pot it will seldom exceed two or three feet (60 or 90 cm).

**Good Care Guide**
*C. terminalis* should overwinter at a minimum temperature of about 60°F (16°C). Water liberally in summer and moderately in winter. Feed every fortnight from April until October. Repot preferably in an all-peat mixture every second spring. Propagate by sucker shoots from the base of the plant or use the tops of old, leggy plants.

## *Euphorbia pulcherrima*
POINSETTIA

The Poinsettia has insignificant flowers surrounded by magnificent red, pink or white leaf-like bracts. The normal flowering season is in winter. To produce flowers at other times, keep the plant in a dark place for fourteen hours a day for eight weeks. About three to six weeks later the flowers will appear.

**Good Care Guide**
In winter the temperature must not fall below 55° to 60°F (13° to 16°C). After the Poinsettia has flowered keep it almost dry until May. Spray in hot weather. Feed every week from June until October. Prune back the top shoots in May and repot in any good proprietary potting compost. To propagate, cut off shoots in early summer and plant in a mixture of sand and peat.

## *Iresine herbstii*
BEEFSTEAK PLANT

The beauty of this South American pot plant lies in its veined, heart-shaped, dark red leaves, for its flowers are small and insignificant. It grows to about twenty inches (50 cm) in height.

**Good Care Guide**
*I. herbstii* requires sunlight to intensify the colour of its leaves. Usually treated as an annual it may be kept for more than one year, but the winter temperature must not fall below 60°F (16°C). Water and spray liberally with tepid water in summer. In winter keep the soil rather dry. Feed fortnightly from March to September. Nip out leading shoots in March to make the plant more bushy. Repot in March in a loam-based compost. Propagate from stem cuttings in March or September.

## *Iresine lindenii*
BLOODLEAF

Another species of *Iresine*, Bloodleaf has narrower pointed leaves of a deep dark red with a paler central vein. One variation has yellow leaves with pale green veins and red stems.

**Good Care Guide**
As with *I. herbstii* this species requires sunlight to bring out the colours of the leaves. Although it is usually grown as an annual it may be kept for two or three years. Overwinter at a temperature above 60°F (16°C). In summer water and spray liberally with tepid water, but in winter keep the soil rather dry. Feed fortnightly from March to September. In March nip out growing shoots and repot in loam-based compost. Propagate from stem cuttings in March or September.

## *Ixora coccinea*
FLAME OF THE WOODS

*I. coccinea* grows to about three feet (90 cm) as a pot plant. It has shiny leaves and clusters of red, orange or pink flowers, which open from May to September. It prefers to remain in one position.

**Good Care Guide**
*I. coccinea* needs good light but must be shaded from the hottest sun in summer. The winter temperature should not fall below 55°F (13°C). Spray and water regularly throughout the summer with tepid, soft water. In autumn gradually reduce spraying and watering. Keep the plant barely moist in winter. From March to September feed fortnightly. Repot in February in an all-peat compost. In March pinch out leading shoots to stimulate flower formation. Propagate by stem cuttings in spring.

### *Hibiscus rosa-sinensis*
ROSE OF CHINA

As its common name implies this attractive shrub is a native of China. It is an evergreen with toothed leaves and lovely large flowers. Colours include red, pink, white and yellow and there are also some double varieties. It can grow to six feet (180 cm) in a tub, but by pruning it can be kept at a more manageable size.

**Good Care Guide**
Rose of China requires light throughout the year, preferably from an east- or west-facing window. In winter the temperature should not fall below 55°F (13°C). Water liberally and spray in summer. Water less in winter. From February to August feed weekly. Prune in February and repot using a loamless mixture. Propagate by cuttings.

### *Impatiens wallerana* 'Holstii'
BUSY LIZZIE

A very popular house plant, Busy Lizzie produces a profusion of red, pink or white flowers throughout the year. It has pale green, pointed leaves and grows to a height of one to two feet (30 to 60 cm).

**Good Care Guide**
In spring and summer shade from the hottest sun and water well. In hot weather it may require more than one watering a day. In autumn and winter put the plant in full light, the temperature can be as low as 50°F (10°C), and water more sparingly. From February to September feed once a week. Repot in a loamless mixture in spring and prune back top shoots to encourage bushiness. To propagate put the pruned top shoots in water or potting compost to root.

### *Jacobinia pauciflora*
JACOBINIA

*J. pauciflora* is a native of Brazil. It grows to two feet (60 cm) and flowers from October to May. The long, tube-like flowers are scarlet tipped with yellow.

**Good Care Guide**
*J. pauciflora* requires sun and fresh air in summer. A winter temperature of 50° to 55°F (10° to 13°C) is desirable. From June to September water only enough to keep the soil moist. From the end of September until the plant stops flowering, water liberally and feed fortnightly. Repot annually in a loam-based compost when flowering has stopped. To promote bushy growth cut the shoots back two weeks after repotting and again when the side shoots are two to three inches (5 to 8 cm) long. Propagate by cuttings in spring.

A plant room or conservatory, far left, can be a delightful addition to a house. *Ananas*, *Clerodendrum* and *Plectranthus* are plants that particularly enjoy a room specially geared to their requirements.

A grape vine trained across the ceiling of a garden room, above, creates a delightful effect and also provides welcome protection from the sun.

With a conservatory it is possible to make palms and other exotic foliage plants part of your life.

## Jacaranda mimosifolia
JACARANDA

Only young specimens of this tropical flowering tree from Brazil can be grown indoors. Therefore it is for its beautiful fern-like foliage that this house plant is cultivated, rather than for the lovely bluey-mauve flowers.

**Good Care Guide**

Light but not too much direct sun, particularly in summer, is what this plant requires. It must be warm—the winter temperature should not fall below 55°F (13°C)—and humid. Water only with tepid, soft water, liberally in summer and sparingly in winter. From April to September feed fortnightly with a liquid fertilizer. Repot in spring when the plant puts out new shoots in any good proprietary potting compost. Propagate by cuttings of young shoots in summer or by seed in spring.

## Jacobinia carnea
JACOBINIA

This tropical, evergreen shrub from Brazil has dark green, pointed leaves and dense terminal heads of pink flowers which open during August and September.

**Good Care Guide**

During the hottest months lightly shade the plant from direct sun. The ideal winter temperature is 50° to 55°F (10° to 13°C). Water well in all seasons except after the plant has been cut back, when it will require a little less. Spray in hot weather. Feed weekly from March to August. Repot in February in any good-quality proprietary potting compost. In March cut back the plant to promote bushy growth and use cuttings of the young shoots that subsequently grow for propagation.

## Jacobinia suberecta

This evergreen plant comes from Uruguay. Suitable for a hanging basket, *J. suberecta* has downy, grey-green stems and leaves and clusters of bright, orange-scarlet flowers which open from July to September.

**Good Care Guide**

This plant should be kept at a temperature of not less than 55°F (13°C) during the winter, when the soil should be just moist. From April to September the plant will thrive best if it is shaded from very hot sun. During the same period water liberally and feed once a week. Although the plant is often discarded when flowering has finished, it can be pruned back rigorously each spring and repotted in any good proprietary potting compost. Propagate by cuttings in spring or summer.

## Pachystachys lutea
LOLLIPOP PLANT

This delightfully decorative house plant inexplicably fell from favour at the beginning of the twentieth century, but fortunately it has recently become available again. *P. lutea* grows to about eighteen inches (45 cm) and bears bright green, oval leaves and bright yellow, erect, cone-shaped clusters of bracts from which little tongue-like, white flowers emerge.

**Good Care Guide**

In winter *P. lutea* requires a temperature no lower than 55°F (13°C), and it should be watered very sparingly. In spring and summer shade from hot sun, water liberally and feed once a week. Repot every spring in loam-based compost. Prune in early spring. Use the new shoots for propagation.

## Pedilanthus tithymaloides 'Variegata'
RIBBON CACTUS, DEVIL'S BACKBONE
REDBIRD CACTUS

In spite of two of its common names, this rather fleshy, bushy plant is not a cactus. It grows about two feet (60 cm) tall, and has branched, greyish-green, zig-zag stems. Oval, reddish-green leaves with white margins develop at each angle along the stems. The eye-catching, scarlet flower heads open in summer.

**Good Care Guide**

In winter the temperature should not fall below 50°F (10°C) and the plant should be watered very sparingly. In spring and summer water moderately, keeping the soil just moist. From May to September feed once a month. Repot every spring in any reliable potting compost. Propagate by cuttings in summer.

## Pentas lanceolata
EGYPTIAN STAR CLUSTER

A native of tropical Africa, *P. lanceolata* has hairy, lance-shaped leaves and dense terminal clusters of starry, pale pink to deep red flowers, which appear at intervals throughout the year. The plant is inclined to become leggy, so it should be pruned hard each year and allowed to grow no taller than about two feet (60 cm).

**Good Care Guide**

The winter temperature should be no lower than 55°F (13°C). In summer water liberally. At other times keep the soil just moist. From April to November feed fortnightly. In March cut back hard and pinch out the tips of young shoots. After pruning repot in any good-quality potting compost. Use the young shoots that arise after cutting back for propagation.

## *Rechsteineria cardinalis*
CARDINAL FLOWER

This plant has tube-shaped flowers which open from May to September and are as scarlet as a cardinal's cassock. *R. cardinalis* has downy, emerald-green leaves and grows about eighteen inches (45 cm) high.
**Good Care Guide**
Water *R. cardinalis* well in spring and summer and feed it once a week during the same period. When it has finished flowering, water sparingly until the leaves and stems have withered. Let the tuber winter in its pot at a temperature no lower than 55°F (13°C) and do not water. In February repot in any good proprietary potting mixture and begin watering. Start feeding six weeks later. To propagate divide the tuber as soon as shoots show, or take cuttings of young shoots.

## *Rechsteineria leucotricha*
BRAZILIAN EDELWEISS

This species of *Rechsteineria* comes from Brazil and grows to about eighteen inches (45 cm). It has exquisitely soft, bright silver-grey leaves which are covered with fine white hairs. The clusters of tube-shaped, coral-coloured flowers open from August until October.
**Good Care Guide**
Treat *R. leucotricha* the same as *R. cardinalis*, keeping it moist and feeding it once a week in spring and summer. When flowering ceases, water sparingly until the leaves and stems have withered. Leave the tuber in the pot and do not water. In February repot in any good proprietary compost. To propagate, divide the tuber when young shoots are visible or take cuttings.

## *Rhoeo spathacea*
BOAT LILY

This Mexican plant has clusters of tiny, white flowers enclosed by purple, boat-shaped bracts. The flowers open from May until July. Its lance-shaped leaves are green, or green with yellow and white stripes on top and reddish-purple underneath.
**Good Care Guide**
Water well in spring and summer and spray regularly or the beautiful leaves will curl up. Give less water in August and September, then very little through the winter, when it should be kept at a minimum temperature of 50°F (10°C). Feed every fortnight from March until September. Repot in spring using, ideally, an all-peat compost. Propagate by basal shoots or from seeds in spring.

## *Rondeletia roezlii*

This evergreen shrub from Guatemala has oval, glossy, green leaves and dense clusters of pinkish-purple flowers with yellow centres which appear during summer and autumn. *R. roezlii* grows to a height of about four feet (120 cm).
**Good Care Guide**
In winter this plant requires a temperature between 55° and 60°F (13° and 16°C). Provide a humid atmosphere at all times by standing the plant on a tray of wet pebbles or moist peat. Water liberally in spring and summer and sparingly in winter. From April to October feed fortnightly. Repot every April in good-quality potting compost. Propagation by cuttings in spring is not easy unless a special heated propagating case is used.

## *Salpiglossis sinuata*
PAINTED TONGUE

A native of Chile, *S. sinuata* is an annual grown for its eye-catching, funnel-shaped flowers, which are borne on delicate, leafy stems and open from July to September. The velvety blooms are either pale purple, red, orange or yellow with contrastingly marked veins and different coloured centres. The plant grows up to two feet (60 cm) tall.
**Good Care Guide**
This plant thrives best on the sill of a south-, east- or west-facing window. Keep the soil moist at all times, and from May to September feed every two weeks. Support the stems with small sticks or canes. Propagate by seed in spring. Plant each seedling in a 5-inch (13-cm) pot containing any reliable potting compost. Discard the plant when flowering ends.

## *Setcreasea purpurea*
PURPLE HEART

This is not a plant for the tidy-minded. Its leafy stems eventually sprawl in all directions unless supported. With its all-over purple colour, however, it looks superb among a group of green plants. Brought from Mexico as recently as 1955, *S. purpurea* has small, deep pink flowers which open from May until December.
**Good Care Guide**
*S. purpurea* must have good light or the intense purple colouring will become green tinted. Water well in summer and feed once a week. In winter keep the soil just moist; the temperature should not fall below 45°F (7°C). It can be repotted every April in any proprietary potting compost, but is best grown annually from cuttings in summer.

In this sumptuous, Edwardian-style room, *Dracaena*, *Begonia*, *Schefflera* and small groups of ferns harmonize with the décor.

In the bathroom, left, a row of *Ficus* plants looks striking against a glass partition.

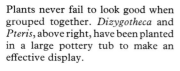

Plants never fail to look good when grouped together. *Dizygotheca* and *Pteris*, above right, have been planted in a large pottery tub to make an effective display.

*Coleus blumei*, right, are seen in a glazed white china container on a window ledge.

# *Plants for temperate rooms*

## *Partial shade*

## *Abutilon megapotamicum*
BRAZILIAN ABUTILON
FLOWERING MAPLE

A versatile plant, *A. megapotamicum* may be cultivated either in a hanging basket or in a pot, where, with support, it can eventually grow to a height of about four feet (120 cm). It has green or green and yellow variegated leaves and fascinating, red and yellow, lantern-shaped flowers which open from spring until autumn.

**Good Care Guide**
Water liberally in summer, sparingly in winter and keep at a minimum temperature of 45°F (7°C). Spray in spring and feed once a week from February until August. Prune a large plant in April and repot at the same time, using a moderate-sized pot containing any good proprietary potting compost. To propagate take stem cuttings in summer.

## *Abutilon striatum* 'Thompsonii'
SPOTTED FLOWERING MAPLE
THOMPSON'S ABUTILON

*A. striatum thompsonii* has green leaves covered with yellow blotches and bell-shaped, orange flowers with dark red veins. The flowers open from late spring through to the autumn.

**Good Care Guide**
In winter keep the plant at a temperature of not more than 55°F (13°C) and water sparingly, keeping the soil just moist. Spray regularly in spring. From March until August water well and feed once a week. Prune in April to encourage bushiness and repot at the same time in a moderate-sized pot containing any good proprietary potting compost. To propagate, take stem cuttings in summer.

## *Acalypha wilkesiana*
COPPER LEAF

Grown for its handsome foliage, there are several forms of *A. wilkesiana*. The leaves, which are often marbled, may be green, red, brown or copper-coloured, with or without white edges.

**Good Care Guide**
If *A. wilkesiana* is kept in heavy shade, the leaves of the red, brown or copper forms may revert to green. Keep the plant in a humid atmosphere at a minimum temperature of 60°F (16°C). Water sparingly, keeping the soil moist, and feed fortnightly from February to August. Prune back side shoots after one year. Beginning in the second year cut back top shoots annually. Repot every February, preferably in an all-peat mixture. Propagate by cuttings of basal or side shoots.

## *Achimenes longiflora*
HOT-WATER PLANT

Although this plant will not provide cheerful greenery through the winter, it produces a wonderful mass of blue, pink, violet or white flowers from June until October. The narrow leaves are hairy and pointed, green above and red-flushed underneath.

**Good Care Guide**
Water sparingly in spring and autumn and more liberally in summer, always using tepid water. After flowering has finished in late summer slowly dry off, cut back the stems and store the tubers in dry sand at a minimum temperature of 45°F (7°C). Repot in an all-peat compost and start watering the plant again the following spring. Feed fortnightly until the first flowers appear. To propagate, separate the tubers before repotting.

## *Adiantum hispidulum*
MAIDENHAIR FERN

Unlike the Common Maidenhair Fern (*A. capillus-veneris*), which grows in many temperate parts of the world, *A. hispidulum* comes from the tropics. It has fronds forked at the base which grow to about twelve inches (30 cm) in length, and hairy leaflets which are reddish-bronze when they first appear, and become mid-green later.

**Good Care Guide**
The temperature in winter should never fall below 55°F (13°C). Water liberally in spring and summer, but keep the soil just moist in winter. Stand the plant on a tray of wet pebbles or moist peat to provide humidity. Feed fortnightly from March to September. Repot every other spring in an all-peat compost and propagate by division.

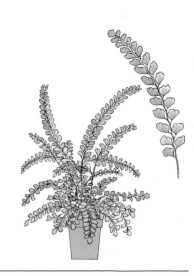

## *Aechmea fasciata*
## *(Billbergia rhodocyanea)*
URN PLANT

*A. fasciata* is from Brazil. Its grey-green and silver-grey striped, arching, strap-shaped leaves form a rosette from which the magnificent flower head protrudes. Protected by long-lasting, pointed, pink bracts, the flowers themselves are small.

**Good Care Guide**
Water the compost moderately in summer and sparingly in winter. Keep the funnel formed by the leaf bases filled with tepid, soft water from late spring to early autumn, but keep dry in winter, when the plant should be kept at a temperature of about 50° to 55°F (10° to 13°C). Feed every three to four weeks from April to October. The main rosette dies after flowering. Propagate from side shoots in an all-peat compost.

## *Aechmea fulgens*
CORAL BERRY

*Fulgens* means shining or glowing and refers to this plant's bright scarlet flower stem and long-lasting, berry-like bracts. The short-lived, blue flowers open in late summer. The flower stem emerges from the centre of a tubular rosette of strap-shaped, slightly prickly, dark green leaves. From French Guiana, it grows fifteen inches (38 cm) tall.

**Good Care Guide**
Overwinter at a temperature no lower than 50°F (10°C). Keep the soil just moist at all times and water even less in winter. Spray often. Feed once a month from April to September. Repot every other April in an all-peat compost mixed with an equal quantity of sphagnum moss. Propagate by removing offsets when they are about six inches (15 cm) tall.

## *Aeschynanthus lobbianus*
LIPSTICK PLANT

A native of Java, *A. lobbianus* is a prostrate or trailing plant which looks at its best in a hanging basket. It has shiny, dark green leaves and terminal clusters of scarlet flowers with purple-brown calyces. The flowers open from May to July and sometimes later.

**Good Care Guide**
Although this plant will survive at a temperature of 45°F (7°C) in winter, it will thrive better if it is kept at about 55°F (13°C). In spring and summer water liberally. At other times keep the soil barely moist. From May to September feed once a month. Spray in hot weather. Repot every second or third spring in three parts peat compost to one part moss. Propagate by cuttings in spring or summer.

## *Alloplectus capitatus*
VELVET ALLOPLECTUS

The beautifully soft leaves of this South American plant are olive green on top and greenish-red underneath. Rather downy, succulent, red stems grow two to three feet (60 to 90 cm) tall and in autumn bear terminal clusters of yellow flowers with deep red centres.

**Good Care Guide**
*A. capitatus* requires a moist atmosphere, so spray regularly. In winter the temperature should not fall below 55°F (13°C) and the plant should be watered sparingly. Water liberally at other times. Feed fortnightly from May to September. Repot every April in any good-quality potting compost. Propagate by cuttings of basal shoots in summer.

## *Amomum cardamom*
CARDAMOM, CARDAMOM GINGER

A native of Java, *A. cardamom* has rather hairy, tough, lance-shaped leaves which give off a deliciously spicy odour if they are rubbed. In its natural state this plant may reach a height of ten feet (3 m), but in a pot it is unlikely to grow taller than about three feet (90 cm), and will not flower.

**Good Care Guide**
In winter provide a temperature of 55° to 60°F (13° to 16°C) and water sparingly. In spring and summer keep the soil moist and spray on hot days. From May to September feed every two weeks. Repot every spring in a good-quality, all-peat potting compost. Propagate by division when repotting.

## *Anthurium andreanum*
PAINTER'S PALETTE

From May to September this splendid plant from Colombia produces waxy, palette-shaped, red or white flowers which have a tail-like spadix growing from the centre. *A. andreanum* grows about eighteen inches (45 cm) tall and has large, heart-shaped, dark green leaves.

**Good Care Guide**
Ideally the plant should be kept at a temperature of 60°F (16°C) in winter, although it will survive at 55°F (13°C). Water liberally in spring and summer and moderately in winter. From May to August feed fortnightly. Provide a humid atmosphere by standing the plant on a tray of wet pebbles or moist peat. Repot every second or third April, preferably in a proprietary all-peat compost, and propagate by division.

**65**

## Acalypha hispida
RED-HOT CAT'S TAIL, CHENILLE PLANT

The two common names of this green-leafed plant from Papua New Guinea perfectly describe the colour, shape and texture of its very decorative flower spikes. The flowering season is from May to September and the dark red "cats' tails" may grow up to twenty inches (50 cm) in length.

**Good Care Guide**

*A. hispida* will thrive in a humid atmosphere at a minimum temperature of 60°F (16°C). It dislikes standing in water, but the soil should be kept moist at all times. Feed every fortnight from February to August. Prune side shoots the first year, then prune top shoots annually. Repot every February in any good proprietary potting compost. Propagate by cuttings of basal or side shoots.

## Anthurium scherzerianum
FLAMINGO FLOWER, FLAME PLANT

Providing a wonderful burst of colour at the end of winter, *A. scherzerianum* has curly, yellow flower tassels and scarlet spathes which grow singly on slender stems from February to July. The dark green leaves are shiny, lance-shaped and leathery.

**Good Care Guide**

*A. scherzerianum* likes a humid atmosphere and a winter temperature not lower than 60°F (16°C). Water judiciously throughout the year, keeping the soil just moist. From February until December feed every three weeks after watering. Repot in spring in a wide, fairly shallow pot containing an all-peat compost. Propagate by division or by seed in spring.

## Aphelandra squarrosa
ZEBRA PLANT, TIGER PLANT

An attractive plant, *A. squarrosa* has large, dark green leaves with creamy-white veins and cone-shaped, red-edged, yellow bracts from which the yellow flowers protrude. It blooms between April and August, sometimes later, and the flowers last for three to six weeks.

**Good Care Guide**

*A. squarrosa* likes a humid atmosphere and a winter temperature no lower than 55°F (13°C). Water and spray liberally in summer, but make sure the soil is never waterlogged. In winter water sparingly. Feed fortnightly from March until August. Pot on in March in any good proprietary potting compost. Prune back top shoots after flowering has finished. Propagate by cuttings in a heated propagating case.

Epiphytic plants growing on a gnarled piece of driftwood make the most beautiful of plant displays.

Many unusual plants are epiphytes including *Vriesea* and *Platycerium*, and the exotic *Aechmea*, above.

# Epiphytes–the hangers-on

The ruggedly handsome Stag's-horn Fern, above, complements the stripped pine of this split-level room.

The strap-like leaves of *Aechmea fasciata*, left, suit the stark simplicity of this bathroom. In contrast to the coarse leaves the pink flower is strikingly delicate.

## *Ardisia crispa*
CORAL BERRY, SPEAR FLOWER

This shrub's tiny, sweet-smelling, reddish flowers open in June and are followed by bright scarlet berries which look as festive as Holly and remain on the plant at least until spring. From the East Indies, *A. crispa* grows about two to three feet (60 to 90 cm) tall and has dark green, glossy leaves.

**Good Care Guide**
Water *A. crispa* freely in summer and spray with tepid water. In winter the temperature should not fall below 45°F (7°C) and the soil should be kept barely moist. Feed fortnightly from April until August. Repot in spring, using any good proprietary potting compost. Prune fairly ruthlessly in February. Propagate by seed in March or by cuttings of lateral shoots in spring or summer.

## *Asparagus densiflorus* 'Sprengeri'
ASPARAGUS

Branches of *A. densiflorus*, and its close relative *A. setaceus* (*plumosus*), are often used in arrangements of cut flowers, but both species make attractive house plants. From Natal, *A. densiflorus* has masses of trailing stems and stiff, green, needle-like leaves. In June it sometimes produces small, greenish-white flowers followed by red berries. Mature plants have somewhat prickly stems.

**Good Care Guide**
Water liberally in summer and sparingly in winter, when the temperature should not fall below 45°F (7°C). Feed fortnightly from May to September and cut off any yellowing branches. Pot on in April in any good potting compost. Propagate by division or by seed in spring.

## *Asparagus setaceus* (*plumosus*)
ASPARAGUS FERN

Have no mouth-watering illusions about this plant, which comes from South Africa. Although it closely resembles culinary asparagus, this species is purely ornamental. It is worth cultivating, however, for its elegant, feathery branches. Scarlet berries are sometimes borne as an added bonus.

**Good Care Guide**
The Asparagus Fern likes to overwinter at a temperature no lower than 45°F (7°C). Water sparingly during this period. Water liberally in summer, when the plant should also be fed fortnightly. Repot in April in any good proprietary potting compost and remove any yellowing branches. Propagate in spring by division or by seed.

## *Asplenium bulbiferum*
HEN AND CHICKEN FERN
MOTHER SPLEENWORT

This feathery green fern, which is indigenous to New Zealand, Australia and India, is remarkable for its method of reproduction. Small plantlets called bulbils develop on the larger fronds. Outdoors the plantlets pull the fronds down to ground level, where they take root. Indoors the plantlets may be removed and planted in separate pots.

**Good Care Guide**
Water *A. bulbiferum* liberally in summer and less often in winter, when it should be kept at a temperature not less than 55°F (13°C). Feed once a week and spray regularly from March to August. Repot in spring using any good proprietary potting compost. Propagate in March by potting the plantlets or by division.

## *Asplenium nidus*
BIRD'S-NEST FERN

From the tropics, *A. nidus* has tough, glossy, green leaves, about two to four feet (60 to 120 cm) long, which form a rosette at the base. The illusion of a bird's nest is much more real when the fern is seen in silhouette high on a tree branch.

**Good Care Guide**
In winter the temperature should not fall below 55°F (13°C) and the soil should be barely moist. *A. nidus* likes a humid atmosphere in spring and summer. Water freely in summer and feed with a weak solution of fertilizer fortnightly from March to August. Repot in spring, preferably using an all-peat compost. Propagation by spores is difficult for the novice. If offsets are formed they may be detached and potted separately in spring.

## *Begonia boweri*
MINIATURE EYELASH BEGONIA

Of the nine hundred species of *Begonia*, *B. boweri*, which grows about six inches (15 cm) high, is one of the smallest. It has little white or shell-pink flowers which open from February to May. The emerald green leaves have purple-brown markings on their hairy margins.

**Good Care Guide**
*B. boweri* requires a humid atmosphere in summer. In winter a temperature of 55° to 60°F (13° to 16°C) is required and the soil must be kept only just moist. Spray, water liberally and feed fortnightly during the growing period from about February to August. Repot every April in a shallow pot or pan containing any proprietary potting compost. Propagate by division when repotting.

## Begonia coccinea
ANGELWING BEGONIA

*B. coccinea* has green leaves with fine red margins and bamboo-like stems which grow about six feet (180 cm) tall in a large pot or tub. Drooping clusters of light red flowers open from May to October. 'President Carnot', a popular hybrid, has silver-spotted leaves and larger pink flowers.

**Good Care Guide**

*B. coccinea* thrives in a humid atmosphere in summer. In winter the temperature should not fall below 50°F (10°C) and the soil should be just moist. From April to September water liberally, spray regularly and feed fortnightly. Cut out two-year-old stems in March. Repot every April in a large pot containing any good proprietary potting compost. Propagate by cuttings in summer.

## Begonia fuchsioides
FUCHSIA-FLOWERED BEGONIA

As the name of this bushy *Begonia* implies, *B. fuchsioides* has drooping clusters of delicate, fuchsia-like, red or pink flowers which open from October to March. The plant has glossy green leaves and grows about four feet (120 cm) tall in a large pot or tub.

**Good Care Guide**

*B. fuchsioides* needs a humid atmosphere in summer. During its winter resting period it should be kept at a temperature of about 50°F (10°C) and watered sparingly. From May to September spray and water liberally, but do not allow the soil to become waterlogged, and feed fortnightly. Cut out two-year-old stems in March. Repot every April in any good proprietary potting compost. Propagate by cuttings in summer.

## Begonia masoniana
IRON CROSS

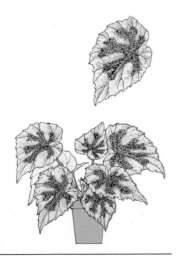

An unusual and splendidly patterned plant, *B. masoniana* has hairy, grey-green, puckered leaves which are marked centrally with a purple-brown cross. Older leaves take on a silvery tinge. This *Begonia* grows to a height of about nine inches (23 cm). It rarely flowers, but with leaves like these, who can complain.

**Good Care Guide**

Like all *Begonia*, *B. masoniana* requires a humid atmosphere in summer, when it should be sprayed often and watered liberally. In winter the temperature must not fall below 55°F (13°C) and be sure the soil is just moist. Feed fortnightly from April to September. Repot every April in a shallow pot containing any good potting compost. Propagate by leaf cuttings in summer.

## Begonia metallica

The leaves of this bushy *Begonia* are olive green with a metallic sheen; crimson veins spread out across the undersides. In September clusters of pink flowers appear. The plant grows to a height of about three feet (90 cm).

**Good Care Guide**

A good-natured plant, *B. metallica* is easy to grow provided it is given a humid atmosphere in summer and a winter temperature of not less than 50°F (10°C). Water liberally, but do not allow the soil to become waterlogged, and feed fortnightly from April to September. In winter keep the soil just moist. In March pinch out top shoots to encourage bushiness. Repot in April in any good proprietary potting compost, preferably an all-peat one. Propagate by stem cuttings in summer.

## Begonia semperflorens

This low, bushy *Begonia* has glossy green or brown-purple-flushed leaves and pretty little white, pink or red flowers which open mainly from May to October, although they may appear, on and off, throughout the year. There are many popular hybrids, ranging in height from six to eighteen inches (15 to 45 cm).

**Good Care Guide**

In summer *B. semperflorens* needs a humid atmosphere. Water freely, but be sure the compost never becomes waterlogged, and feed once a fortnight from May to September. In winter the plant requires a temperature of about 50°F (10°C) and just enough water to keep the soil moist. Pinch out top shoots in March. Repot in April in a loam-based compost. Propagate by seed in spring or stem cuttings in summer.

## Begonia serratipetala

As its name suggests, *B. serratipetala*'s pink flowers have serrated, or notched, edges. The flowers open from spring until autumn and look beautiful against the plant's glossy, pink-spotted, dark green leaves. It is a bushy plant rarely exceeding a height of twelve to eighteen inches (30 to 45 cm).

**Good Care Guide**

Be sure to keep *B. serratipetala* in a humid atmosphere in summer, when it should be watered liberally and fed once a fortnight. In winter do not let the temperature fall below 50°F (10°C) and water sparingly, keeping the soil just moist. Prune in March. In April repot in any good proprietary potting compost, preferably an all-peat one. Propagate by stem cuttings in summer.

In a kitchen where space is limited a group of plants, can be planted together in a pottery tub.

A butcher's chopping table, top, makes an appropriate stand for *Asparagus* and *Nephrolepis* ferns in a country kitchen.

Small arrangements of plants, above, can be placed on out-of-the-way shelves in a busy kitchen. The bright colours of *Sinningia*, *Calathea* and *Nephrolepis* harmonize with the rich colouring of the walls.

## Begonia (socotrana hybrids) Hiemalis

Many hybrids have been developed from *B. socotrana*, but the Hiemalis group are the most beautiful. They have large pink, white, yellow or orange flowers which open in winter.

**Good Care Guide**

Water sparingly after flowering has finished in January. When the green leaves discolour, prune the plant and move it to a cool—45°F (7°C)—position. In April give more water and warmth. When new shoots are three inches (8 cm) long, cut them off at the base and plant in separate pots preferably containing an all-peat compost. Discard the parent plant. Pot the cuttings on until they are in 6-inch (15-cm) pots, pinching out top shoots to encourage bushiness. Feed fortnightly, spray and water freely until flowering is over.

## Billbergia nutans

ANGEL'S TEARS, QUEEN'S TEARS

Put up with *B. nutans*'s dullish silvery-bronze-tinted, dark green, narrow, arching leaves for most of the year and from winter until early summer you will be rewarded with a show of violet-blue and green flowers which protrude from pink bracts. The plant grows about eighteen inches (45 cm) tall and comes from South America.

**Good Care Guide**

Ideally, this plant needs a temperature of about 60°F (16°C) in winter, when it should be watered sparingly, but it is very tolerant of neglect and will endure temperatures as low as 35°F (2°C) for short periods of time. Water liberally and feed fortnightly from May to October. In June or July repot in an all-peat compost and propagate by division.

## Biophytum sensitivum

LIFE PLANT

The oval, green leaves of this fascinating, umbrella-shaped plant fold back if they are touched or if they are exposed to bright sunshine or a sudden blast of air. Cup-shaped flowers, which are pale purple at first, becoming yellowish-orange, open in summer. A tropical plant, *B. sensitivum* grows about six inches (15 cm) tall.

**Good Care Guide**

In winter the temperature should not fall below 60°F (16°C) and the plant should be watered sparingly. In spring and summer keep the soil moist and spray regularly. From April to September feed fortnightly. Repot every spring in any good-quality potting compost. Propagate by seed in spring, at a temperature of 65°F (18°C).

## Brunfelsia calycina

YESTERDAY, TODAY AND TOMORROW

*B. calycina* has tough, rather glossy green leaves and sweet-smelling, purplish-violet flowers which fade to almost white and are profuse from March to September or even longer. It can grow to a height of about two feet (60 cm) and comes from Brazil.

**Good Care Guide**

This shrub likes a lot of light in winter, when it should be kept at a temperature of not less than 50°F (10°C) and watered sparingly. In summer keep in the shade, water liberally and spray. Feed monthly from March to September. If pot-bound, repot in spring using any good all-peat potting compost. Pruning is seldom necessary unless stems get bare and leggy. Propagate by cuttings in summer, ideally in a propagating case with bottom heat.

## Calathea insignis

RATTLESNAKE PLANT

This Brazilian plant has wavy edged, lance-shaped, velvety, medium green leaves with oval, olive markings. The undersides of the leaves are the colour of port wine. If the plant is kept in a small pot the leaves rarely exceed six inches (15 cm) in length.

**Good Care Guide**

Always shade *C. insignis* from direct sunlight or the leaves will discolour. In summer keep in a humid atmosphere and water liberally. During the winter the temperature should not fall below 55°F (13°C) and the plant should be watered sparingly. Feed fortnightly from May to September. Repot in early summer, preferably using an all-peat potting mixture. Propagate by division when repotting.

## Calathea makoyana

PEACOCK PLANT

The long-stemmed, broad, oval leaves of this Brazilian plant look as though they have been hand-painted. They are silvery-green with dark green markings along the main veins. On the undersides of the leaves the pattern is repeated, but the dark areas are a purplish colour. In a small pot *C. makoyana* rarely exceeds nine inches (23 cm) in height.

**Good Care Guide**

Always keep this plant in the shade. In summer it needs a humid atmosphere and plenty of water. In winter keep at a temperature of not less than 55°F (13°C) and water sparingly. Feed fortnightly from May to September. Repot in early summer in an all-peat potting compost. Propagate by division when repotting.

## Calathea ornata

Pairs of pink stripes, which gradually fade to cream, curve between the main veins of *C. ornata*'s dark green, oval leaves. The undersides of the leaves are dark purple. A native of Colombia, this plant will grow to eight feet (240 cm) in its natural habitat, but indoors in a pot it is unlikely to grow taller than eighteen inches (45 cm).

**Good Care Guide**
Shade from the sun and keep in a humid atmosphere in summer. In winter the temperature should not fall below 60°F (16°C). Water liberally during the March-to-September growing season. In winter keep the soil just moist. Feed fortnightly from May to September. Repot in early summer, preferably using an all-peat potting compost. Propagate by division when repotting.

## Calathea zebrina
ZEBRA PLANT

As its name implies this Brazilian plant's emerald-green, oblong leaves are boldly striped with bands of a darker green. On the undersides of the leaves the bands are a purplish colour. *C. zebrina* grows about eighteen inches (45 cm) tall, but in a large pot or tub may reach three feet (90 cm).

**Good Care Guide**
Protect from bright sun. Keep in a humid atmosphere in summer and at a temperature not less than 60°F (16°C) in winter. Water liberally except during the winter, when the soil should be kept barely moist. Feed fortnightly from May to September. Repot in early summer, preferably using one of the all-peat composts. Propagate by division when repotting.

## Chamaedorea elegans
DWARF MOUNTAIN PALM

Also known as *Collinia elegans* and *Neanthe bella*, this graceful little Mexican palm rarely grows more than four feet (120 cm) tall in a pot and takes several years to do so. Each of its green leaves has an arching stalk from which many very narrow leaflets grow.

**Good Care Guide**
In winter the temperature should not fall below 50° to 55°F (10° to 13°C) and the soil should be kept just moist. Spray and water freely in summer. Feed once a month from April to September. Repot annually in spring for the first three years and thereafter every two years in an all-peat potting compost. Propagate by seed sown in spring. A temperature of 75°F (24°C), however, must be maintained for good germination.

## Cissus discolor
REX BEGONIA VINE

Climbing or trailing, *C. discolor* is a sensational-looking plant. Its richly coloured leaves are a bright metallic green marbled with purple and white with a hint of crimson and peach. The undersides are deep crimson. From the East Indies, it is a semi-evergreen and, therefore, loses only some of its foliage in winter.

**Good Care Guide**
The temperature should not fall below 55°F (13°C) in winter, when the soil should be kept just moist. In spring and summer water liberally. Feed fortnightly from May to September. Prune in February. Repot every March or April in any good-quality potting compost, preferably an all-peat kind. Propagate by cuttings of lateral shoots in June or July.

## Cissus striata
MINIATURE GRAPE IVY

*C. striata* is a delicate plant from South America that looks particularly graceful if it is allowed to trail. The leaves, which are pink when young and dark green later, are made up of five leaflets, each barely one inch (2 cm) long.

**Good Care Guide**
*C. striata* needs a well-lit position, but it should be shaded from direct sun at all times. In winter the temperature should not fall below about 45°F (7°C). Water liberally in spring and summer, sparingly in winter. Feed once a month from the time when new shoots begin to grow until September. Repot in March in any good proprietary potting compost. Pinch out new shoots occasionally. Propagate by cuttings of stem pieces in summer.

## Clivia miniata
KAFFIR LILY

*C. miniata* has trumpet-shaped, orange flowers and shiny, dark green leaves. It grows eighteen to twenty-four inches (45 to 60 cm) tall and usually flowers in March.

**Good Care Guide**
The winter temperature should not fall below 40°F (4°C), but can rise to 55°F (13°C) or a little higher. There is no need to feed *C. miniata* the first year, but thereafter use a liquid fertilizer once a month from April to August. Water moderately in summer. The rest of the year water only when the soil dries out completely. Repot in any good proprietary potting compost only when the pot is congested. After flowering propagate by division or detach the offsets from the base of the plant when they show four or five leaves.

### Begonia rex

*B. rex*, king of the *Begonia*, has magnificent, dark green, wrinkled leaves with silver markings. It is seldom seen today, but many hybrids and cultivated varieties, sold under the name of *B. rex*, have been developed. Their green leaves have beautiful silver, cream, pink, red, purple or copper markings. Mature plants may produce pink flowers in the summer.

**Good Care Guide**

Provide a humid atmosphere in summer. In winter maintain a temperature of not less than 55°F (13°C). Water liberally and feed fortnightly from April to September. In winter keep the compost just moist. Pruning is not necessary. Repot every April preferably in an all-peat compost. Propagate by leaf cuttings in summer.

### Begonia × tuberhybrida

*B. × tuberhybrida* is an umbrella title for a large group of tuberous hybrids. They have green leaves and rose-like or pendulous flowers in many colours which open in summer.

**Good Care Guide**

In September, when flowering has finished, water sparingly. When the stems wither, overwinter the tuber in dry peat at a temperature of 45°F (7°C). In April repot in any good potting compost, start watering gradually and move to a warmer room—about 65°F (18°C). Shoots will soon appear. Water more liberally when the plant is in full leaf and feed fortnightly from the time when the buds are just visible until the flowers are over. Propagate by cuttings from newly sprouted tubers or by cutting the tubers into two or more pieces, each with at least one shoot.

### Beloperone guttata
SHRIMP PLANT

Down-curving, shrimp-like flower heads composed of overlapping, pinkish-brown bracts, from which narrow white flowers emerge, give this bushy, evergreen shrub its common name. It flowers from April to December and rarely exceeds eighteen inches (45 cm) in a 5- or 6-inch (13- or 15-cm) pot.

**Good Care Guide**

The Shrimp Plant needs fresh air in summer. Although it will survive a temperature of 45°F (7°C) in winter, the most suitable temperature is 55° to 60°F (13° to 16°C). Water liberally from April to November and sparingly in winter. Feed fortnightly from May to September. Prune rigorously in February. Repot in March. Propagate by stem cuttings in spring or summer.

The range and quality of colour of *Begonia* is unsurpassed. 'Fireglow', with its brilliant red flowers, above, is one of the most striking examples.

The blowzy beauty of the cultivated varieties of *Begonia*, left, suit the atmosphere of this country-style kitchen.

An unusual Indian wood carving of a winged Krishna playing his flute, right, is poised above a banked mass of splendid *Begonia rex*.

### Coffea arabica
COFFEE PLANT

The Coffee Plant is grown for its glossy, dark green leaves. The clusters of star-shaped, fragrant, white flowers and red berries which contain the coffee "beans", or seeds, are rarely seen on a pot plant. A native of Africa, it grows up to four feet (120 cm) in height indoors.

**Good Care Guide**
Provide the Coffee Plant with a winter temperature of not less than 45°F (7°C). Water liberally in summer and sparingly in winter. Spray occasionally. Feed every two weeks from March to October. Repot every other February in any good proprietary potting compost. In March prune back the top shoots to encourage bushiness. Propagate by lateral stem cuttings, preferably with a heel of old wood, in summer.

### Columnea microphylla
GOLDFISH VINE

This trailing plant from Costa Rica looks magnificent tumbling out of a hanging basket. It has tiny, hairy, dark coppery-green leaves and scarlet and yellow hooded flowers which appear between November and April.

**Good Care Guide**
Provide a temperature no lower than 55° or 60°F (13° or 16°C) in winter and keep the soil moist. Spray and water moderately in summer. Feed every ten days from May to September. Repot every other June in a 10-inch-wide (25-cm) hanging basket containing an all-peat potting compost. Cut out any dead or bare stems. To propagate, plant three-inch-long (8-cm) stem sections as cuttings in pots in spring after flowering.

### Convallaria majalis
LILY OF THE VALLEY

As Lord Byron wrote, ". . . 'tis very silly 'To gild refined gold, or paint the lily,'" and indeed few plants are more perfect than the sweet-smelling Lily of the Valley with its tiny, white, waxy textured, bell-shaped flowers and slender green leaves. It grows about eight inches (20 cm) tall.

**Good Care Guide**
The Lily of the Valley is a short-term pot plant. In October or November plant a dozen single crowns in a 6-inch (15-cm) pot containing any good-quality potting compost. The tops of the crowns should be visible. Place in an unheated but frost-free room. Keep the soil moist. In January bring the plant into a warm—55° to 65°F (13° to 18°C)—room and water freely. Discard after flowering.

### Cyperus alternifolius
UMBRELLA GRASS

Slender, arching, leaf-like, green bracts radiate at the end of long stems, giving this African plant the appearance of a bunch of umbrella frames. In summer small, insignificant, yellowish-brown or green flowers appear from the base of the bracts. The plant rarely exceeds a height of two feet (60 cm) in a pot.

**Good Care Guide**
Provide a winter temperature of about 50° to 55°F (10° to 13°C). Appropriately, the Umbrella Grass loves water, so keep the pot standing in a water-filled saucer. Feed fortnightly from April to September. Repot in April in any good proprietary potting compost. If many new stems appear repot again in the autumn. Cut off old stems. Propagate by division when repotting.

### Cyrtomium falcatum
HOLLY FERN, FISH-TAIL FERN

A native of the Far East, this long-living and attractive fern is a surprisingly tolerant house plant. The arching fronds are about eighteen inches (45 cm) in length and the dark green, glossy pinnules (the leaflets which form the fronds) are about three inches (8 cm) long.

**Good Care Guide**
Protect this fern from sunlight at all times and provide a winter temperature between 45° and 50°F (7° and 10°C). During the April to August growing period feed fortnightly and water liberally. Spray in hot weather. From October to February water sparingly. Repot every other March in any good proprietary potting compost, preferably an all-peat one. Propagate by division when repotting.

### Dichorisandra thyrsiflora
BLUE GINGER

In Brazil this exotic plant reaches a height of about four feet (120 cm), but in a pot it is unlikely to grow taller than about two feet (60 cm). It has shiny, lance-shaped, green leaves with purplish undersides and clusters of blue and yellow flowers, which open in summer.

**Good Care Guide**
This plant requires a temperature of not less than 60°F (16°C) in winter, when the compost should be kept almost dry. From spring to autumn water liberally, feed every two weeks and provide a moist atmosphere by standing the pot on a tray of wet pebbles. Repot every spring in any good proprietary potting compost. Propagate by division when repotting, or by cuttings in summer.

## Dieffenbachia picta
DUMB CANE

*D. picta* has oblong, green leaves which are spattered with large, creamy-white blotches. The plant, which comes from Brazil, grows two to four feet (60 to 120 cm) tall and is highly poisonous. There are several handsome cultivated varieties with different leaf markings.

**Good Care Guide**
If possible provide a winter temperature of not less than 60°F (16°C). *D. picta* will survive at a somewhat lower temperature, but the bottom leaves may yellow and sag dispiritedly. Keep the soil moist at all times, spray regularly and feed every week from March to August. Repot every spring in good-quality potting compost. Propagate by tip or stem-section cuttings if you have a heated propagator.

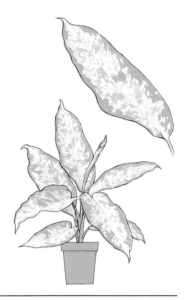

## Dipladenia splendens
PINK ALLAMANDA

This glossy leaved, climbing plant from Brazil may grow more than fifteen feet (4.5 m) tall. When it is only about twelve inches (30 cm) high, large heads of trumpet-shaped, pink flowers appear from June to September.

**Good Care Guide**
The temperature should not fall below 55°F (13°C) in winter. In March, when the new growth begins, move the plant to a warmer room with a temperature not lower than 60°F (16°C). In spring and summer water liberally and spray often. In winter keep the soil just moist. Feed once a week from June to September. Repot every March in any reliable proprietary potting compost. Cut the stems back after flowering. Propagate by cuttings in summer.

## Dizygotheca elegantissima
FALSE ARALIA, FINGER ARALIA

When young, this most elegant plant from the New Hebrides has coppery-red leaves which are divided into several three-inch-long (8-cm), narrow, tooth-edged leaflets. As the plant grows—it can reach a height of up to five feet (150 cm)—the leaves become coarse and dark green.

**Good Care Guide**
In winter provide a temperature of not less than 50°F (10°C) and water sparingly. In summer water moderately. Spray all year round and feed fortnightly from May to August. Repot every other May in any good proprietary potting compost. In March the trunk of an old leggy plant may be cut back to a few inches to induce the formation of young shoots. Propagate by seed in spring.

## Dracaena deremensis
DRAGON PLANT

Each glossy, dark green leaf of this palm-like plant from eastern Africa has two silver stripes running from the base to the tip. The sword-shaped leaves grow up to eighteen inches (45 cm) long, and the plant can eventually reach a height of four feet (120 cm) or more. 'Bausei' and 'Warneckii' are two popular cultivated varieties.

**Good Care Guide**
In winter, do not let the temperature drop below 55°F (13°C). Water liberally during spring and summer and more sparingly in winter. Feed fortnightly from May to September. Repot every other April in any good-quality proprietary potting compost. Propagate by tip or stem-section cuttings in summer, preferably in a heated propagating case.

## Dracaena godseffiana
GOLD-DUST DRACAENA

Quite different in appearance from most other *Dracaena*, this central African shrub has wiry, branching stems bearing three-inch-long (8-cm), oval leaves which are dark green with creamy-yellow spots. Small, pale yellow flowers may appear in spring, followed by red berries. The plant grows to a height of about two feet (60 cm).

**Good Care Guide**
Provide a winter temperature of not less than 45°F (7°C). Keep the soil just moist from spring to autumn. In winter water even less. Feed fortnightly from June to September. Pinch out top shoots in spring. Repot every other April in any good-quality proprietary potting compost. Propagate by cuttings in early summer using a heated propagator.

## Dracaena marginata
'Variegata'
MADAGASCAR DRAGON TREE

This is a tree-like species but it grows very slowly and takes many years to reach a height of four feet (120 cm). The hard, narrow leaves grow up to eighteen inches (45 cm) long and are dark green with pink-tinted, cream stripes.

**Good Care Guide**
Although this plant will tolerate a winter temperature of 50°F (10°C) it prefers it to be between 55° and 60°F (13° and 16°C). Water sparingly in winter, more liberally in spring and summer and feed fortnightly from June to September. Repot every other April in any good-quality proprietary potting compost. Propagate by tip or stem-section cuttings in March or April, preferably in a heated propagator.

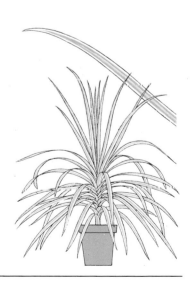

77

An unused fireplace, above left, once the focal point of the room, now provides an excellent setting for a carefully composed arrangement of *Dracaena*, *Dieffenbachia* and sea shells.

Towering *Ficus*, left, add interest to the subtle, neutral tones of this room—a perfect background for plants.

Maximum use is made of the split-level design of this house. *Schefflera* and *Dracaena*, right, and *Dieffenbachia*, above, are positioned to create a visual flow across the room's different levels.

## Fuchsia magellanica
FUCHSIA

*F. magellanica* is an easy plant to grow indoors. It has green leaves and clusters of delicate, half-red and half-purple flowers. There are numerous hybrid cultivated varieties in different colour combinations —the most common are pink and white, pink and red and red and purple.

**Good Care Guide**
In winter the temperature should not fall below 45°F (7°C) and the plant should be watered sparingly. In summer water moderately and spray often. Feed once a week from April to September. Fuchsia likes fresh air on warm days but shield it from direct sunlight. Prune lightly in February then repot in any good-quality proprietary potting compost. Propagate by cuttings in March.

## Fuchsia triphylla
FUCHSIA

Growing to a height of about two feet (60 cm), *F. triphylla* has lance-shaped leaves which are green on top and purplish-red underneath. The dazzling, orange-scarlet flowers grow in pendant clusters and open from July to October. This species is less hardy than *F. magellanica*.

**Good Care Guide**
In winter the temperature should not fall below 50°F (10°C) and the soil should be kept just moist. Spray regularly and water liberally during spring and summer, and feed once a week from April to September. Give the plant plenty of fresh air on warm days. Cut out dead stems and prune leggy plants in February before repotting in any good-quality potting compost. Propagate by cuttings in March.

## Gardenia jasminoides
GARDENIA, CAPE JASMINE

Indigenous to China, the *Gardenia* is a plant that has everything—glossy, dark green leaves all year round and white, waxy, double flowers which open in summer and have a glorious, heavy scent. Growing to a height of two to four feet (60 to 120 cm), the *Gardenia* is fussy in its demands.

**Good Care Guide**
In winter the temperature should be between 55° and 60°F (13° and 16°C). Water liberally in summer, sparingly in winter. If the buds fall it means that you are over- or underwatering. Feed fortnightly and spray often from May to October. Repot every other April in good-quality potting compost. Prune after flowering. Propagate by cuttings in spring or summer, preferably in a heated propagating case.

## Geogenanthus undatus
SEERSUCKER PLANT

The uneven texture of this Peruvian plant's oval leaves is perfectly described by its common name. Mid-green with dark green stripes on top, the leaves are brownish-red underneath. *G. undatus* grows up to a height of twelve inches (30 cm).

**Good Care Guide**
In winter the temperature should not fall below 55°F (13°C). Water liberally in spring and summer and sparingly in winter. All year round spray often with tepid water. Feed once a fortnight from March to August. Repot every April in any good-quality proprietary potting compost. Propagate by cuttings in summer or by division in late spring.

## Graptophyllum pictum
CARICATURE PLANT

An amusing shrub from the East Indies, *G. pictum* has hard, oval, green leaves with white markings which sometimes resemble human faces. The plant grows to a height of two feet (60 cm) or more and bears small clusters of bright crimson flowers which open in summer.

**Good Care Guide**
In winter provide a temperature of about 55°F (13°C) and as much light as possible. Water liberally in spring and summer and keep the soil just moist in winter. Spray in warm weather and shade from the hottest summer sun. Feed once a fortnight from April to September. Repot every April in any good-quality potting compost. Propagate by cuttings from April to June.

## Guzmania lingulata
SCARLET STAR

This plant from the South American rain forests has hard, spear-shaped, eighteen-inch-long (45-cm), green leaves which grow in a funnel-forming rosette. A cluster of yellow-white flowers surrounded by crimson bracts appears in winter.

**Good Care Guide**
Provide a humid atmosphere and a winter temperature of not less than 60°F (16°C). Water liberally in summer, sparingly in winter, preferably using tepid, soft water. Keep the centre of the rosette filled with water except during the winter months. Feed once a month with dilute liquid fertilizer. Repot every second or third spring. To propagate, detach offsets in April and plant in a good-quality potting compost mixed with sphagnum moss.

## Gynura aurantiaca
VELVET PLANT

Brilliant violet hairs cover the stems and velvet-textured, dark green leaves of this Javanese shrub, which grows up to three feet (90 cm) tall. The clusters of small orange flowers, which appear on erect stems in February, have such a strong and pungent scent that some people remove them before they open.

**Good Care Guide**
In winter the temperature should not fall below 55°F (13°C), the plant should be kept in a well-lit position and must be watered sparingly. In summer water liberally. Feed fortnightly from June to September. Repot in April in any good-quality proprietary potting compost. Prune rigorously in March. Propagate by cuttings in summer.

## Howea forsteriana
KENTIA PALM, PARADISE PALM

This is the palm beside which orchestras played in luxury hotels before the Second World War. It has graceful, long-stemmed, dark green leaves, which are divided into numerous slender leaflets. *H. forsteriana*, which comes from the Lord Howe Islands in the Pacific, grows up to ten feet (3 m) tall in a tub.

**Good Care Guide**
Overwinter at about 55°F (13°C) and keep the soil just moist. Water liberally from April to July, then moderately until October. Feed fortnightly from April to September. Cut out any dead leaves. Repot every other April in good-quality potting compost. Propagate by seed in spring; for the best results use a heated propagating case with a temperature of 75° to 80°F (24° to 27°C).

## Hoya bella
MINIATURE WAX PLANT

This sweet-scented plant from India looks at its best in a hanging basket. It has arching branches bearing oval, green leaves which are occasionally spotted with silver. Clusters of small, waxy, white flowers with red-purple centres open from May to September.

**Good Care Guide**
In spring and summer spray regularly and do not let the temperature fall below 60°F (16°C). In winter a temperature of about 55°F (13°C) is ideal. Water liberally in summer, sparingly in winter. Feed fortnightly from March to September. Pinch out the tops of new shoots to encourage bushiness. Repot every other year in April in good-quality potting compost. Propagate by cuttings in summer.

## Hoya carnosa
WAX PLANT

A vigorous climber from Queensland, *H. carnosa* clings on to bark or a moss-covered stick by means of aerial roots. In a tub it can reach a height of twenty feet (6 m). New stems often remain bare for some time before the fleshy green leaves appear. Umbels of pinkish-white, sweet-smelling, star-shaped flowers open from May to September.

**Good Care Guide**
A humid atmosphere and a temperature of not less than 60°F (16°C) is required in spring and summer. In winter keep at about 50°F (10°C). Water liberally in summer, sparingly in winter. Feed fortnightly from May to September. Repot in April in good-quality potting compost. Propagate by cuttings of mature stems in summer.

## Hypocyrta nummularia
MINIATURE POUCH FLOWER

This curiously attractive creeping or hanging plant from Central America has red, hairy stems and fleshy, glossy green leaves. Each red flower is tubular at the base, expanding into a broad pouch with five yellow petals at the mouth. The flowers open in summer.

**Good Care Guide**
In winter the temperature should not fall below 55°F (13°C) and the plant should be watered sparingly. In spring and summer keep the soil just moist and spray regularly. Feed once a month from April to September. Repot every second spring preferably in a peat compost, although any good-quality potting mixture will do. Propagate by shoot-tip cuttings in spring or summer.

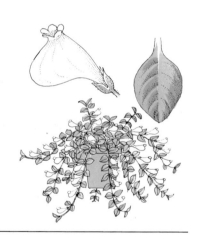

## Kohleria eriantha

From June to September *K. eriantha* bears clusters of partly spotted, scarlet flowers. The stems and leaf margins of this one- to three-foot-tall (30- to 90-cm) plant are covered with purplish-red hairs.

**Good Care Guide**
*K. eriantha* is grown from a rhizome which is planted in February or March in shallow peat. A temperature of 70°F (21°C) is necessary to initiate growth. When the new shoots are a few inches high plant in potting compost, start watering moderately and keep at about 60°F (16°C). Feed fortnightly and spray until flowering finishes. Stop watering when the leaves turn yellow. Cut back the stems and store the rhizome in its pot at a temperature of about 55°F (13°C). Propagate by dividing the rhizome when repotting in spring.

### Manettia bicolor
FIRECRACKER PLANT

With a profusion of fleshy textured, tubular, half-red, half-yellow flowers, which are borne on twining stems like the lights on a Christmas tree, this plant from Brazil will trail or climb as you wish. The flowering season lasts from early spring through to late autumn.

**Good Care Guide**

*M. bicolor*'s resting period begins after flowering has finished, when it should be moved to a room where the temperature is about 50°F (10°C). Water liberally in spring and summer and sparingly in winter. Feed once a week from April to October. Repot every March in any good-quality potting compost. Propagate by cuttings of young shoots in summer.

### Calceolaria × herbeohybrida
SLIPPERWORT, SLIPPER PLANT

This group of hybrids produces a mass of curious, but colourful, pouch-shaped flowers which open from May to July. The flowers are yellow, red or orange with crimson blotches or spots. The green leaves are soft and hairy. Some hybrids grow eighteen inches (45 cm) tall; the dwarf plants attain half this height.

**Good Care Guide**

The Slipperwort is grown in an open cold frame or well-ventilated greenhouse until September, then kept at a temperature of about 50°F (10°C) until in flower. It is then suitable as a house plant until it finishes flowering, when it is discarded. Shade from the hottest sunshine and keep moist. Leave propagation to the professionals.

### Camellia japonica
### 'Adolphe Audusson'
CAMELLIA

The *Camellia* comes from Japan and has glossy, dark green, laurel-like leaves and rose-like, single or double, white, pink, red or variegated flowers which open from February to May. It will reach two to three feet (60 to 90 cm) by the time it is three.

**Good Care Guide**

*C. japonica* needs a temperature of 50° to 55°F (10° to 13°C) when in bud, not more than 60°F (16°C) when in flower and not less than 45° to 50°F (7° to 10°C) the rest of the year. Water liberally from May to July; keep just moist at other times. Feed once a fortnight from December to July. In May prune lightly and repot in an all-peat potting compost. Propagate by stem cuttings or leaf-bud cuttings in summer.

Airy and delicate ferns and palms will look graceful in almost any setting. The elegant fronds of *Howea forsteriana*, above, echo the shape of the arch.

A farmhouse doorway, left, leads into a comfortable room in which glossy, broad-leaved *Asplenium* ferns have the place of honour.

The cool and shadowy greenness of the bedroom, above right, is enhanced by fragile *Dizygotheca* and *Pteris* ferns.

Jardinières with or without matching stands were the Victorians' favourite receptacles for palms. A modern touch, right, is the addition of variegated leaves to the palm.

## Liriope muscari
BLUE LILY TURF

Much admired in the United States, where it is known as the Big Blue Lily Turf, this plant is easy to grow indoors and deserves to be better known in Europe. *L. muscari*, which comes from China and Japan, has broad, grass-like leaves. Spikes of violet-mauve, bell-shaped flowers are borne on twelve-inch-long (30-cm) stems. The flowers open from August to November.

**Good Care Guide**
Provide a winter temperature between 45° and 50°F (7° and 10°C). Water liberally in spring and summer, sparingly in winter. Feed once a fortnight from June to October. Repot every April in any good-quality proprietary potting compost. To propagate, divide the roots of the plant when repotting.

## Maranta leuconeura 'Erythrophylla'
PRAYER PLANT
RED HERRING-BONE PLANT

Sometimes sold as *M. leuconeura* 'Tricolor', this plant has dark green leaves with yellowish-green margins and crimson veins. The plant is small—about eight inches (20 cm) tall—and very decorative.

**Good Care Guide**
In winter provide a temperature of about 55°F (13°C) and water sparingly, but be careful not to let the soil dry out completely. In spring and summer spray and water liberally. Always use tepid, soft water. Feed fortnightly from April to August. No pruning is necessary. Repot every other spring in any good-quality proprietary potting compost. Propagate by dividing the rhizome when repotting.

## Maranta leuconeura 'Kerchoveana'
PRAYER PLANT, RABBIT'S TRACKS

This is a fascinating plant—by day its leaves lie horizontally, but at night they become upright like folded hands. It also has a strangely attractive colour scheme; the leaves are greyish-green with lighter veins and big brown blotches which in time turn dark green. The plant grows to a height of about eight inches (20 cm).

**Good Care Guide**
In winter the most suitable temperature is between 55° and 60°F (13° and 16°C). In spring and summer, spray regularly and water freely with tepid, soft water. Give a fortnightly feed from April to August. Repot every other spring in good-quality potting compost. Propagate by division when repotting.

## Nephrolepis exaltata
SWORD FERN, LADDER FERN

Provided it is protected from draughts, this fern will live for a long time—twelve years or more—indoors. It looks at its best in a hanging basket. The species plant has stiff green fronds which grow about two feet (60 cm) long. There are several cultivated varieties with feathery, arching or spiralling fronds which vary in colour from pale to bright green.

**Good Care Guide**
Provide a winter temperature of not less than 50°F (10°C). Water freely in summer and keep the soil just moist in winter. Feed once a fortnight from March to August. Repot every other year in good-quality potting compost. Propagate by division or by removing the new plants which appear on the runners.

## Nidularium innocentii
BIRD'S NEST

This Brazilian plant blooms in the autumn when a cluster of small white flowers, surrounded by orange bracts, emerges from the centre of the eighteen-inch-high (45-cm) rosette of green, strap-shaped leaves flecked with purple. The undersides of the leaves are deep red.

**Good Care Guide**
In winter the temperature should not drop below 50°F (10°C). Spray often, keep the soil moist and feed once a week from April to September. In autumn and winter keep the soil barely moist. Keep the centre of the rosette filled with water from spring to autumn but allow it to dry out during the winter. Repot every other April in good-quality potting compost. Propagate from well-grown basal offsets in spring or summer.

## Ochna serrulata

A native of Natal, *O. serrulata* is a decorative shrub which grows about four feet (120 cm) tall, but can be kept smaller in a pot. It has glossy, green leaves with serrated edges. The flowers, which open in summer, are yellow and green. The shiny black berries develop several weeks later and are borne on the red and swollen flower centres.

**Good Care Guide**
Weak sun will do no harm to this plant, but it should be kept in light shade and sprayed occasionally during the hottest months. In spring and summer water moderately. In winter keep in a cool but frost-free room and water sparingly. From April to September feed fortnightly. Repot every other spring in any reliable potting compost. Propagate by seed in spring or by cuttings in summer.

## Pellaea rotundifolia
BUTTON FERN, CLIFF BRAKE FERN

A most untypical-looking fern, *P. rotundifolia* has twelve-inch-long (30-cm), dark brown, arching stalks on which waxy, green leaflets grow. These are round on young plants, but oval to oblong on mature ones.

**Good Care Guide**

Although this plant tolerates quite heavy shade it can be kept in a well-lit position if it is shaded from direct sunshine. Overwinter at a temperature of not less than 50°F (10°C). Ventilate and water freely in summer. In winter water sparingly, but never let the soil dry out completely. There is no need to spray. Feed once a fortnight from March to August. Repot every other April in any good proprietary potting compost. Propagate by division when repotting.

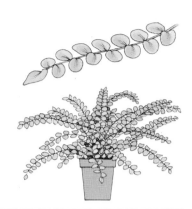

## Pellionia pulchra
DARK NETTING

This plant from the Far East is really a creeper, but is quite happy to trail from a hanging basket. It has purplish, succulent stems and small, silvery-green leaves with red, turning to dark green, markings along the veins.

**Good Care Guide**

Keep in a draught-free position at all times. During the October to January resting period, provide a temperature between 50° and 55°F (10° and 13°C) and water sparingly, never letting the soil dry out completely. In spring and summer water liberally. Feed fortnightly from April to September. Repot every March or April in any good proprietary potting compost. Propagate by division when repotting or by cuttings in spring or summer.

## Phoenix roebelenii
PIGMY DATE PALM

This graceful subtropical palm is a slow-growing and undemanding house plant. After fifteen to twenty years it may grow too large to remain indoors and will then have to be moved to a conservatory.

**Good Care Guide**

The Pigmy Date Palm requires plenty of light, but should not have direct sunlight in summer. In winter the temperature should not fall below 50°F (10°C). Using soft, tepid water, water liberally in summer and sparingly in winter. Never let the soil dry out. From March to October feed weekly after watering. Spray throughout the year. Repot in loamless potting compost every March for the first three years, then repot every two or three years. Propagate by seed.

## Pilea cadierei
ALUMINIUM PLANT

Introduced from Indo-China in 1938, the species plant has dark green, quilted leaves marked with shining, silvery patches. The plant grows about twelve inches (30 cm) tall and tends to become leggy. *P. cadierei* 'Nana', a cultivated variety, is a more compact plant with similarly marked leaves.

**Good Care Guide**

Provide a temperature of not less than 50°F (10°C) in winter, when the plant should be watered moderately. Water freely in spring and summer. Feed once a fortnight from March to September. Spray occasionally. Cut back leggy stems and pinch out new shoots in spring. In April repot in any good proprietary potting compost. Propagate by cuttings in late spring or summer.

## Pilea muscosa (microphylla)
GUNPOWDER PLANT
ARTILLERY PLANT

From May to September *P. muscosa* produces insignificant greenish-yellow flowers which puff out tiny clouds of pollen when the plant is touched. Small, rich green leaves grow profusely on many-branched stems, giving *P. muscosa* a mossy appearance. The plant comes from tropical America and grows six to nine inches (15 to 23 cm) tall.

**Good Care Guide**

A temperature of not less than 50°F (10°C) is desirable in winter. Water freely in spring and summer, moderately in winter, never letting the soil dry out completely. Feed fortnightly from March to September. Spray occasionally. Repot every other April in a good-quality potting compost. Propagate by cuttings in summer.

## Piper ornatum
ORNAMENTAL PEPPER

The pepper we use for seasoning comes from the species *P. nigrum*. *P. ornatum* is, as its name implies, purely ornamental. It has heart-shaped, shiny green leaves, with pale pink dots along the main veins. It comes from Sulawesi (Celebes) and is a plant that will trail or climb.

**Good Care Guide**

*P. ornatum* prefers a winter temperature of not less than 60°F (16°C), but it will survive in slightly cooler conditions, although some leaves may fall. Water moderately all year round and spray regularly. Feed fortnightly from March to August. Repot every other April in good-quality potting compost. Propagate by cuttings in summer, using a propagating case.

85

# The scene-stealers

A windowless bathroom need not be without plants. Here *Saintpaulia ionantha* and *Pilea cadierei* grow successfully in artificial light and bring colour to the room.

Clusters of *Saintpaulia* grace almost any container. A Portuguese soup tureen, top, adds height to these lovely, low-growing plants.

A brass box, the lid propped open with a stick or pencil, makes an unusual, but temporary, container for two *Saintpaulia*.

## Pitcairnia xanthocalyx

*P. xanthocalyx* is native to Mexico and the West Indies and grows about eighteen inches (45 cm) tall. It has rosettes of arching, strap-shaped leaves, which are green on top and white underneath. Tall spikes of yellow flowers open in summer.

### Good Care Guide

Keep this plant either in partial shade or full light but protect it from strong sunshine. Although it can survive a temperature of 50°F (10°C) in winter it will do better at 55° to 60°F (13° to 16°C). Water moderately in spring and summer and sparingly in winter. Spray on hot days. From April to September feed once a month. Repot every second spring in equal parts of potting compost and moss. Propagate in summer by detaching offsets and treating them as cuttings.

## Polystichum acrostichioides

CHRISTMAS FERN, SHIELD FERN

A native of North America, where it is used to decorate homes at Christmas, *P. acrostichioides* has glossy, dark green, feathery fronds which are up to three feet (90 cm) long in the wild. The fronds grow in a dense clump and keep their colour throughout the year. In pots they rarely exceed one to two feet (30 to 60 cm).

### Good Care Guide

Overwinter at a temperature of not less than 50°F (10°C). Water freely from spring to autumn, and keep the soil just moist in winter. Feed once a month from April to September. Repot every second or third April in any good-quality proprietary potting compost. Propagate by division in spring.

## Platycerium bifurcatum

STAG'S-HORN FERN

A humorous and exotic substitute for the stuffed stag's head on the wall, *P. bifurcatum* has antler-shaped fronds which grow up to thirty inches (75 cm) long, and smaller, round, shield-like, supporting fronds. In its natural habitat in Australia this fern grows in trees. Indoors, grow it in a hanging basket.

### Good Care Guide

Provide a winter temperature of not less than 55°F (13°C). Water liberally in spring and summer, and sparingly in winter. Spray regularly in hot weather. Feed fortnightly from April to August. Repot every second or third spring in peat preferably mixed with an equal amount of sphagnum moss. In spring or summer propagate by detaching the plantlets which develop on the roots.

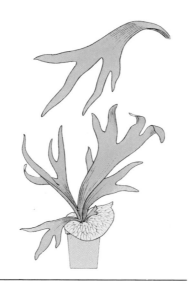

## Primula malacoides

FAIRY PRIMROSE, BABY PRIMROSE

From December until April this native of China, with its rosettes of pale green, oval leaves, is a mass of scented, star-like flowers which range in colour from carmine to dark purple to white.

### Good Care Guide

*P. malacoides* requires a winter temperature between 45° and 55°F (7° and 13°C). It prospers in a semi-shaded location, but needs more light in winter so that the colour of the flowers will not fade. Keep the soil moist at all times. Provide a humid atmosphere by standing the plant on a tray of wet pebbles. Feed every two weeks with liquid fertilizer. Once flowering has ended, the plant is discarded. Propagate by seed in late June or early July.

## Plectranthus oertendahlii

PROSTRATE COLEUS, SWEDISH IVY

Immensely popular in Scandinavia, this creeping plant from South Africa will trail attractively from a hanging basket. The almost round leaves are dark green with silvery-white veins on top and purple underneath. From late winter to early summer loose clusters of bottle-shaped, very pale violet flowers appear on erect stems.

### Good Care Guide

*P. oertendahlii* can survive a temperature of 45°F (7°C) in winter, although a slightly higher temperature is desirable. Water liberally from spring to autumn, but keep the soil only barely moist in winter. Feed fortnightly from March to September. Repot every April in any good potting compost. Propagate by division in spring or by cuttings in spring or summer.

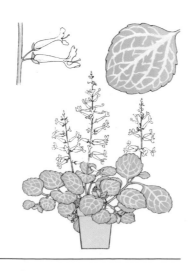

## Primula obconica

PRIMULA

*P. obconica* has umbels of up to fifteen flowers that range in colour from pale pink to blue-purple, and open from December to May. Unfortunately, the large, rounded leaves are covered with short glandular hairs that can cause severe dermatitis to those with sensitive skin.

### Good Care Guide

Overwinter this perennial at a temperature between 50° and 55°F (10° and 13°C). Although it likes a half-shaded position in summer, give it more light in winter. Keep the air humid and the soil fairly damp, but do not spray. Feed with dilute liquid fertilizer every two weeks from August to March. Repot in May after flowering has ceased, using a light, loamless mixture. Propagate by seed at the end of May.

## Pteris cretica
RIBBON FERN

The Ribbon Fern is much admired for its graceful fronds, deeply divided into ribbon-like strips, that can grow as long as twelve inches (30 cm).

**Good Care Guide**

*P. cretica* is a tough plant which makes few demands. It requires a winter temperature no lower than 50°F (10°C). Spray daily to ensure that a moist atmosphere is maintained or stand on a tray of wet pebbles. Water liberally from March to July, but moderately in winter. From March to October feed every two to three weeks with liquid fertilizer. Repot in any good proprietary potting compost in spring, although rapid growth may necessitate a second repotting later in the year. Propagation is usually by division in spring.

## Pteris ensiformis
'Victoriae'
VARIEGATED SWORD BRAKE

*P. ensiformis* 'Victoriae' is a cultivated variety that has arisen from the species plant, *P. ensiformis*, which is found in India, Sri Lanka and Australia. It is an unusual fern because it has green- and white-variegated leaflets. The slender stems grow about eighteen inches (45 cm) tall; some are arched while others are erect.

**Good Care Guide**

In winter the temperature must never fall below 55°F (13°C) and the soil should be kept just moist. In spring and summer water liberally. From April to September feed once a month. Cut out any dead leaves. Repot every other April in any good-quality potting compost. Propagate by division when repotting.

## Quesnelia liboniana

Indigenous to South America, *Q. liboniana* has one- to two-foot-tall (30- to 60-cm) tubular rosettes of tough, slightly serrated leaves, which are green on top and greyish-green underneath. Spikes of red and dark blue flowers open in winter.

**Good Care Guide**

Provide a temperature not lower than 50°F (10°C) in winter. At all times water moderately, keeping the soil just moist. *Q. liboniana* requires a humid atmosphere in hot weather, so spray regularly in summer. From May to September feed once a month. Repot every second spring in equal parts of a good-quality potting compost and moss. Propagate in summer by detaching offsets and treating them as cuttings.

## Rhoicissus rhomboidea
GRAPE IVY, NATAL IVY

This attractive climbing plant from Natal reaches a height of four to six feet (120 to 180 cm) in a pot. The toothed trifoliate leaves of the mature plant are green and shiny, but are covered with hairs when young.

**Good Care Guide**

A spacious north-facing window sill with a temperature no lower than 45°F (7°C) is ideal for *R. rhomboidea*. Give it plenty of fresh air in summer and water moderately all year round. Use a liquid fertilizer fortnightly from April to September. Spray the leaves regularly and sponge them occasionally. Repot in a loam-based compost in April. Pinch out young shoots to encourage bushy growth. Propagation is by cuttings of lateral shoots in spring.

## Saintpaulia ionantha
AFRICAN VIOLET

A native of eastern Africa, the *Saintpaulia* produces long-lasting, violet-like, deep purple, pink or white flowers which peer just above velvety, green, heart-shaped leaves.

**Good Care Guide**

Plenty of light but no direct sun, a temperature between 60° and 70°F (16° and 21°C) all year round and high humidity are required for the African Violet. To keep the soil moist pour tepid water into the base dish and empty the excess after half an hour. Try to avoid wetting the leaves or heart. Use a liquid fertilizer every three or four weeks from April to September. Repot every other April in shallow pots preferably using an all-peat compost. Propagate by seed or leaf cuttings in March or April.

## Sansevieria hahnii
DWARF MOTHER-IN-LAW'S TONGUE
BIRD'S NEST, BOWSTRING HEMP

The four-inch-long (10-cm), dark green leaves of this plant from western Africa form a rosette and are decoratively marked with wavy grey and yellow bands. The leaves of the cultivated variety 'Golden Hahnii' have yellow margins.

**Good Care Guide**

This good-natured plant will tolerate either a shady or sunny position, although it will not thrive in deep shade. In winter keep at a temperature of not less than 50°F (10°C) and water very sparingly. Water more liberally in summer. Feed once a month from May to September with a liquid fertilizer. In spring repot in an all-peat potting compost, but only when the pot is congested or you want to divide the roots.

## Neoregelia carolinae

A spectacular plant from Brazil, *N. carolinae* has a rosette of shiny, green, sword-shaped leaves. At any time of the year a cluster of insignificant flowers may emerge from the centre of the rosette, while the surrounding leaves open out and turn red or purple. The plant grows up to twelve inches (30 cm) tall.

**Good Care Guide**

Provide a winter temperature of not less than 55°F (13°C). Spray the plant and water the compost moderately in summer. Water less in winter. Keep the centre of the rosette filled with water from spring to autumn, but allow it to dry out in winter. Feed fortnightly from April to August. Repot every other April in good-quality potting compost. Propagate by detaching rooted offsets in June.

## Pseuderanthemum kewense (Eranthemum atropurpureum)

The oval, four- to six-inch-long (10- to 15-cm) leaves of this Pacific islands shrub are a striking shade of near black-purple. Springtime sees the arrival of tubular-shaped, red-spotted white flowers in erect spikes.

**Good Care Guide**

The temperature in winter must not fall below 60°F (16°C). A north-facing window sill is best for it. In summer keep the air humid and the soil moist, but water moderately from October to February. Feed every three weeks from April to August with a liquid fertilizer. Repot in early spring using any good proprietary potting compost. To encourage bushiness, pinch out leading growths. Propagate in spring or summer by cuttings of lateral shoots.

## Tillandsia lindeniana
BLUE-FLOWERED TORCH

This Peruvian native is a handsome ornamental plant. It has a rosette of narrow, green leaves and violet-blue flowers that emerge from coral pink bracts. Each flower is short-lived, but there is a continual succession during the summer and the bracts keep their colour for six weeks.

**Good Care Guide**

A winter temperature of not less than 55°F (13°C) and a well-lit, airy location are essential. Water well in hot weather, but keep the soil just moist at other times. In spring and summer give a dilute liquid feed fortnightly. Spray frequently from April to September and daily during the hottest weather. Repot in spring, using equal amounts of sand and leaf-mould or osmunda fibre. Propagate by removing offsets.

A dish garden provides great fun for adults and children alike. Plants that have the same growing requirements can be planted together to create a miniature garden.

A variety of plants can be successfully grown together in a bottle or terrarium. Such gardens make few demands, requiring little or no watering or attention.

## Sansevieria trifasciata 'Laurentii'
MOTHER-IN-LAW'S TONGUE
SNAKE PLANT

Creamy-yellow margins and greyish-green or yellow cross-bandings characterize the fleshy, green, sword-shaped leaves of this ornamental plant from western Africa. When pot grown it rarely exceeds a height of eighteen inches (45 cm).
### Good Care Guide
This plant will grow in sun or shade and tolerates dry air. But do not let the winter room temperature fall below 50°F (10°C). Water moderately in summer, but no more than once a month in winter. Repotting is seldom required, but when it is necessary, do so in spring using any good proprietary potting compost. Propagate by division of the root-stock when repotting.

## Schefflera actinophylla (Brassaia actinophylla)
QUEENSLAND UMBRELLA TREE

The glossy, mid-green leaves of this Australian and Polynesian native are elegant. They divide into long oval, pointed leaflets which increase in number from three to five and eventually to sixteen. This slow-growing plant can reach a height of eight feet (240 cm) in a tub.
### Good Care Guide
The beautiful foliage will drop if the temperature falls below 55°F (13°C). Protect from direct sunlight, but place it in a well-lit position. Keep the air moderately humid and the soil moist all year round. Use a dilute liquid fertilizer once a month from March to September. Repot in any good proprietary potting compost every alternate April. Propagate by seed in February or March.

## Scirpus cernuus (Isolepis gracilis)
SLENDER CLUB RUSH

This small marsh plant from western and southern Europe and northern Africa is an excellent hanging plant, for as it grows its dark, shiny thread-like blades begin to curve over the edges of the pot.
### Good Care Guide
A semi-shaded location suits the Slender Club Rush in summer. To prevent the leaves from acquiring brown tips, spray daily and keep the air moist in spring and summer. In winter give it full light, but the temperature may fall to 40°F (4°C) without harm. The base dish should always contain soft water. Feed every two weeks from March to September. Repot in February in a good potting compost. Propagate by division when repotting.

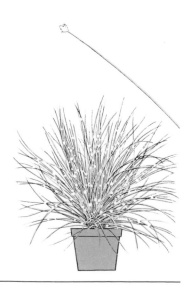

## Selaginella kraussiana
SPREADING CLUB MOSS
CREEPING CLUB MOSS

With its branching filigree of yellow-green, prostrate stems, this little plant from South Africa is both fern-like and mossy in appearance. It looks delightful in a hanging basket, but it may also be grown in a pot.
### Good Care Guide
*S. kraussiana* will survive a winter temperature of 40°F (4°C), but it will thrive if the temperature does not drop below 50° to 55°F (10° to 13°C). Spray often and water moderately in spring and summer, sparingly in winter. Feed once a month from April to October. Repot every April in any good-quality potting compost. Discard the plant when it becomes thin and straggly. Propagate by cuttings in spring or summer.

## Sinningia speciosa
GLOXINIA

The large, velvety, bell-shaped flowers of Gloxinia open from May until October. They vary in colour from crimson to violet and white.
### Good Care Guide
A humid atmosphere is best for Gloxinia. Until flowering ceases, keep the soil moist, then reduce the water and stop completely as leaves turn yellow and the plant dies down. Overwinter the tuber in the pot at 50°F (10°C). Repot it in February, preferably using a proprietary all-peat compost, and keep at a temperature of about 65°F (18°C). When the plant begins to grow water sparingly, increasing the amount as growth strengthens. When the plant is established feed weekly with liquid fertilizer until it flowers. Propagate by seed or leaf and stem cuttings.

## Smithiantha zebrina
TEMPLE BELLS

Indigenous to Mexico, *S. zebrina* has velvety, heart-shaped, reddish mottled leaves and bell-shaped, scarlet flowers with yellow throats which open from June to October.
### Good Care Guide
Give *S. zebrina* liquid fertilizer every two weeks from March until the flowers open. Water liberally in summer; then reduce and finally stop watering a month or so after flowering ceases. Remove the dead leaves and flowers and overwinter the tubers in their pot at a temperature between 50° and 55°F (10° and 13°C). In February repot several tubers together in a 5- or 6-inch (13- or 15-cm) pot using all-peat potting compost. Propagate by division of rhizomes in spring.

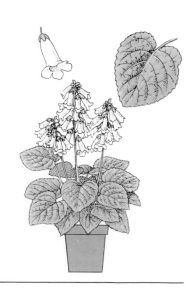

## Spathiphyllum wallisii
PEACE LILY, WHITE SAILS

Here is a house plant grown for its long-lasting flowers and for its attractive, lance-shaped leaves. A pure white spathe encloses the yellow spadix of flowers that first appear in spring and continue off and on until autumn.

**Good Care Guide**
*S. wallisii* appreciates a winter temperature of at least 50°F (10°C) and a light but not sunny position. Spray frequently to provide a humid atmosphere. Keep the soil moist throughout the year. Give a liquid feed every two weeks from April to September, then a weaker mixture monthly. Vigorous growth demands annual repotting in any good potting compost in March or April. Propagation can be carried out at the same time by division.

## Tetrastigma voinieriana
CHESTNUT VINE

This is an imposing climbing plant with exceedingly large, toothed leaves, composed of five dark green leaflets, which is reminiscent of the foliage of the Horse Chestnut tree. *T. voinieriana* is indigenous to Southeast Asia.

**Good Care Guide**
*T. voinieriana* appreciates a well-lit situation, but cannot tolerate direct light or a winter temperature below 55°F (13°C). Spray in spring. Water liberally in summer, but keep almost dry in winter. A dilute liquid feed is advisable weekly from April to August. Repot in a generous-sized pot, using any good proprietary potting compost. Propagate by cuttings in early summer, preferably in a heated propagating case.

## Stephanotis floribunda
MADAGASCAR JASMINE

Bridal bouquets are likely to contain the fragrant, waxy, white flowers of the Madagascar Jasmine. It has glossy, green, oval leaves and blooms indoors from May to October; its vigorous growth should be trained along a secure framework.

**Good Care Guide**
*S. floribunda* will grow spindly unless it overwinters between 55° and 60°F (13° and 16°C) and is given ample light. Spray often to ensure a humid atmosphere and water well from March to September; thereafter keep the soil just moist. Feed generously every fortnight from May to September. Repot in April in a large pot using any good proprietary potting compost. When flowering ends cut back shoots. Propagate by cuttings in summer.

## Tradescantia fluminensis
SPEEDY JENNY

This South American native is an ideal plant for those who claim they cannot grow anything. Its green or purplish stems bear long-lasting, bright green, cream- or white-striped, oval leaves that look attractive in a hanging basket.

**Good Care Guide**
*T. fluminensis* makes very few demands. Place it in good light, but protect it from direct sun. Water liberally during summer and moderately in winter, when the temperature should not fall below 50°F (10°C). Feed every two weeks from March to August. Repot in April, using any good proprietary potting compost. Pinch out the stem tips of the young plant to induce bushiness. Propagate by cuttings of stem tips from April to September.

## Streptocarpus × hybridus
CAPE PRIMROSE, CAPE COWSLIP

The popularity of the Cape Primrose can be attributed to its long flowering season—from May to October. Small clusters of foxglove-like flowers in shades of red, purple and white are borne at the top of wiry stems; at the base is a rosette of wrinkled leaves.

**Good Care Guide**
This group of hybrids prefers a lightly shaded, moist situation with a winter temperature of not less than 50°F (10°C) and with good ventilation in the hottest weather. Water well in summer, but moderately between November and March. Apply a weak liquid feed fortnightly from May to September. Repot every March in a shallow pot filled with any good proprietary potting compost. Propagate by seed in spring or by leaf cuttings in summer.

## Zebrina pendula
WANDERING JEW, ZEBRA PLANT

*Z. pendula*, which comes from Mexico, is easily propagated and virtually indestructible. The green leaves have silvery stripes down the middle. The plant is seen to best advantage in a hanging basket so that the purple and green undersides of the leaves are visible.

**Good Care Guide**
An east- or west-facing window and a winter temperature not lower than 45°F (7°C) will benefit this Mexican species. Give it plenty of water in summer, but practise moderation in winter. A weak liquid feed once a fortnight from March to October is sufficient. Repot in any good potting compost in spring. Pinching out tips of the young plant will induce bushiness. Propagate by cuttings of top shoots in spring.

The decision of where to put your plants is a very personal one and sometimes a difficult one, especially when space is limited. Placing ferns among the crockery on a dresser, top, is one effective idea.

The modern table, above, makes an ideal home for a plant. An Asparagus Fern nestles comfortably in one of the compartments.

Antique wrought-iron oil heaters, right, make magnificent plant stands. An upright plant, such as the Umbrella Grass, is as successful in this setting as the Asparagus Fern which trails over the stand.

# *Fitting in with the furniture*

This attractive wooden planter has been specially designed to show plants to their best advantage. For maximum versatility it is mounted on castors so that it can be moved about easily.

A carved wooden camel makes an exotic stand for an *Asplenium* fern.

# Plants for warm rooms

Warmth and humidity are necessary if tropical plants are to thrive. Tropical flowering plants also require plenty of light. Although such conditions are more easily provided in a conservatory, these plants can be successfully cultivated in well-heated homes. Regular mist spraying, however, will have to be provided to make up for the lack of moisture in the air. There are two striking climbers that like warm and light conditions—the yellow *Allamanda cathartica* and the scarlet and white *Clerodendrum thomsonae*. Among the invaluable shade-loving plants in this group are the various *Ficus*, *Monstera deliciosa* and the *Philodendron*. The delicate *Adiantum raddianum* and the very bold *Blechnum gibbum* are two lovely ferns. And there is *Mimosa pudica*, which more than two centuries ago reduced the Chinese Emperor Ch'ien Lung to fits of laughter when first he saw it.

## Direct light

### Clerodendrum thomsonae
BLEEDING HEART VINE

This evergreen climber from western Africa has deep green, oval leaves and clusters of blossoms consisting of creamy-white, heart-shaped calyces enclosing bright red, starry flowers.

**Good Care Guide**
This plant likes plenty of light but not direct hot sun in summer. From October to February keep it in a light place at 50°F (10°C) and water sparingly. Move to a warmer room and begin watering in mid-February. In summer water well, then lessen the water gradually from September. Spray regularly in the spring. Feed fortnightly from March to September. Prune old branches right back in spring and repot in any good-quality proprietary potting compost. Propagate by cuttings in the spring.

### Clianthus formosus (C. dampieri)
GLORY PEA

This eye-catching prostrate plant has a short life, but it is worth growing for its furry, silver leaves and stems and its extraordinary, claw-shaped flowers, which are bright red with black blotches. The flowers open from June to September. A native of Australia, *C. formosus* looks at its best trailing from a hanging pot or basket.

**Good Care Guide**
Although a short-lived perennial this plant is best treated as an annual because it usually dies after flowering. Keep in full light in a warm, airy room and water sparingly from below. From May to September feed every two weeks. Propagate by seed in spring in a heated propagator at a temperature of 75°F (24°C).

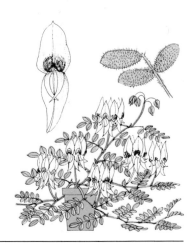

### Clerodendrum speciosissimum
JAVA GLORYBEAN

In summer tiered clusters of bright scarlet flowers are borne on long stems which rise above the hairy, heart-shaped, green leaves of this Javanese shrub. Grown in a pot, *C. speciosissimum* reaches a height of about three feet (90 cm).

**Good Care Guide**
Although this plant needs plenty of light, it should be shaded from very hot sunshine. It will thrive best if it is kept at a temperature of not less than 55°F (13°C) in winter, when it should be watered sparingly. In spring and summer water liberally. From May to September feed fortnightly. Repot every April in any good-quality potting compost. Prune rigorously after flowering ends. Propagate by cuttings in summer.

### Crossandra undulifolia (infundibuliformis)

This plant has vivid orange-red flowers which appear from spring until autumn. Native to Sri Lanka and India, it can grow to a height of three feet (90 cm), but it seldom exceeds half this size in a pot.

**Good Care Guide**
The winter temperature should not fall below 60°F (16°C). Shade from the hottest sun in summer, but give the plant plenty of direct light in winter. Always maintain a humid atmosphere by standing the plant on a tray of wet pebbles. Water liberally from March to September and moderately for the rest of the year. From April to August feed fortnightly with liquid fertilizer. Repot in spring preferably using an all-peat compost. Propagate by cuttings in summer.

## Euphorbia fulgens
SCARLET PLUME

Scarlet, petal-shaped bracts surround insignificant orange flowers which cover the slender, arching branches of this elegant, four-foot-tall (120-cm) Mexican shrub from November to February.
**Good Care Guide**
In winter the temperature should be between 55° and 60°F (13° and 16°C) and the plant should be watered sparingly. About a month after flowering ceases gradually dry the plant off. In April move to a warmer room, about 65°F (18°C), moisten the soil and increase humidity. From June to September feed every two weeks. Repot every other March in any good potting compost. Prune during the dry dormant period. Propagate from young shoots that arise on the plant after pruning.

## Musa velutina

A dramatic-looking plant which could be the dominant feature of a large room, *M. velutina*, from Assam, grows four feet (120 cm) tall and five feet (150 cm) wide. The large leaves, which are pure green or green blotched with maroon, grow on pink stems in clumps. Clusters of yellow flowers with red bracts open from June to August, followed by enticing but inedible red fruit.
**Good Care Guide**
In winter the temperature should never fall below 60°F (16°C) and the soil should be kept barely moist. In spring and summer water liberally. From May to September feed fortnightly with dilute fertilizer. Cut out dead flower stems. Repot every other March in any good-quality potting compost. Propagate by division before repotting.

## Pandanus veitchii
SCREW PINE

The Pacific islands of Polynesia are home to this *Pandanus*. Arranged in a large rosette its narrow, evergreen leaves grow to a length of two to three feet (60 to 90 cm) in a pot. The leaves are spiny margined and strikingly tipped and bordered with creamy-white bands.
**Good Care Guide**
*P. veitchii* demands a winter temperature no lower than 65°F (18°C). Use tepid water liberally in spring and summer, but moderately in winter. It should be fed every fortnight from March until October and sprayed in summer. Repot in any good proprietary potting compost in March. To propagate, remove suckers from the base of the plant when they have about six leaves and treat as cuttings.

## Plectranthus coleoides
'Marginatus'
CANDLE PLANT

This low, bushy plant from India has oval, rich green leaves with irregular white margins. The white and purple flowers are insignificant.
**Good Care Guide**
If the sun is particularly fierce during the summer months, shade *P. coleoides* during the hottest part of the day. In winter the ideal temperature for this plant is between 55° and 60°F (13° and 16°C). Water well in summer, but the soil should be only just moist in winter. In March prune vigorously to improve the shape of the plant. Repot in April using any good proprietary potting compost. The best time to propagate is in spring, either by stem-tip cuttings or by division.

## Sanchezia nobilis

The eye is immediately attracted to the bold, yellow, vein pattern on the long, oval leaves of *S. nobilis*. In late autumn clusters of handsome yellow flowers emerge from the bright red bracts of this South American shrub.
**Good Care Guide**
Overwinter at not less than 50°F (10°C), and always shade from the hottest sun. To ensure humid conditions, spray daily with tepid water or stand on a tray of moist peat or pebbles. Always keep the soil moist but less so during the winter months. Feed every two or three weeks throughout the year with dilute liquid fertilizer. Prune adult plants heavily in early spring, then repot, using any good proprietary compost. Propagate by stem cuttings in summer.

## Tacca chantrieri
BAT FLOWER, CAT'S WHISKERS

This bizarre and intriguing South-east Asian plant has a tuft of long-stalked, corrugated, olive-green, lance-shaped leaves. The clusters of maroon-black flowers also grow on long stalks. They are protected by dark purple bracts and have whiskery filaments which are up to twelve inches (30 cm) long. The plant grows about two feet (60 cm) tall.
**Good Care Guide**
Ideally the temperature in winter should not fall below 60°F (16°C). Water liberally in spring and summer, but keep the soil just moist in winter. Feed every two to three weeks from April to September. Repot every other April using any good-quality potting compost. Propagate by division in spring.

## *Allamanda cathartica*
COMMON ALLAMANDA

A native of Brazil, this vigorous tropical climber with its brilliant yellow, trumpet-shaped flowers, which open from June to October, can grow to a height of twenty feet (6 m) or more, but can be kept less than half this size in a large pot.

**Good Care Guide**

*A. cathartica* requires a humid atmosphere and a winter temperature no less than 55°F (13°C). In summer protect from sun during the hottest part of the day. Water liberally during warm weather, but sparingly in autumn and winter. From April to September feed fortnightly. Repot in February or March in any good proprietary potting compost. To encourage bushiness prune in February. Propagate by cuttings in late spring in a heated propagator.

## *Ananas comosus* 'Variegatus'
PINEAPPLE

Indigenous to South America, the centre of *A. comosus* 'Variegatus' is flushed red and the leaves are striped creamy-white. It bears dense spikes of purple flowers that give way to fruit.

**Good Care Guide**

*A. comosus* thrives in a warm, draught-free room whose winter temperature must not fall below 55°F (13°C). Keep the plant moist throughout the year, although less so in winter. It should flower when it is two or three years old. Once flowering has ended, use liquid fertilizer sparingly. Suckers then develop while the parent stem dies; these can be removed with roots and repotted in any good proprietary potting compost.

## *Ruellia macrantha*
CHRISTMAS PRIDE

The large, trumpet-shaped, purple flowers of *R. macrantha* appear mainly in clusters, from late autumn to spring. The plant, a perennial, grows to about three feet (90 cm).

**Good Care Guide**

To encourage flowering keep *R. macrantha* at a winter temperature of 55° to 60°F (13° to 16°C). In summer shade lightly during the sunniest time of the day. Water regularly throughout the year. After the first year feed fortnightly with weak liquid fertilizer from October to June. In September repot in any good proprietary potting compost. When flowering ceases cut back the shoots to within three inches (8 cm) of the base. Propagate in spring using the shoots that grow after pruning as cuttings.

Plants used temporarily as the centrepiece of a table setting can be grouped for their visual qualities rather than for their growing requirements. Variegated Ivy, white African Violets and the Button Fern, top, echo the green and white of the patterned curtains.

The exciting appliqué wall-hanging in the modern dining-room, above, is complemented by a group of Kentia Palms and a simple table arrangement of African Violets.

In a skilfully arranged table decoration, right, *Dracaena*, *Maranta* and *Begonia* effectively repeat the colours of this beautiful period room.

# Plants for warm rooms

## Partial shade

## Adiantum raddianum (A. cuneatum)
DELTA MAIDENHAIR

The Delta Maidenhair has light green, finely dissected fronds. Often reaching a height of eighteen inches (45 cm) it is a perfect fern for a hanging basket.

**Good Care Guide**
Although it is indigenous to Brazil, this species will tolerate a winter temperature as low as 50°F (10°C). Place it in a north-facing window or semi-shaded situation. Spray often, particularly from March to August, to ensure a humid atmosphere. Water liberally during summer and never allow the soil to dry out. Apply a very dilute fertilizer monthly from April to August. Repot in spring, preferably using a proprietary all-peat compost. At the same time propagate by division.

## Aeschynanthus speciosus

A hanging planter is ideal for this Indonesian perennial. It has pale green leaves and long, trailing stems which carry terminal clusters of bright orange, tubular-shaped flowers from July to September.

**Good Care Guide**
A. speciosus should be positioned in partial shade throughout the year. The winter temperature must not fall below 55°F (13°C). To maintain a humid environment during its growing season in spring and summer, spray frequently with tepid water. Water sparingly from November to February; thereafter use tepid water to keep the soil moist. Feed occasionally from March to August. Repot every two to three years in March or April using an all-peat compost. Propagate by tip cuttings in summer.

## Aglaonema commutatum
CHINESE EVERGREEN

Reaching a height of about six inches (15 cm), this compact Southeast Asian perennial has attractive, dark green, lance-shaped leaves with silvery markings. Very small, waxy, white spathes, appear in July.

**Good Care Guide**
A. commutatum will thrive if it is protected from direct sunlight and if it overwinters at a temperature not lower than 50°F (10°C). It appreciates a moist atmosphere and will do well on a tray of wet pebbles or moist peat. Water well from April to August, but sparingly in winter. Give a liquid feed every two weeks during the growing season. Repot every other spring using a proprietary all-peat compost. Propagate by cuttings in summer.

## Aglaonema pictum
CHINESE EVERGREEN

Malaya and Borneo are home to this elegant plant with its magnificent foliage. Each leaf, up to eight inches (20 cm) long, is covered with irregular patches in three different shades of green. Creamy-yellow spathes are borne in August.

**Good Care Guide**
This evergreen perennial will not tolerate a winter temperature below 50°F (10°C), needs to be shaded from direct light and kept away from oil and gas fumes. It thrives in a moist atmosphere; if possible stand it on a tray of wet pebbles or moist peat. Water liberally and feed fortnightly from April to August, but keep the soil only just moist during winter. Repot in April, preferably in a proprietary all-peat compost. Propagate by cuttings in summer.

## Bertolonia marmorata
JEWEL PLANT

The bright green leaves of this small, beautiful, Brazilian plant are heavily splashed with silvery-white on top and flushed with purple underneath. Tiny purple flowers sometimes appear in summer.

**Good Care Guide**
Keep at a temperature not lower than 60°F (16°C) at all times. Provide a humid atmosphere by standing the plant on a tray of wet pebbles or moist peat. Water moderately in spring and summer. In winter keep the soil barely moist. From April to September feed once a month. Repot every second May or June in pans containing an all-peat potting compost. Propagate by careful division or by cuttings in summer; a heated propagating case gives best results.

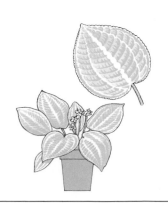

## Blechnum gibbum

*B. gibbum* is a handsome fern from New Caledonia (Western Pacific) which may reach a height of three feet (90 cm) at maturity. Its large fronds are divided into narrow, stiffly held segments that give the appearance of a palm-like crown.

**Good Care Guide**
This fern is accustomed to a warm climate and, therefore, the winter temperature should not fall below 55°F (13°C). It benefits from a humid atmosphere in spring and summer. From March to July feed fortnightly with dilute liquid fertilizer and water liberally; at other times water sparingly. Repot preferably in a proprietary all-peat compost. Propagation is by offsets when these occur or by spores in spring or summer.

## Campelia zanonia
### 'Mexican Flag'

Striking, green- and cream-striped leaves with red margins grow in clusters on this Mexican plant's erect stems. Small white flowers, sometimes spotted or flushed with purple, appear in summer.

**Good Care Guide**
Never let the temperature drop below 50°F (10°C). Provide a humid atmosphere by standing the plant on a tray of wet pebbles or moist peat. In spring and summer water moderately. In winter keep the soil just moist. From April to September feed fortnightly. Discard the plant after one or two years when it is about three feet (90 cm) tall and bare at the base. Take cuttings in summer, plant them in any good-quality potting compost and keep humid until rooted.

## Codiaeum variegatum pictum
CROTON, SOUTH SEA LAUREL

The leaves of this Malaysian evergreen come in many shapes; common colour combinations include green and pink, scarlet and orange or nearly black and orange.

**Good Care Guide**
*C. variegatum pictum* is fairly demanding. It should be placed on the sill of an east- or west-facing window to ensure ample light. In winter see that the temperature does not fall below 60°F (16°C) and water sparingly. Water liberally and feed fortnightly from April to September. Spray regularly all year. In spring repot in a proprietary all-peat potting compost. Pinch out shoot tips to encourage bushiness. Propagate by tip cuttings using a heated propagating case.

## Cryptanthus acaulis
GREEN EARTH STAR

Although it is only three inches (8 cm) tall, *C. acaulis* will enhance any arrangement of small indoor plants. Indigenous to Brazil, it has a compact rosette of broad, prickle-toothed leaves that are mid-green above and white and scaly beneath.

**Good Care Guide**
The Green Earth Star is easy to grow. See that it has plenty of light, although no direct sun. Humidity and a winter temperature that remains between 55° and 60°F (13° and 16°C) are also necessary. Keep the soil moist in summer, almost dry in winter. Feeding is not essential. Repot in April and May using a proprietary all-peat compost and a small or shallow pot. Propagate by offsets in April.

## Cryptanthus bromelioides
### 'Tricolor'
RAINBOW STAR

Prominent cream-and-white-striped leaves with pink-tinged margins characterize this stemless plant from Brazil. Although its flowers are insignificant, *C. bromelioides* 'Tricolor' produces handsome offsets.

**Good Care Guide**
Overwinter at a temperature of about 60°F (16°C) and place in a humid, well-lit situation out of direct sunlight. In summer water moderately to prevent the soil ball drying out and keep the leaf rosette filled with tepid water. Very little water is required in winter. Feed once a month from April to September. Repot in April and May in a small pot or shallow bowl ideally using a proprietary all-peat compost. Propagate by offsets in late spring.

## Ctenanthe oppenheimiana
### 'Variegata'
NEVER-NEVER PLANT

This attractive foliage plant from Brazil bears somewhat fan-shaped sprays of oblong to oval leaves. The upper surface of each leaf is boldly splashed with white and has silver-grey bands; the lower surface is purple-red.

**Good Care Guide**
This species needs shading from direct sunlight and benefits from a humid environment in summer. Keep the soil just moist at all times, but water even less in winter and see that the temperature does not fall below 55°F (13°C). Feed every two weeks from spring to autumn. Repot in any good proprietary potting compost, preferably an all-peat one. Propagate by division in late spring.

The simplicity of stone-coloured, hand-thrown pottery contrasts with the intricate markings of *Calathea*, the colouring of *Begonia* and the grass-like texture of *Scirpus*.

Mixing plants and paintings demands a sense of visual balance and the courage of your convictions. *Dracaena*, *Anthurium* and *Pellaea rotundifolia* are an unlikely but successful combination.

A simple group of mixed *Peperomia* brings out the richness of the muted pinks and golds of the Victorian-style wallpaper and draws attention to the accessories on the table.

The extraordinary white-veined leaves of *Fittonia argyroneura*, grouped in and around Indian brass-bound coconut shells on a coffee table, invite closer inspection.

## Episcia cupreata
FLAME VIOLET

Only when *E. cupreata* is placed in a hanging basket can its magnificent foliage be fully appreciated. Its downy, oval, mid-green leaves have a red and silver band down the centre. From June to September it bears bright red flowers.

**Good Care Guide**
In winter the temperature should ideally not fall below 55°F (13°C). Stand on a tray of wet pebbles or moist peat or, if you are growing the plant in a hanging basket, regularly spray the basket and undersides of the leaves. Always keep the soil moist, but water less in winter. Apply a dilute liquid fertilizer every two weeks from April to September. Repot in April in a pan or basket, using a proprietary all-peat compost. Propagate by runners in summer.

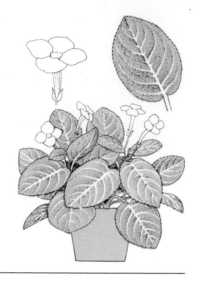

## Episcia dianthiflora
LACE FLOWER

This Mexican evergreen with lovely, dark green, oval leaves is eminently suitable for a hanging basket. Its beauty is enhanced by the summertime blooming of its delicately fringed white flowers.

**Good Care Guide**
*E. dianthiflora* needs a winter temperature of not less than 50°F (10°C). Stand the plant on a tray of wet pebbles or moist peat. If you are growing the plant in a hanging basket spray the basket and the undersides of the leaves. Water regularly throughout the year but less in winter. Every two weeks, from April to August, feed with a dilute liquid fertilizer. In April repot in a basket or pan, using a proprietary all-peat compost. Propagate by runners in spring or summer.

## Ficus benjamina
WEEPING FIG

A graceful tree with arching or pendulous side branches, *F. benjamina* has slender, pointed leaves which are grass green when they first appear and become darker later. In the Indian jungle it grows to forty feet (12 m) in height. Indoors in a large pot it is unlikely to grow taller than six feet (180 cm).

**Good Care Guide**
*F. benjamina* appreciates a humid atmosphere at all times. Do not let the temperature fall below 50°F (10°C) in winter, when the soil should be kept just moist. In spring and summer water liberally. Feed fortnightly from May to September. Pruning is seldom necessary. Repot every other April in any good-quality potting compost. Propagate by cuttings in summer.

## Ficus elastica decora
RUBBER PLANT

The dignified *F. elastica*, much loved by the Victorians, is seldom seen today. It is the cultivated variety, *F. elastica decora*, with its single stem and large, glossy, dark green leaves, which keeps vigil in so many office reception rooms. In tropical Asia it may reach one hundred feet (30 m). Indoors it grows to about six feet (180 cm) in a large pot.

**Good Care Guide**
Overwinter at not less than 60°F (16°C) and keep the soil just moist. In spring and summer water liberally. Feed fortnightly from May to September. Sponge the leaves regularly. Repot every other April in any good-quality proprietary potting compost. Propagate by leaf-bud or stem-tip cuttings in summer, using a heated propagating case.

## Fittonia argyroneura
SILVER NET LEAF

An exquisitely delicate network of white veins covers the bright green leaves of this low-growing plant from Peru. Occasionally inconspicuous flowers develop, but they are best pinched out before they open.

**Good Care Guide**
A suitable plant for modern heated houses, *F. argyroneura* needs a temperature of not less than 60°F (16°C) in winter, when it should be watered sparingly. In spring and summer water liberally and spray regularly. Feed once a fortnight from June to September. Cut back untidy stems in March. Repot in April in any good-quality potting compost, preferably an all-peat kind. Propagate by cuttings or by division in late spring or summer.

## Fittonia verschaffeltii
PAINTED NET LEAF

From a distance the leaves of this creeping plant look purple, but this is just an illusion created by the network of red veins which spreads across the dark green leaves. *F. verschaffeltii* comes from Peru and is easier to grow than its relative *F. argyroneura*.

**Good Care Guide**
The temperature should not fall lower than 55°F (13°C) in winter. In spring and summer water liberally and spray often. In winter water sparingly, but never let the soil dry out completely. Give a fortnightly feed from June to September. Prune lightly in spring. Repot in April preferably using an all-peat compost. Propagate by cuttings or by division in late spring or summer.

## Hemigraphis colorata
RED IVY

A native of Malaysia, *H. colorata* is seen at its best in a hanging basket. The leaves are metallic violet-purple on top and reddish-purple underneath. Small white flowers open in summer.

**Good Care Guide**
Like many tropical plants, *H. colorata* requires warmth and a humid atmosphere throughout the year, so do not let the temperature drop below 55°F (13°C) and spray regularly all year round. In spring and summer water liberally. In winter keep the soil just moist. Feed once a fortnight from May to September. In late winter cut back any straggling stems. Repot every March or April using any good-quality potting compost. Propagate by cuttings in late spring or summer.

## Hypoestes sanguinolenta
FRECKLE-FACE

In comparison to its downy, dark green leaves, which have numerous pink spots and red veins, this plant's pale lilac, white and purple flowers, which open in summer, are insignificant and may be pinched out. *H. sanguinolenta*, which comes from Madagascar, grows about twenty inches (50 cm) tall.

**Good Care Guide**
Overwinter at a temperature of not less than 55°F (13°C). Water liberally in spring and summer. In winter water judiciously, keeping the soil just moist. Spray regularly. Feed once a week from June to September. In spring cut back leggy stems and pinch out top shoots to encourage bushiness. Repot in April in any good-quality potting compost. Propagate by cuttings in summer.

## Hypoestes taeniata

Indigenous to Madagascar and very similar in habit to *H. sanguinolenta* this species has glamorous purple flowers which are protected by pink bracts and grow at the end of long stems. The flowers, which look down on the mid-green leaves, open in autumn and early winter.

**Good Care Guide**
In winter the temperature should not fall below 55°F (13°C) and the plant should be watered sparingly. In spring and summer water liberally. Spray regularly or stand on a tray of wet pebbles or moist peat. Feed once a week from June to October. Pinch out top shoots in spring to keep the plant bushy. Repot every April in any good-quality potting compost or propagate annually by cuttings in spring.

## Medinilla magnifica
ROSE GRAPE

*M. magnifica* comes from the Philippines and Java. It has large, boldly veined, leathery, green leaves and clusters of rose-pink and purple flowers, which are borne on long pendulous stems and open from April to August. In a large pot or tub it grows to a height of four or five feet (120 or 150 cm).

**Good Care Guide**
In winter the temperature should not fall below 60°F (16°C). Water liberally in spring and summer and more sparingly in winter. Spray regularly. Feed once a fortnight from April to September. If the plant becomes straggly, cut it back after flowering. Repot every other April in an all-peat proprietary potting compost. Propagate by cuttings in late spring in a heated propagator.

## Microcoelum martianum (Syagrus or Cocos weddelliana)
DWARF COCONUT PALM
TERRARIUM PALM

The ideal palm for a small room, *M. martianum* takes about twenty years to reach its full height of six feet (180 cm). It has elegant, arching stems bearing long, narrow, green leaflets.

**Good Care Guide**
In winter the temperature should never fall below 60°F (16°C). Spray often throughout the year. From May to September feed fortnightly and water liberally. At other times keep the soil just moist—the leaves will turn brown if the soil dries out completely. Repot every other April in any reliable proprietary potting compost. Propagate in spring by seed, using a heated propagator.

## Mimosa pudica
SENSITIVE PLANT, HUMBLE PLANT

From Brazil, here is the performing plant! Touch its feathery green leaves in daylight hours and watch them fold and droop. After about thirty minutes they rise and spread again. Cultivated as an annual, this intriguing plant grows about two feet (60 cm) tall and bears small, ball-like, pink flower clusters in summer.

**Good Care Guide**
Keep the soil moist at all times. From June to September spray regularly and feed fortnightly with liquid fertilizer. Discard the plant in late autumn, when it becomes unsightly. Propagate by seed in spring in a temperature of 65° to 70°F (18° to 21°C). The seedlings should be planted in any good-quality potting compost.

## Peperomia caperata
### 'Emerald Ripple'

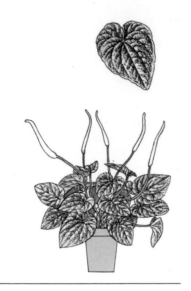

Heart-shaped and deeply corrugated, the leaves of this small plant grow in a dense clump on pinkish stems which are rarely more than three inches (8 cm) long. The leaves are dark green with a silvery-grey sheen. Six-inch-long (15-cm), slender, white flower spikes, which are sometimes branched, are borne on long stems from April to December.

**Good Care Guide**
Overwinter at a temperature not lower than 50°F (10°C). Water moderately in spring and summer and sparingly in winter, always letting the soil dry out between watering. Spray on hot days. Feed once a month from May to September. In April repot in any good-quality potting compost. Propagate by leaf cuttings from April to August.

## Sonerila margaritacea
### 'Argentea'
PEARLY SONERILA

Heavily speckled with silvery-white spots, the four-inch-long (10-cm), dark green, oval leaves of this low-growing, Javanese plant have purple undersides and red stems. Clusters of purplish-pink flowers open from May to September.

**Good Care Guide**
The leaves of this plant may fall if it is kept at a temperature lower than 60°F (16°C) in winter. Always keep the soil just moist, but water even less in winter. From May to September feed fortnightly. Provide a humid atmosphere by standing the plant on a tray of wet pebbles or moist peat. Repot every other April in any good-quality potting compost. Propagate by cuttings taken in April, May or June.

## Vriesea splendens
FLAMING SWORD

Indigenous to Guyana, *V. splendens* has strap-shaped, dark green leaves with brown-purple cross bands. The leaves are fifteen inches (38 cm) long and grow in a rosette. In late summer an eighteen-inch (45-cm) sword-like spike emerges from the centre of the rosette, bearing small yellow flowers enclosed in red bracts.

**Good Care Guide**
Keep in a humid atmosphere at a temperature not less than 60°F (16°C) at all times. In spring and summer water the compost liberally. In winter keep it barely moist. Pour a little water into the centre of the rosette in summer. From April to September feed fortnightly. Repot every second March in equal parts of sand, peat and sphagnum moss. Propagate from offsets in spring.

*Philodendron* and *Fittonia* brighten a dark bathroom, above. The brass containers echo the fittings.

The glossy leaves of *Fatsia japonica*, × *Fatshedera lizei* and *Cissus antarctica*, left, add the finishing touch to this charming bathroom.

The traditional white enamel of a bathroom, right, provides an excellent backdrop to the richly coloured foliage of such plants as *Dracaena*, *Begonia*, *Maranta* and *Tradescantia*.

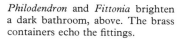

*Asplenium* ferns, top, and the delicate coloured Maidenhair Ferns, above, contrast well with cork-lined walls. These shade-loving plants particularly enjoy the humid atmosphere of the bathroom.

## Monstera deliciosa
SWISS CHEESE PLANT

Large holes naturally occur in this popular Mexican plant's deeply slashed, shield-shaped, leathery, green leaves. After many years it may reach a height of twenty feet (6 m) in a large tub. Arum-like, creamy-white, flowering spathes appear on the mature plant, followed by edible pineapple-flavoured fruit. Grow it up a moss-covered stick so that its aerial roots can find support.

**Good Care Guide**
Overwinter at not less than 55°F (13°C). In spring and summer water liberally and spray often. Keep the soil just moist in winter. From April to September feed fortnightly with dilute fertilizer. Repot every second or third April in an all-peat compost. Propagate by stem-tip or leaf-bud cuttings in summer.

## Oplismenus hirtellus 'Variegatus'
BASKET GRASS

This creeping grass from the West Indies has slender stems which root easily at the joints where the white-and-pink-striped, narrow, lance-shaped leaves appear. O. hirtellus will trail attractively from a hanging basket or a wall pot, or will provide attractive ground-cover.

**Good Care Guide**
Although O. hirtellus will tolerate a temperature of 45°F (7°C), for good winter growth 55°F (13°C) is necessary. In spring and summer water liberally. In winter keep the soil just moist. Feed fortnightly from May to September. In April repot in any good-quality potting compost. Propagate by division when re-potting or by removing rooted shoots in spring or summer.

## Peperomia argyreia
WATERMELON PEPEROMIA

From a distance the red stems of this Brazilian plant appear to be bearing strange-looking, round fruit. This is an illusion created by the pattern on the leaves—curved, silver-grey, feathery edged bands lead from a point just off-centre to the tip of each dark green leaf. The plant grows about nine inches (23 cm) tall.

**Good Care Guide**
In winter the temperature should not be lower than 55°F (13°C) and the plant should be watered very sparingly. Water moderately in spring and summer. Always let the soil dry out between watering. From May to September feed once a month. Spray in hot weather. In April repot in any good-quality potting compost. Propagate by leaf cuttings in summer.

## Peperomia hederifolia
IVY-LEAVED PEPEROMIA

A restrained little plant from Brazil, P. hederifolia grows to a height of about six inches (15 cm). Borne on pink stems, the heart-shaped, quilted-looking leaves of this species are a subtle silver-grey with dark green veins.

**Good Care Guide**
In winter provide a well-lit position at a temperature of about 50°F (10°C) and water sparingly, keeping the plant almost dry. In spring and summer water moderately, allowing the compost to dry out between watering. Provide a humid atmosphere by standing the plant on a tray of wet pebbles or moist peat. Feed fortnightly from April to September. Repot annually or biennially in April in good potting compost. Propagate by leaf cuttings in summer.

## Peperomia magnoliifolia
DESERT PRIVET

The species plant, which has glossy green leaves borne on purplish stems, is not often seen today, but two variegated cultivated varieties, 'Variegata' and 'Green Gold', which have green-and-cream leaves, are excellent substitutes. They grow to about six inches (15 cm) in height.

**Good Care Guide**
Overwinter at not less than 50°F (10°C) and keep the soil barely moist. In spring and summer water moderately. Provide a humid atmosphere by standing the plant on a tray of wet pebbles or moist peat. Spray in hot weather. From March to September feed fortnightly. Repot every April in any good potting compost. Pinch out tips of new shoots in summer to promote bushiness. Propagate by stem cuttings from April to August.

## Philodendron andreanum (P. melanochryson)
VELOUR PHILODENDRON

This handsome climber from Colombia grows to a height of four to six feet (120 to 180 cm) in a large pot and needs support. The heart-shaped, white-veined, velvety green leaves have purplish undersides.

**Good Care Guide**
In winter the temperature should not fall below 55°F (13°C). From April to October water liberally. At other times keep the soil just moist. From May to September feed fortnightly. Provide a humid atmosphere by standing the plant on a tray of wet pebbles or moist peat. Spray in hot weather. Repot every second April in one of the proprietary all-peat composts. Propagate by stem-tip or leaf-bud cuttings in summer.

## Philodendron oxycardium (P. scandens)

PARLOUR IVY

HEART-LEAF PHILODENDRON

Tolerant of deep shade and polluted air, *P. oxycardium*, from Panama, is one of the easiest plants to grow. Its heart-shaped, green leaves are borne on thin stems which will climb to a height of six feet (180 cm).

**Good Care Guide**

Overwinter at 55° to 60°F (13° to 16°C). From November to March keep the soil just moist. At other times water liberally. Provide a humid atmosphere by standing the plant on a tray of wet pebbles or moist peat. From May to September feed fortnightly. Pinch out new shoots occasionally to encourage bushiness. Repot every second April in an all-peat compost. Propagate by stem-tip cuttings in summer.

## Philodendron selloum

LACY TREE PHILODENDRON

This species from Brazil gradually develops a trunk which eventually may reach a height of five feet (150 cm) in a tub. The deeply lobed, dark green leaves can grow up to three feet (90 cm) in length and are borne on long stalks.

**Good Care Guide**

Do not let the winter temperature drop below 55°F (13°C). From April to October water liberally. At other times keep the soil just moist. From May to September feed fortnightly. Provide a humid atmosphere by standing the plant on a tray of wet pebbles or moist peat. Spray in hot weather. Repot every other April, preferably in an all-peat compost. Propagate by stem-tip or leaf-bud cuttings in May or June, using old leggy plants.

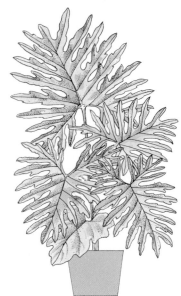

## Polyscias balfouriana

DINNER PLATE ARALIA

In its natural habitat in Africa, *P. balfouriana* reaches a height of twenty-five feet (7.5 m), but in a pot it is unlikely to grow taller than about four feet (120 cm). Each leaf is composed of one to several large, round, green leaflets with serrated edges.

**Good Care Guide**

Although this plant will survive a winter temperature of 55°F (13°C), it will thrive better at 60°F (16°C) or higher. In spring and summer water moderately. At other times keep the soil just moist. From April to September feed fortnightly and spray regularly. Repot every other spring in an all-peat potting compost. Propagate by stem-tip, leaf-bud or root cuttings in early summer, preferably using a heated propagating case.

## Scindapsus aureus

DEVIL'S IVY, GOLDEN POTHOS

The young plant has four-inch-long (10-cm), oval leaves which are bright green splashed with yellow. As the vine matures the leaves become heart-shaped. *S. aureus* comes from the Solomon Islands and climbs to a height of six feet (180 cm) or more in a pot. Support it with canes or a trellis.

**Good Care Guide**

The temperature should not fall below 50°F (10°C) in winter, when the soil should be kept barely moist. At other times water moderately. From May to September feed once a month with a liquid fertilizer. Repot every second April in any good-quality potting compost. Remove stem tips in summer to promote branching and use the pruned shoots for propagation.

## Siderasis fuscata

BROWN SPIDERWORT

A low-growing plant from South America, *S. fuscata* has oval, light-green leaves thickly covered with reddish-brown hairs. The leaves grow in rosettes and have a buff-coloured central stripe. Small, pinkish-purple flowers may open in summer.

**Good Care Guide**

In winter *S. fuscata* requires a temperature of not less than 55°F (13°C). In spring and summer keep the soil moist. At other times water sparingly. Provide a humid atmosphere by standing the plant on a tray of wet pebbles. From April to September feed once a month. Repot every spring in any good-quality potting compost. Propagate by division when repotting.

## Syngonium podophyllum

AFRICAN EVERGREEN, GOOSEFOOT PLANT

When young this native of Central America has arrow-shaped, green leaves borne on long, straight stems which contain a milky sap. In time it develops into a climber, with lobed leaves which are said to resemble a goose's foot. The mature plant can be trained up a trellis or potted in a hanging basket.

**Good Care Guide**

The winter temperature should not be lower than 60°F (16°C). Water liberally in spring and summer and more sparingly in winter, making sure the soil never dries out completely. From March to September apply a liquid feed fortnightly. Repot every February in any good proprietary potting compost. Propagate by cuttings in summer.

A plant can be kept anywhere, as long as its basic requirements are considered. These wide steps, for example, are excellent for displaying *Monstera* and *Philodendron*.

Although traditionally plants are not kept in the bedroom, there is no reason why a plant such as this *Philodendron*, right, should not share a well-ventilated room with you.

A dramatic *Philodendron*, far right, transforms an otherwise unremarkable corner into a point of interest.

# Bulbs

Of all the bulbous-rooted plants those most widely grown as house plants are the spring-flowering Narcissus, Hyacinth and Tulip. Unfortunately, one season's flowering is all they manage indoors and they are then usually thrown away. But their exotic relations in the *Liliacae* and *Amaryllidaceae* families, to which most of the bulbs and tubers in this section belong, will flower year after year if given proper care.

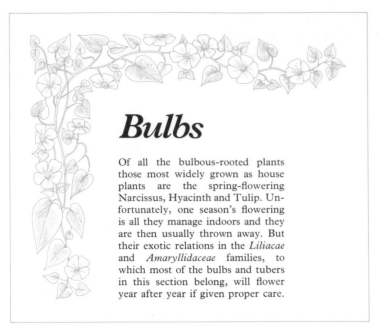

## Amaryllis belladonna
BELLADONNA LILY, CAPE BELLADONNA

*A. belladonna* comes from South Africa and grows from a large bulb. Beautiful, trumpet-shaped, pink or reddish-pink flowers are borne on stout stalks in autumn before the strap-shaped, green leaves appear. It grows up to two feet (60 cm) tall.
### Good Care Guide
In October start the bulb into growth at a temperature of 55° to 60°F (13 to 16°C). Keep in a sunny position and water sparingly. When the leaves appear water liberally and feed once a week. During the resting period, which begins when the leaves turn yellow, keep the soil dry. Repot every other October in any good proprietary potting compost leaving the top half of the bulb uncovered. Propagate by removing offsets when repotting.

## Caladium × hortulanum

This South American plant has long-stemmed leaves that are shaped like arrow heads and grow from a tuber. They are usually two-coloured—red and white, green and white or green and red—with white, cream or red veins. *C. × hortulanum* grows about fifteen inches (38 cm) tall.
### Good Care Guide
In March pot the tuber in any good potting compost. Keep at a temperature of 70°F (21°C) and water sparingly. When the leaves are well developed move the plant to a cooler room, water liberally, spray daily and feed once a week. Gradually stop watering as the leaves wilt in autumn. Overwinter the tuber at 55°F (13°C) in barely moist soil. Propagate by removing offsets from the tuber when repotting.

## Canna × hybrida
CANNA

Developed from *C. flaccida* and other species these hybrids have broad, green, bronze or purple leaves which appear in spring, followed by clusters of long-stemmed, orchid-like yellow, orange or red flowers. The hybrids grow from tuber-like rhizomes and reach a height of three to four feet (90 to 120 cm).
### Good Care Guide
In spring start the rhizome into growth by providing a temperature of 55° to 60°F (13° to 16°C). Keep in good light and water sparingly. When shoots appear, water liberally and feed once a fortnight. In autumn cut the plant back, move it to a cool but frost-free room and keep almost dry. Repot each spring in any good potting compost. Propagate by division when repotting.

## Crocus vernus
CROCUS

Of the many cultivated varieties developed from *C. vernus* the pale blue and silver-grey 'Vanguard', the pure white 'Joan of Arc' and the deep purple 'Purpureus Grandiflorus' are recommended for indoor cultivation. The flowers, which are four to five inches (10 to 13 cm) high, open in February.
### Good Care Guide
In October plant half a dozen Crocus corms in a shallow pan containing any good potting compost. Water once, then put in a cool, dark cupboard. In mid-January, when shoots appear, move to a well-lit, cool position and water moderately. After flowering discard the old corms or plant them out in the garden. For a good display of blooms indoors buy fresh corms each year.

## Freesia × kewensis
## (Freesia × hybrida)
FREESIA

These exquisitely scented hybrids have narrow, green, sword-shaped leaves and funnel-shaped flowers in a variety of colours which open in early spring.
### Good Care Guide
In October plant a dozen corms in a 5-inch (13-cm) pot containing any good potting compost. Keep in a sunny position and water moderately. As soon as each corm has three to four leaves, and until the flower buds appear, apply a liquid feed fortnightly. The temperature should not drop below 45°F (7°C) nor rise above 65°F (18°C). When the leaves yellow after flowering, dry off and store the corms in a cool, dry place. Repot only the largest corms in autumn. Propagate by offsets.

## *Gloriosa rothschildiana*
GLORY LILY

A native of tropical Africa, this climbing lily grows from a tuber to a height of four feet (120 cm) or more. It has lance-shaped leaves and wavy edged, crimson and yellow flowers which open from June to August.
**Good Care Guide**
In spring plant the tuber in a 6-inch (15-cm) pot containing any good potting compost. Keep in a humid atmosphere at a temperature not lower than 60°F (16°C) and water sparingly. When stems develop, support with canes or twiggy sticks. Water freely and feed once every two weeks. After flowering, reduce watering until leaves yellow, then dry off. Store the tuber in its pot at a temperature of about 50°F (10°C). Propagate from offsets removed from the tuber when repotting.

## *Habranthus robustus*

A native of Argentina, this handsome plant grows from a bulb to a height of about two feet (60 cm). Narrow, strap-shaped leaves appear first, followed by long-stemmed, trumpet-shaped flowers, which are purplish-pink fading to white. The flowers open in June and July.
**Good Care Guide**
In spring bring the bulb into growth by watering moderately. Keep in good light but protect from strong sun. From March to May feed fortnightly. When flowering finishes and the leaves turn yellow, stop watering and move to a cool but frost-free room. Repot every other spring in good-quality potting compost. Propagate by removing offsets from the bulb when repotting.

## *Haemanthus multiflorus*
SALMON BLOOD LILY

This central African plant grows to about two to three feet (60 to 90 cm) in height. It has lance-shaped leaves and large, round flower heads which are pink or red and open in spring.
**Good Care Guide**
In March give this bulb light, a temperature of 55° to 60°F (13° to 16°C) and a moderate amount of water. From May to August feed every two weeks. After flowering, gradually reduce the water. Overwinter at a temperature of 50° to 55°F (10° to 13°C) and keep almost dry. Repot every third March in a 6-inch (15-cm) pot containing any good potting compost. Propagate by offsets when repotting.

## *Hippeastrum*
AMARYLLIS

With their trumpet-shaped flowers these hybrids closely resemble *Amaryllis belladonna*. There is, however, a far wider choice of colours—pure white, white with orange streaks, pure pink, pink with orange veins, pure red and orange-red. The flowers open from December to May.
**Good Care Guide**
In October start the bulb into growth at a temperature of 55° to 60°F (13° to 16°C). Place in a well-lit position and water sparingly. When the foliage appears water more liberally and feed once a week. Stop watering and feeding when the leaves turn yellow. Repot the bulb every other October in any good potting compost leaving the top half of the bulb uncovered. Propagate by removing any offsets when repotting.

## *Hyacinthus orientalis*
HYACINTH

The cultivated varieties known as Dutch Hyacinths have strap-shaped, green leaves and dense spikes of sweet-scented, waxy, bell-shaped flowers, which open in winter or spring. The most popular colours are blue, pink or white. Roman Hyacinths have loose, blue or white flower spikes, several to each bulb.
**Good Care Guide**
In September or October plant the bulbs in moist potting compost or bulb fibre. Leave the tops of the bulbs uncovered. Keep in a cool, dark place until shoots appear, then move to a well-lit position in a cool room. Water sparingly. When the leaves are well developed the Hyacinths may be kept at a higher temperature, about 65°F (18°C). Discard the bulbs after flowering.

## *Hymenocallis calathina*
*(H. narcissiflora)*
SPIDER LILY

A sweet-scented, deciduous species from Peru, *H. calathina* grows from a bulb to a height of two feet (60 cm) or more. It has arching green leaves and large, somewhat daffodil-like white flowers, which have slender, pointed petals. They open either in spring or summer.
**Good Care Guide**
From November to January plant in moist potting compost leaving the top of the bulb uncovered; the temperature should not fall below 55°F (13°C). When shoots appear water moderately and feed once a fortnight. Shade from strong sunshine. After flowering, stop feeding and keep the soil just moist. Repot every second April and propagate by removing offsets from the bulb.

Purple Crocus in a terracotta bowl, top, herald spring. The compost in the bowl is covered with moss to hold the moisture and to make the arrangement look more attractive.

Delicate Snowdrops with their green, blade-like leaves are set in front of a round, white-framed window, above. The container is an old salt jar.

*Caladium* grow in every shade from white to deep red with a lace-like tracery of delicate green veins. The subtle colours of the curtains and rug, right, are matched by the leaves.

Three Hyacinths flower on a window
sill, above. They have been planted,
along with grass, in a white tureen.

## Lachenalia aloides
CAPE COWSLIP

*L. aloides* grows about twelve inches (30 cm) tall. It has strap-shaped, green leaves, which are sometimes flecked with purple, and loose spikes of pendant, tubular, yellow flowers with red and green markings which open between December and March.

**Good Care Guide**
In late August plant six bulbs in a 6-inch (15-cm) pan or half pot using any reliable potting compost. Water well once. Keep the pot in good light at a temperature of 50° to 55°F (10° to 13°C). When shoots appear water moderately and feed fortnightly. About a month after flowering ceases gradually stop watering. Keep the soil dry until the bulbs are repotted in August. Propagate by detaching bulblets or offsets from the parent bulb when repotting.

## Lilium longiflorum
EASTER LILY

In spite of its common name this Japanese lily produces its magnificent, heavily scented, trumpet-shaped, white flowers in July and August. The flowers are borne on three-foot-tall (90-cm) stems, which are covered with narrow, pointed, green leaves.

**Good Care Guide**
In autumn plant each bulb in a 6-inch (15-cm) pot containing any good-quality potting compost. Put the pot in a cool, dark place and keep the soil moist. When shoots appear move to a well-lit position. Water liberally and feed every two weeks. Shade from strong sunshine. After flowering keep the soil just moist until the bulb is repotted in autumn. Propagate by offsets when repotting or by seeds in autumn or spring.

## Lycoris aurea
GOLDEN SPIDER LILY

This lily comes from China and grows from a bulb to a height of about twelve inches (30 cm). It has strap-shaped leaves which die before the deep yellow, funnel-shaped flowers open in August and September.

**Good Care Guide**
*L. aurea* should be kept in good light at a temperature no lower than 60°F (16°C). Bring the bulb into growth by watering moderately after flowering finishes. Once the plant is in full leaf, spray regularly and feed fortnightly. When the leaves turn yellow, stop watering and keep dry until flowering is over. Repot every other summer in any good-quality potting compost. Propagate by removing offsets from the bulbs when repotting.

## Narcissus
NARCISSUS, DAFFODIL

The *Narcissus* genus, which includes the familiar Daffodil, embraces a great many species and hybrids with strap-shaped leaves and predominantly yellow, red or white flowers, each with a central cup or trumpet borne on stiff stems. They grow between fifteen and eighteen inches (38 and 45 cm) tall.

**Good Care Guide**
In early autumn plant the bulbs close together in moist potting compost or bulb fibre, leaving the tops uncovered. Keep in a cool, dark place. When shoots appear move to a well-lit position in a cool room. Water moderately. As soon as the flower buds are well developed the bulbs may be moved to a warmer room—about 60°F (16°C). Discard after flowering or plant outdoors.

## Nerine flexuosa

From September to November this strikingly beautiful South African bulb produces large, pink flower heads composed of up to twelve frilly-petalled blooms, on two- to three-feet-tall (60- to 90-cm) stems. The arching, strap-shaped leaves develop at the same time.

**Good Care Guide**
In August plant each bulb, leaving the top uncovered, in a 3- or 4-inch (8- or 10-cm) pot in any reliable potting compost. Begin to water moderately when leaves appear and feed every two weeks. The bulb should be kept in a well-lit position at a temperature of 50° to 55°F (10° to 13°C) all through the winter. When the leaves begin to yellow stop watering and feeding. Repot every three years and propagate by removing offsets from the bulb.

## Ornithogalum thyrsoides
CHINCHERINCHEE

From May to July twenty to thirty star-shaped, white, cream or yellow flowers are borne in a dense spike at the top of each of this bulb's twelve- to eighteen-inch-tall (30- to 45-cm) stems. *O. thyrsoides* comes from South Africa and has rather fleshy, strap-shaped, green leaves.

**Good Care Guide**
In October plant four to six bulbs in a 6-inch (15-cm) pot containing a reliable potting compost. Maintain a temperature of not less than 45°F (7°C) and keep in a well-lit place. Keep the soil moist and feed every two weeks. After flowering finishes in July, stop feeding and gradually cease watering. Repot every autumn. Propagate by removing offsets from the bulbs when repotting.

## Sparaxis tricolor
HARLEQUIN FLOWER, VELVET FLOWER

A native of South Africa, *S. tricolor* grows from a corm to a height of eighteen inches (45 cm). Sword-shaped leaves form narrow fans, from the centres of which appear several flat-petalled, multicoloured blooms in May and June. Several cultivated varieties are available. The flowers are combinations of orange, red, purple, yellow and white.

**Good Care Guide**

In September plant six corms in a 6-inch (15-cm) pot containing any good potting compost. Water well once and keep at a temperature not lower than 45°F (7°C). When shoots appear keep the soil moist. When the leaves yellow at the tips stop watering and dry out; store the corms in a dry, frost-free place. Propagate by offsets when repotting in autumn.

## Tulipa
TULIP

Tulip bulbs were first brought to Europe from Turkey in the sixteenth century. Today hundreds of cultivated varieties with stiff stems, narrow, often grey-green leaves and goblet- or cup-shaped flowers in numerous colours are available. Early-flowering Tulips are particularly suitable for indoor cultivation.

**Good Care Guide**

Plant several bulbs almost touching each other in pots or bowls containing moist bulb fibre or potting compost. Keep in a cool, dark place until shoots appear, then move to a well-lit position in a cool room. Water liberally. When the leaves are a few inches tall, move to a warmer room, about 65°F (18°C). Discard the bulbs after flowering or plant in the garden.

## Vallota speciosa
SCARBOROUGH LILY

Like many of the more spectacular flowering bulbs, *V. speciosa* comes from South Africa. Clusters of up to ten bright scarlet, funnel-shaped flowers, which open from July to September, grow at the top of one- to two-foot-long (30- to 60-cm) stems. The erect to arching evergreen leaves are strap shaped.

**Good Care Guide**

In August or March plant the bulbs singly in 4- or 5-inch (10- or 13-cm) pots of any good-quality potting compost, leaving the tops of the bulbs uncovered. Keep at a temperature not lower than 55°F (13°C) on a sunny window sill. Water moderately throughout the year. Remove dead flowers and leaves regularly. Repot every second or third year and propagate by removing offsets.

## Veltheimia viridifolia (Veltheimia capensis)
FOREST LILY

Few bulbs have longer lasting flowers than this handsome South African lily. From the centre of a rosette of wavy margined, glossy green leaves, a red-flecked, twelve- to eighteen-inch (30- to 45-cm) stem emerges in spring bearing a dense spike of up to sixty pendant, tubular, pink flowers, which last for at least a month.

**Good Care Guide**

In August or September plant the bulb in any reliable potting compost. Water sparingly until leaves develop, then water liberally. Keep in light shade and maintain a temperature not lower than 50°F (10°C). Let the soil dry out during the June to August resting period. Propagate by offsets from the bulb when repotting.

## Zantedeschia aethiopica
ARUM LILY, CALLA LILY

The two- to four-foot-tall (60- to 120-cm) flower stem of this lily, bearing the white lily spathe with its bright yellow spadix, emerges from the middle of a clump of long-stemmed, arrow-shaped, dark green leaves. The flowers open from March to June.

**Good Care Guide**

In September or October plant the rhizome in a good-quality potting compost. Water liberally. Place in good light and provide a winter temperature not lower than 45°F (7°C). Keep the soil just moist. When shoots appear, water frequently. From May to August feed every two weeks. After flowering, gradually stop watering and feeding. Propagate by dividing the rhizomes or by offsets when repotting in autumn.

## Zephyranthes grandiflora
ZEPHYR LILY

This small, lily-like plant from Central America grows from an oval bulb to a height of about eight inches (20 cm). It has narrow, green leaves and six-petalled, funnel-shaped, luminous pink flowers borne on hollow stems. The flowers open in June and July.

**Good Care Guide**

In March or April plant half a dozen bulbs in a 6-inch (15-cm) pot containing any reliable potting compost. Place in a well-lit position in a cool room and water sparingly. When shoots appear, start watering freely and feed fortnightly. After flowering, stop feeding and keep the soil barely moist. Overwinter the bulb at a temperature of not less than 50°F (10°C). Propagate by detaching bulbils when repotting in spring.

# Succulents

All cacti are succulents but not all succulents belong to the cactus family. Although they may resemble each other a true cactus can be identified by the little cushion-like tufts called areoles from which spines and barbed hairs sometimes grow. Success with cacti, especially if they are to flower well, depends on providing them with cool and dry conditions during their seasonal resting period.

## *Lithops lesliei*
LIVING STONES, PEBBLE PLANT

This succulent from the deserts of South Africa can easily be mistaken for a pebble because of its colouring and its shape. Its reddish-brown upper surface is marked with green-brown grooves and its pair of thick leaves is joined together to form a single body with a slit across the top.

**Good Care Guide**
Maximum sunlight and a winter temperature of about 40°F (4°C) is advisable. Withhold water from October to April. When the old leaves have completely dried up and the new ones appear, keep the soil just moist. Repot every third April in a pan or half pot filled with any reliable potting compost mixed with an equal amount of coarse sand. Propagate by seed in spring.

## *Chamaecereus silvestrii*
GHERKIN CACTUS, PEANUT CACTUS

In summer the finger-length, cylindrical, almost gherkin-like, branched stems of this low-growing Argentinian cactus bear several handsome scarlet flowers.

**Good Care Guide**
For the Gherkin Cactus to flower plenty of light in winter is essential. The winter temperature should not fall below 40°F (4°C) or rise above 60°F (16°C). Water regularly in summer, but allow the soil to dry out between waterings. At other times water very sparingly to prevent shrivelling. Use a liquid fertilizer once a month from April to August. Repot carefully in any good potting compost, but those with extra gritty sand added are best. Propagate by using the separate stems as cuttings.

# Stylish succulents

Dark green succulents planted in a bright yellow casserole, above, make an intriguing miniature garden.

The unusual shapes of succulents deserve equally interesting containers. The wine glass, left, is the perfect home for a single cactus.

Cacti and other succulents make eye-catching groups on shelves and tables, right. Ivy softens the formality of the arrangement.

## Agave americana
CENTURY PLANT

In spite of its common name this Mexican plant reaches maturity well before its hundredth year. Its decorative rosette of grey-green, leathery, spine-tipped leaves dies after flowering. Flowering, however, rarely or never takes place indoors. A young plant can be as small as six inches (15 cm) across, but if potted on it could eventually grow to four feet (120 cm) across.

**Good Care Guide**

This plant prefers dry air and welcomes a well-lit position with a winter temperature not lower than 40°F (4°C). Water regularly in summer but sparingly in winter. Apply a liquid feed once a month from April to September. Repot every two years in spring, in a good potting compost. Propagate from offsets in spring.

## Aloe variegata
PARTRIDGE-BREASTED ALOE

Unlike most succulents, this South African species has a winter growing season and, consequently, produces upright spikes of pale orange, tubular flowers in spring. But its widespread popularity can be attributed to its rosette of attractive, triangular, dark green leaves banded with white markings.

**Good Care Guide**

A. variegata is perfectly at home on a sunny window sill in the dry air of a living-room. The winter temperature, however, should not fall below 40°F (4°C). Water very sparingly in summer and moderately in winter and spring, but never in the rosette. Repot every other year in spring, using any good proprietary potting compost. Propagate by removing offsets in summer.

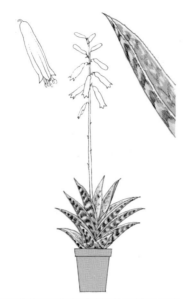

## Aporocactus flagelliformis
RAT'S-TAIL CACTUS

Although it is frequently grafted on to a tall cactus, this Mexican species with its trailing, mid-green, spiny stems looks best in a hanging basket. Spring-opening, bright pink flowers add to its appeal.

**Good Care Guide**

The Rat's-tail Cactus is ideal for the novice for it requires little care. To ensure flowering, overwinter at a temperature not lower than 40°F (4°C), provide plenty of light and a dry atmosphere. From April to August give the plant a liquid feed once a month and water regularly, allowing the compost to dry out between each watering. See that the compost is just moist at other times. Repot annually in potting compost when flowering has ceased. Propagate by cuttings between April and July.

## Astrophytum myriostigma
BISHOP'S CAP, BISHOP'S MITRE

The name Bishop's Cap seems quite appropriate for this globular, spineless, Mexican cactus with its arrangement of five, sharply edged ridges. An overall covering of small tufts of white hair and yellow flowers, which develop from the centre of the plant, enhance its appearance. It grows to a height of six inches (15 cm).

**Good Care Guide**

A. myriostigma is well suited to indoor culture. It thrives in full light and plenty of air. See that the winter room temperature does not fall below 41°F (5°C). Water only when the soil is dry from March through to October. Do not spray. Repot in early spring, using any proprietary compost mixed with equal parts coarse sand or grit. Propagate by seed in spring.

## Cephalocereus senilis
OLD MAN CACTUS

Long, silky white hairs crown this imposing pillar cactus. It grows slowly and, unfortunately, its nocturnal, summer-opening flowers do not appear until the plant is several feet tall. In its natural habitat it can grow to forty feet (12 m) in height.

**Good Care Guide**

C. senilis needs attention. Position it in a dry, sunny location and see that the winter room temperature is not lower than 40°F (4°C). Keep the soil moist in summer and dry from November to February. Take care not to wet the hairs too often. Apply a liquid fertilizer once a month from May to August. Repot every two years in spring, using any good potting compost mixed with equal parts of limestone grit. Propagate by seed in spring.

## Crassula argentea
JADE PLANT, SILVERY SUCCULENT
MONEY TREE

This small, tree-like succulent from South Africa is prized chiefly for its thick, green, oval leaves, which have an almost metallic gloss. Indoors it rarely produces its white flowers.

**Good Care Guide**

To ensure healthy growth, place C. argentea on the sill of a sunny south-facing window. A dry atmosphere and a winter temperature that does not drop below 40°F (4°C) is best. In summer water sparingly; keep the soil dry during the rest of the year. From April to July use a dilute liquid feed once every month. Spray only if the leaves are dusty. Repot every second April in any good potting compost. Propagate by leaf cuttings in spring and in summer.

## Echeveria gibbiflora
### 'Carunculata'

From Mexico comes this attractive *Echeveria* with its rosette of fleshy, spoon-shaped, blue-mauve leaves, each curiously branded with wart-like blisters. Occasionally sprays of bell-shaped scarlet and yellow flowers are borne on long arching stems, from autumn to winter.

**Good Care Guide**

Overwinter the plant at a temperature not lower than 40°F (4°C) and place it in a situation that affords full sunlight all the year round. Water regularly in summer, sparingly in winter. But keep moisture away from the leaf rosette. Apply liquid feed once a month from April to August. Repot annually or every other year in April, using any good potting compost. Propagate by leaf or stem cuttings in summer.

## Echinocactus grusonii
GOLDEN BARREL, GOLDEN BALL
MOTHER-IN-LAW'S CHAIR

This popular, pale green, globular cactus has a handsome covering of golden-yellow spines. A slow grower, it rarely produces its small, yellow flowers indoors.

**Good Care Guide**

To ensure good spine colour, place *E. grusonii* in a spot where it will receive strong light and good ventilation. Do not let the temperature fall below 40°F (4°C) in winter. It appreciates being kept moist in summer, but must be kept dry from October to March. Apply liquid fertilizer once a month from March to mid-August. Repot every two to three years in any reliable potting compost mixed with extra coarse sand. To propagate, sow seeds in spring.

## Echinocereus pectinatus

*E. pectinatus* is a popular house cactus which grows to eight inches (20 cm) in height. The oval stems are set with star-like patterns of white spines and in summer long, funnel-shaped flowers open widely to show that they are bright pink inside.

**Good Care Guide**

Cultivation is easy for this rapid-growing central Mexican cactus. A winter temperature of about 40°F (4°C) and a location offering maximum sunlight are advisable. Water well in summer, but keep absolutely dry from October to March. The plant should prosper if it is repotted in a wide, shallow pan filled with any reliable potting compost which is mixed with extra grit or coarse sand. Propagate by seed in early spring or by stem cuttings between April and August.

## Echinopsis rhodotricha

This cactus from Argentina and Paraguay has oval or cylindrical stems with between eight and thirteen ribs, which bear yellowish, black-tipped spines. Magnificent, funnel-shaped, six-inch-long (15-cm), white flowers open in summer.

**Good Care Guide**

*E. rhodotricha* will thrive if placed in full light, although some shade from the hottest sun is advisable. To guarantee successful flowering, the winter temperature should be about 40°F (4°C) and the compost should be kept moist in summer, but almost dry in winter. A fortnightly application of liquid fertilizer from April to August is beneficial. Repot every alternate year in April, using any reliable potting compost. Propagate by offsets in summer or by seed in spring.

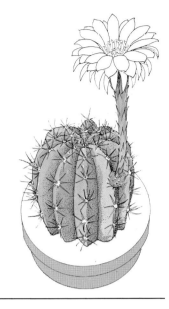

## Epiphyllum × ackermannii
ORCHID CACTUS

*Epiphyllum* hybrids are frequently called *E. × ackermannii*. Those bearing fragrant, scarlet flowers, which open in daytime in May and June, bloom more profusely than the evening-flowering white and yellow forms.

**Good Care Guide**

*Epiphyllum* require a well-lit, airy position that offers shelter from direct sunshine. Overwinter at a temperature of 45° to 50°F (7° to 10°C). Water liberally in summer but moderately in winter. When the flower buds begin to form, give a high-potassium fertilizer every two weeks. Repot annually after spring flowering in a mixture of loam, sphagnum moss, peat fibre and sand. Propagate by seed in spring or by cuttings in summer.

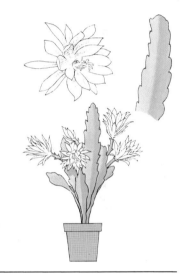

## Euphorbia milii (E. splendens)
CROWN OF THORNS

This shrub from Madagascar is named the Crown of Thorns because its angular branches are covered with sharp thorns. Clusters of green-yellow flowers are borne on long, scarlet stems in spring, but it is the showy blood-red bracts surrounding the blooms which are so appealing.

**Good Care Guide**

*E. milii* enjoys hot sun, dry air and good ventilation. In winter the temperature should not fall below 55°F (13°C). Water moderately from May to August, but keep barely moist at other times. Use a liquid fertilizer every two weeks from June to August. Repot in any good potting compost mixed with extra sand every second year in spring. Propagate by cuttings in spring or summer.

This simple way of displaying plants is ideal for a collection of small cacti and other succulents. The plants, above, have been placed in the pigeonholes of an antique desk in a well-lit room.

A small group of *Kalanchoe blossfeldiana* in full flower, right, provides colour and makes a charming arrangement in a corner or on a shelf.

Cacti are easy to care for and well suited to the hustle and bustle of a kitchen, right.

## *Euphorbia obesa*
TURKISH TEMPLE

A native of Cape Province, *E. obesa* looks like a spineless sea urchin. It is globular in shape, six inches (15 cm) tall and its grey-green, leafless stem has eight broad ribs covered with brown-purple bands. Minute, sweet-scented, bell-shaped flowers appear in summer.

### Good Care Guide
This succulent appreciates dry air and a very sunny situation. In winter the temperature should be about 45°F (7°C). From April to early autumn keep just moist, but allow the compost to dry out from late autumn to spring. Use a dilute fertilizer every three weeks from May to August. Repot every second or third year in May using any reliable compost with extra sand. Propagation from seed is not easy.

## *Faucaria tigrina*
TIGER'S JAWS, CAT'S JAWS

Only two inches (5 cm) tall, *F. tigrina* is easily recognized because of the distinctive criss-cross arrangement of its fleshy, thick, grey-green leaves with their covering of white dots and sharply toothed margins. In autumn large, bright yellow, daisy-like flowers appear.

### Good Care Guide
This South African succulent does best in full sunlight, but it must be overwintered at a temperature no lower than 40°F (4°C). Keep the compost moist during the growing season in late summer and autumn, but allow it to dry out in winter. Repot every third year in April, using any reliable potting compost mixed with equal parts of sharp sand. Propagation is by seed in spring or by cuttings from June to August.

## *Gasteria verrucosa*

This South African succulent has dark green, fleshy leaves, which grow opposite one another in two ranks, are handsomely marked with pearly-white warts and grooved upper surfaces. Twelve-inch-long (30-cm) stems bear orange-red, tubular flowers in spring and summer.

### Good Care Guide
*G. verrucosa* thrives in a sunny, airy position, preferably near a south-facing window. In winter the room temperature must not fall below 40°F (4°C). Keep the compost moist from March to September, but almost dry in winter. Feed every three weeks from April to August. Repot every second or third year in spring or after flowering, using any good potting compost mixed with extra sand. Propagate by seed, leaf cuttings or division in summer.

## *Haworthia margaritifera*
PEARL PLANT

This small South African succulent has broad rosettes of tapering, dark green leaves, which are thickly covered with large, white nodules. The flowers are insignificant.

### Good Care Guide
*H. margaritifera* makes few demands. It favours full light but can tolerate some shade. See that the temperature in winter does not fall below 40°F (4°C). In spring and summer the compost should be kept moist, but in autumn and winter keep the compost almost dry. Give a dilute liquid fertilizer every two weeks from April to August. Repot annually, in spring, in pans or half pots using equal parts of loam-based compost and sharp sand. Propagate by removing offsets in summer or from seed in spring.

## *Kalanchoe blossfeldiana*
TOM THUMB

If the short-day treatment is applied to this leaf succulent from the highlands of Madagascar its clusters of orange-red, scented flowers can be made to appear nearly all year round. But several plants are needed for an all-year succession. The dark green, notched leaves are edged with red.

### Good Care Guide
*K. blossfeldiana* should be placed in full light. The winter temperature must be at least 40°F (4°C). Water liberally in summer but sparingly in winter. Apply a dilute fertilizer every two weeks from May until August. To encourage bushiness, pinch out shoot tips when young. Repot every spring in any reliable potting compost. Propagate by seed in spring or by stem cuttings in summer.

## *Mammillaria bocasana*
POWDER PUFF

An undemanding cactus, *M. bocasana* has silvery-white spines and hairs that handsomely cover its blue-green globular body. It depends to a great extent upon the summer sun for its colour and beauty. In June small, cream flowers encircle the crown; these are later followed by purple berries.

### Good Care Guide
Maximum sunlight is essential and the plant must be turned occasionally to prevent lopsided growth. In winter the temperature should not fall below 40°F (4°C) and the compost should remain dry. In summer water liberally and use a liquid fertilizer once a month. Repot annually in April using a finely sieved potting compost. Propagate by seed in April or by offsets in summer.

## Opuntia microdasys
BUNNY EARS, INDIAN FIG
PRICKLY PEAR

Found throughout the Americas, *O. microdasys* is distinguished by its jointed, flattened stems. It must be handled with care because its yellow areoles are covered with numerous glochids, or barbed bristles, which can easily break off and painfully penetrate the skin.
**Good Care Guide**
This slow-growing species prefers a light, airy position. In winter it requires a temperature no lower than 45°F (7°C). Keep the compost moist during the summer, but water sparingly in winter. From spring until August use a liquid fertilizer every two weeks. Repot every other spring in reliable potting compost mixed with extra sand. Propagate by cuttings in summer.

## Rebutia kupperiana
RED CROWN

From May to July brilliant red, trumpet-shaped flowers emerge from areoles at the base of this Bolivian clump-forming cactus with its spherical red-green stems. In bloom for only a week, the flowers open each morning and close each evening.
**Good Care Guide**
*R. kupperiana* flourishes in a well-ventilated, sunny location. In winter the temperature should not fall below 40°F (4°C). In spring and throughout the summer, while the buds are developing, keep the compost moist, but in winter provide just enough moisture to prevent the plant from shrivelling. Repot in any reliable potting compost mixed with extra sand. Propagate by sowing seeds in spring or by detaching offsets during the summer.

## Rhipsalidopsis gaertneri
EASTER CACTUS

In spring the Easter Cactus bears a profusion of scarlet, tubular flowers, which emerge from the areoles on top of its jointed stems. It grows eighteen inches (45 cm) tall.
**Good Care Guide**
Since *R. gaertneri* is indigenous to the forests of Brazil, it favours a humid, warm environment. In summer partial shade is needed, but a light position is advisable in winter, when the temperature should be about 55°F (13°C). Feed monthly and water liberally from August to December. Then water sparingly until new buds form. Spray frequently in spring and summer. Repot after flowering in any reliable potting compost mixed with an equal part of sphagnum moss. Propagate by cuttings in summer.

## Schlumbergera truncata
CHRISTMAS CACTUS, CRAB CACTUS

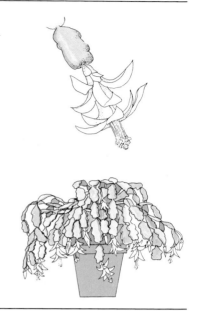

When *S. truncata* is displayed in a hanging basket its red, trumpet-shaped flowers can be seen to full advantage. From November to January they emerge at the tips of the bright green, flat, leaf-like branches.
**Good Care Guide**
Christmas Cactus prefers a light position that provides some shading from the summer sun. A winter temperature of not less than 55°F (13°C) is advisable. When the flower buds form, water well and feed once a week with a dilute liquid fertilizer. In summer, when the plant is resting, keep the soil almost dry. Frequent spraying in the growing season is important. Repot in a compost containing equal parts of loam, peat, moss and sand. Propagate by cuttings during the summer.

## Senecio rowleyanus
STRING OF BEADS

Show off this South West African succulent, with its decorative mat of creeping stems and globular leaves with pointed tips, in a hanging basket. Sweet-scented, daisy-like heads of white florets with deep purple stigmas appear from September to November. Two inches (5 cm) tall, this plant has a spread of two to three feet (60 to 90 cm).
**Good Care Guide**
Always give *S. rowleyanus* plenty of sunlight and do not let the winter temperature fall below 50°F (10°C). From March to September water liberally, otherwise the compost should remain just moist. Repot in March in any reliable potting compost with extra sand added. Propagate by stem cuttings from spring to autumn.

## Trichocereus chiloensis

*T. chiloensis* sometimes produces magnificent, large, white, scented flowers with reddish-rimmed outer petals. They make their appearance in summer, opening only in the evenings. This Chilean cactus grows to a height of two to three feet (60 to 90 cm) indoors.
**Good Care Guide**
This slow-growing columnar cactus enjoys a very sunny situation and should be overwintered at 40°F (4°C). Water liberally in summer, but withhold all water in winter. Use a liquid fertilizer at monthly intervals throughout the summer. Repot annually in March in any reliable potting compost mixed with sand. To reduce particularly vigorous growth, take stem-tip cuttings in summer. Propagate by cuttings or seed in April.

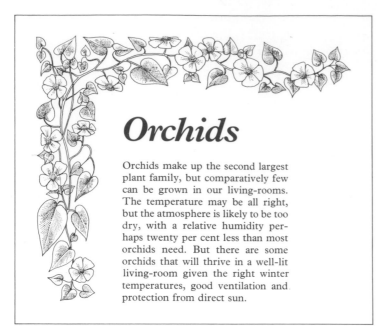

# Orchids

Orchids make up the second largest plant family, but comparatively few can be grown in our living-rooms. The temperature may be all right, but the atmosphere is likely to be too dry, with a relative humidity perhaps twenty per cent less than most orchids need. But there are some orchids that will thrive in a well-lit living-room given the right winter temperatures, good ventilation and protection from direct sun.

### Dendrobium nobile

This winter-blooming orchid can be found from northeastern India to southern China. Each blossom consists of white petals shaded with pink or lilac, a rounded white or yellow lip with a deep purple blotch in the throat and pink to purple margins.

**Good Care Guide**
Give *D. nobile* direct light from September to March but shade it the rest of the year. In winter keep it at a temperature between 45° and 60°F (7° and 16°C) and provide fresh air. Water liberally and feed every three weeks with liquid fertilizer from April to October. Keep the compost almost dry in winter. Every two to three years repot in a very small pot after flowering. Use equal parts of sphagnum moss and osmunda fibre. Propagate by division when the young shoots show roots at the base.

### Paphiopedilum insigne
SLIPPER ORCHID, LADY'S SLIPPER

The flowers of this Himalayan plant are borne singly on twelve-inch (30-cm) stems. They have large, yellow-green dorsal petals with purple-brown veining and a pale green, slipper-shaped lip netted with brown, and appear from November to March.

**Good Care Guide**
The winter temperature should not fall below 40°F (4°C). Shade from direct sun from March to October and give plenty of fresh air. Provide humidity and keep compost moist throughout the year. Apply a dilute liquid feed every two weeks from May to September. Repot in a mixture of equal parts osmunda fibre, sphagnum moss and loam every second or third spring. Propagate by division at the same time.

Orchids thrive best in the controlled conditions of a conservatory, but some can be grown in your own living-room. They have an unusual beauty and an air of extravagance unsurpassed by any other indoor plant. The *Paphiopedilum*, left, and *Cymbidium*, right and far right, display the subtleties of shade and pattern that epitomize the orchid.

## Calanthe vestita

This deciduous Malaysian plant bears three-foot (90-cm) spikes of up to twenty-five handsome pure white flowers, each with a pink or red lip, from October to February.

**Good Care Guide**

*C. vestita* must be shaded from the hot sun between April and September and must have a winter temperature no lower than 55°F (13°C). Water well as the leaves expand, but stop watering completely when the foliage turns yellow. Little water is needed during flowering. As soon as the leaves are half grown begin to apply a dilute liquid feed every two weeks and continue until the leaves are mature. Repot the silver-grey pseudobulbs singly, preferably in a loam-based compost, when flowering has stopped. Propagate by separating offsets at the same time.

## Coelogyne cristata

*C. cristata*, an extremely tolerant orchid from Nepal, has pendulous clusters of up to seven fragrant, yellow-centred, white flowers which open successively from December to March.

**Good Care Guide**

This species is best grown in an orchid basket in a semi-shaded position. The winter temperature should not fall below 55°F (13°C). From April to October give plenty of fresh air, spray often and water well, preferably with rain or lime-free water; then gradually reduce the amount of water towards autumn. Use a dilute liquid feed every three weeks from May to September. Repot every two or three years in spring in equal parts of osmunda fibre, sphagnum moss and peat or leaf mould. Propagate by division at the same time.

## Cymbidium × Rosanna
'PINKIE'

This classic orchid hybrid has erect eighteen- to twenty-four-inch (45- to 60-cm) spikes of white, pink-flushed flowers which open in spring. The arching leaves are strap shaped.

**Good Care Guide**

This hybrid should be kept in a cool, airy room. Provide a winter temperature of 45° to 55°F (7° to 13°C). Protect the plant from strong summer sun, but expose it to autumn and winter sunshine. Water liberally in summer but sparingly in winter. From April to August spray regularly and feed fortnightly with half-strength liquid fertilizer. About every three years repot after flowering finishes. Use equal parts of fibrous loam or peat, osmundà fibre and sphagnum moss. Propagate by division when repotting.

## Epidendrum prismatocarpum
RAINBOW ORCHID

This epiphytic orchid from Central America bears two mid-green leaves and fifteen-inch (38-cm) spikes of ten to twenty waxy flowers from May to August. The petals are yellowish-green with maroon spots. The pointed lip is rosy-purple with a yellow tip and white margin.

**Good Care Guide**

*E. prismatocarpum* is moderately easy to cultivate if the winter temperature does not fall below 55°F (13°C) and if it is shaded from the sun from April to October. Keep the compost moist from April to September, water sparingly at other times. Repot from March to May in a mixture of two parts osmunda fibre to one part sphagnum moss. Propagate by division when repotting.

## Laelia pumila

This autumn-flowering species from Guyana is ideal for the novice. Its six-inch (15-cm) spikes carry one or two bright rose-purple flowers. The lip of the flower is deep crimson-purple with raised yellow stripes.

**Good Care Guide**

The requirements of *L. pumila* are not exacting. Protect from the hottest sun but see that it gets ample sunlight. Overwinter at 55°F (13°C) and ventilate freely during warm weather. Water liberally during the growing season from April to September, and sparingly from November to March. Repot in a small perforated pot, using a compost of equal parts osmunda fibre and sphagnum moss. Propagation is by division when new root activity is apparent.

## Lycaste deppei

This Mexican orchid produces fragrant winter and spring flowers on six-inch (15-cm) stems, which grow directly from the furrowed and flattened pseudobulbs. The yellow-crested flowers have white petals and jade sepals mottled with crimson.

**Good Care Guide**

Keep in partial shade from April to September, then place in a sunny position. The winter temperature should not fall below 55°F (13°C). In warm weather give the plant plenty of fresh air. Keep the compost moist from May to September; otherwise supply just enough moisture to prevent the pseudobulbs from shrivelling. In spring repot in compost made up of two parts loam, one part osmunda fibre, one part sphagnum moss and one part peat or leaf mould and propagate by division.

## Miltonia vexillaria
PANSY ORCHID

In May and June, when the flowering of most other tropical orchid groups has ceased, the slender, arching spikes of this Colombian native bear fragrant, flat, pansy-like, rose-mauve blooms with distinctive yellow veining on the lips.
**Good Care Guide**
Shade *M. vexillaria* from bright summer sunshine but expose it to full light from November to February. Overwinter at 55°F (13°C). In summer spray the plant frequently and give it fresh air. The compost should always be kept slightly moist. Repot after flowering every July in a small pot, using a mixture of two parts osmunda fibre and one part sphagnum moss. Propagate by division every two or three years in spring or late summer.

## Odontoglossum grande
CLOWN ORCHID, TIGER ORCHID

Between August and November this Guatemalan plant usually bears up to seven large, cinnamon-barred, bright yellow flowers on each of its twelve-inch-high (30-cm) spikes.
**Good Care Guide**
In winter the Clown Orchid should have ample light and the temperature should not fall below 45°F (7°C). In summer shade from the hot sun and provide plenty of fresh air. The compost should be moist, except after flowering, when water should be withheld until new bulb growth starts to develop. Spray frequently throughout the summer. Repot every two or three years in a mixture composed of two parts osmunda fibre to one part sphagnum moss. Propagate by division when repotting.

## Oncidium varicosum

This elegant Brazilian orchid can reach three feet (90 cm) in height and has lance-shaped, green leaves. From September to November a many-branched stem bears a profusion of blooms. Each flower has tiny, greenish-yellow and brown petals and sepals, and a large lip which is deep yellow blotched with red.
**Good Care Guide**
In summer keep in a humid atmosphere and protect from strong sun. From May to September feed with dilute fertilizer once a month. Overwinter at 45° to 50°F (7° to 10°C). Keep the soil just moist at all times. Repot every second or third spring when new shoots are visible. Use one part sphagnum moss to two parts osmunda fibre and add a little sand. Propagate by division when repotting.

## Paphiopedilum venustum
SLIPPER ORCHID, LADY'S SLIPPER

This Nepalese orchid bears flowers singly on ten-inch (25-cm) stems from October to January. Each blossom consists of white sepals and petals striped with green and flushed palest purple. These surround a highly polished, yellow-green pouch with magnificent green marbling.
**Good Care Guide**
Do not allow the winter temperature to fall below 45°F (7°C). From March to October shade from hot sun and provide fresh air and humidity. Keep the compost moist, but never wet, at all times. Use a dilute liquid feed once a month from May to September. Every second or third spring repot in equal parts of osmunda fibre, sphagnum moss and fibrous loam. At the same time propagate by division.

## Pleione formosana
INDIAN CROCUS

This small orchid, native to the high altitudes from Tibet to Formosa, will flower freely between January and May. The petals range from white to deep mauve-pink; the paler lip is marked with brick red, magenta or yellow blotches.
**Good Care Guide**
In winter the temperature may fall to 40°F (4°C). In summer, it needs protection from direct sun and should have plenty of fresh air. From May to September apply a dilute liquid fertilizer monthly and keep moist, but withhold water when leaves turn yellow. Repot every two years, after flowering, in a mixture of two parts of any proprietary potting compost and one part sphagnum moss. Propagate by offsets or bulbils when repotting.

## Vanda tricolor

This robust Indonesian orchid grows to a height of seven feet (210 cm). It bears thick, strap-shaped leaves and up to twelve pale, creamy-pink flowers with distinctive brown spots on a curving stem.
**Good Care Guide**
*V. tricolor* does best in a generous-sized hanging basket or pot kept in a room with a winter temperature that does not fall below 55°F (13°C). Protect from hot sunshine and give plenty of fresh air. Spray regularly with soft or rain water in summer. Keep the soil moist from March to October and almost dry for the rest of the year. Apply a half-strength liquid feed once a month from April to September. Repot every third year in two parts osmunda fibre to one part sphagnum moss. Propagate by removing side shoots.

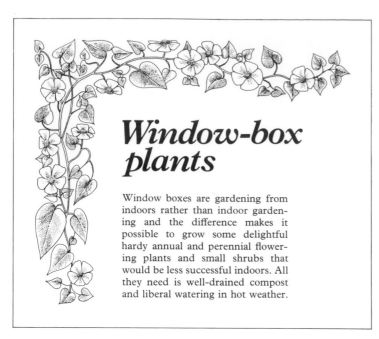

# Window-box plants

Window boxes are gardening from indoors rather than indoor gardening and the difference makes it possible to grow some delightful hardy annual and perennial flowering plants and small shrubs that would be less successful indoors. All they need is well-drained compost and liberal watering in hot weather.

## *Antirrhinum*
SNAPDRAGON

Long-lasting, colourful and hardy, Snapdragons, particularly such dwarf cultivated varieties as 'Floral Carpet' or 'Tom Thumb', are excellent window-box plants. Grown annually from seed, the six-inch-tall (15-cm) stems bear narrow leaves and numerous round-lipped, tubular flowers in various colours including red, orange, yellow and white. The flowers open from summer until early autumn.

**Good Care Guide**
Sow seeds in February or March at a temperature of 60°F (16°C). From March to May harden off the seedlings in a cool, frost-free room before planting in a south-, east- or west-facing window box. Water liberally. Pinch out shoot tips of the taller cultivated varieties.

## *Tagetes patula*
FRENCH MARIGOLD

Even on a grey day this charming Mexican annual looks encouragingly cheerful. The twelve-inch-tall (30-cm) stems, which grow in bushy clumps, bear dark green leaves and, from mid-summer until autumn, bright yellow or brownish-crimson flowers. A box in front of a large window needs a more imposing plant, such as *T. erecta* (African Marigold) which grows two to three feet (60 to 90 cm) tall.

**Good Care Guide**
In March or April sow the seed and keep at a temperature of 60° to 65°F (16° to 18°C). In May harden off the seedlings in a cool room before planting about nine inches (23 cm) apart in a sunny window box containing any good potting compost. Water liberally in dry weather.

*Hydrangea* make a splendid show in a window box, top. The rich colour of the flower heads contrasts well with the plain white walls surrounding the window.

The sophisticated display of foliage plants, above, has the advantage of remaining green for most of the year. Subtle variations in the plants' colour, tone, shape and texture provide interest.

Window boxes bring delight, not only to their owners but to passers-by as well. Even a simple box filled with *Pelargonium*, right, will give pleasure to anyone who sees it.

# WINDOW-BOX PLANTS

## *Chamaecyparis lawsoniana* 'Ellwoodii'
LAWSON CYPRESS

In time this hardy, evergreen, dwarf conifer grows to a height of ten feet (3 m). It can, however, spend its youth in a window box. After a few years transfer it to a tub and put it next to the front door—its neat, classical shape gives style to the most insignificant entrance. The species plant, which comes from North America, grows to a height of one hundred and fifty feet (45 m) or more.

**Good Care Guide**

In October plant *C. lawsoniana* 'Ellwoodii' in a window box or tub containing any reliable potting compost. It will thrive in a sunny situation or in light shade. In late summer propagate by heel cuttings of one-year-old stems. Replant every three or four years.

## *Dianthus chinensis*
CHINESE or INDIAN PINK

Several cultivated varieties have been developed from this clove-scented plant from eastern Asia. The best choice for a sunny window box is 'Heddewigii', an annual which has small, narrow, green leaves and nine-inch-tall (23-cm) stems bearing single or double, flat-petalled flowers in white and various shades of pink and red. The flowers open from summer until autumn.

**Good Care Guide**

In mid-April sow the seeds in a window box containing any good-quality potting compost. When the seedlings are large enough to handle, thin them out to six inches (15 cm) apart. Water well in dry weather. Cut off dead flower heads. Discard the plants after flowering.

## *Erica carnea*
HEATH, HEATHER

Here is a compact, low-growing, winter-flowering shrub which comes from the European Alps and is easy to grow in a south-, east- or west-facing window box. The six-inch-long (15-cm) branches are covered with needle-like green leaves, and from November to May a profusion of pink or white, tiny, bell-shaped flowers are borne on terminal spikes.

**Good Care Guide**

In spring or autumn set several plants twelve inches (30 cm) apart in a window box containing any reliable potting compost. Water liberally in dry weather. Prune when flowering finishes. From July to September propagate by cuttings of one-year-old shoots with a heel. Replant every few years. Discard any thin, straggly plants.

## *Euonymus japonicus* 'Microphyllus Variegatus'
JAPANESE SPINDLE TREE

This attractive, bushy shrub has slightly serrated, tough, green leaves with white margins. Clusters of greenish-white flowers open in May and June and, on mature plants, are sometimes followed by orange and pink fruit. The young plant can be grown in a window box. When it reaches a height of two to three feet (60 to 90 cm) it may be transferred to a tub and kept in a sheltered situation.

**Good Care Guide**

In spring or autumn plant in a window box containing any reliable potting compost. Water liberally in dry weather. Pinch out top shoots to encourage bushiness. Replant every few years. In August propagate by cuttings of lateral shoots.

## *Godetia grandiflora* (*G. amoena whitneyi*)

Producing a dense mass of showy flowers with a delicate fragrance, *G. grandiflora* is a popular California annual. The fifteen-inch-tall (38-cm) stems bear pointed, green leaves and, from June to August, spikes of rose-purple, poppy-like flowers. Several dwarf varieties are available with flowers of white, lilac and shades of pink and red.

**Good Care Guide**

In March sow the seed in a south-, east- or west-facing window box containing potting compost. In April or May thin the seedlings four to six inches (10 to 15 cm) apart. Keep the soil moist at all times. Unless the compost has been used previously to grow other plants, do not feed because fertilizer encourages too much leaf growth.

## *Hebe rakiensis*

This bushy shrub from New Zealand is one of the hardiest *Hebes* and can survive at temperatures below freezing. It has oval, rather glossy ever-green leaves. Clusters of pure white flowers open from late spring to early summer but only appear on un-pruned plants. Left to its own devices it will reach a height of eighteen inches (45 cm) or more, but it can be pruned back regularly to about twelve inches (30 cm).

**Good Care Guide**

For best results, plant *H. rakiensis* in an east- or west-facing window box. Keep the soil moist at all times. From April to September feed once a month. Replant every other spring in a good-quality potting compost. Propagate by cuttings in late summer.

## Heuchera sanguinea
CORAL BELLS

Spikes of pink, bell-shaped flowers, which open from June to September, grow in loose clusters on this Mexican perennial's delicate, twelve- to eighteen-inch-long (30- to 45-cm) stems. Round or heart-shaped, ever-green leaves grow at the base of the plant. Several hybrids and cultivated varieties have been developed with pink, red or white flowers, some of which grow on slightly longer stems.

**Good Care Guide**
In autumn, winter or spring, plant in a sunny or partially shaded window box containing any good potting compost. Water liberally in dry weather. Cut off dead stems when flowering finishes. Replant every other year at any time from autumn to spring. Propagate by division when replanting or by seed in spring.

## Juniperus communis 'Compressa'
JUNIPER

Developed from the species plant *J. communis*, which is found in many places including Britain and North America, *J. communis* 'Compressa' is a slow-growing, columnar, dwarf conifer, which only reaches a height of about two feet (60 cm) after many years. The close-growing branches are covered with grey-blue, awl-shaped foliage.

**Good Care Guide**
In April plant in a sunny or partially shaded window box containing good-quality potting compost. Water liberally in dry weather. No pruning is necessary. Replant every few years or when the plant gets too large for the window box. In autumn propagate by cuttings with a heel. Over-winter cuttings in a cool room.

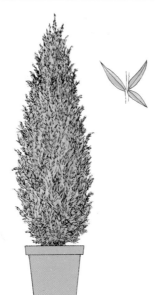

## Linaria maroccana
TOADFLAX

This slender annual comes from Morocco. In June and July flowers blotched white or yellow develop at the top of leafy stems, which grow eight to fifteen inches (20 to 38 cm) tall. There is a wide choice of colours ranging from yellow to various shades of blue and pink.

**Good Care Guide**
In March or April sow the seed in a window box that has several hours of sunshine each day. The box should be filled with any good-quality pro-prietary potting compost. When the seedlings can be handled easily thin them out to six inches (15 cm) apart. Water liberally in dry weather. There is no need to feed the plants. Discard them when flowering finishes.

## Malcolmia maritima
VIRGINIA STOCK

*M. maritima* comes from the south-ern Mediterranean area and thrives best in a sunny situation. It is, how-ever, a good-natured, hardy annual which will not object to a certain amount of shade. The tiny, white, pink, red or lilac, sweet-scented, long-lasting flowers open about six weeks after sowing and are borne on delicate, leafy, eight-inch-tall (20-cm) stems. They look effective when planted in front of a row of taller plants.

**Good Care Guide**
From March to July sow the seed thinly in a window box containing potting compost. Water freely in dry weather. There is no need to feed the plants. Discard when flowering finishes.

## Phlox drummondii
DWARF ANNUAL PHLOX

There are dozens of species and cultivated varieties of *Phlox*, but the most suitable for a window box is *P. drummondii*, an annual from Texas. It has leafy, fifteen-inch-long (38-cm) stems bearing dense clusters of flowers which open from July to September. The purple varieties look superb against white walls. Other colours include red, pink, white and lavender.

**Good Care Guide**
In March sow the seed and keep at a temperature of about 60°F (16°C). In late April harden off the seedlings in a cool but frost-free room. In May plant them in a south- or west-facing window box containing any good potting compost. In dry weather water the plants liberally. Cut off dead flower heads.

## Viola
PANSY

The Pansy, with its appealing open face only a few inches off the ground, makes an excellent edging plant for window boxes. They can also be used to fill the gaps between larger plants. Grown as an annual or short-lived perennial in a shady or sunny situa-tion, the pansy produces a profusion of blooms in many colours at almost any time of the year, depending on the temperature and the variety.

**Good Care Guide**
Sowing and planting dates differ from variety to variety so follow the instructions on the seed packet. Pansies thrive best in a good-quality potting compost that is kept moist at all times. Cut off dead flowers. Discard the plants after flowering, which may, with short lulls, continue for two years.

### Aster novi-belgii 'Lady in Blue'
MICHAELMAS DAISY

Michaelmas Daisies are hardy perennials with stiff, branched stems bearing narrow, pointed, green leaves. The daisy-like flowers, which open in September and October, come in a wide range of colours but usually have yellow centres. The best choice for a window box is the deep blue, dwarf 'Lady in Blue', which grows ten inches (25 cm) tall.
**Good Care Guide**
In winter or spring plant in a south-facing window box which contains any good-quality potting compost. The plants should be set at least twelve inches (30 cm) apart. Water liberally in dry weather. Prune back hard after flowering. Replant every winter or spring and propagate by division at the same time.

### Iris pumila
BEARDED DWARF IRIS

This dwarf Iris from southern Europe grows from a rhizome to a height of only four inches (10 cm). A sun-loving, hardy perennial, *I. pumila* has sword-shaped leaves and white, yellow or purple flowers with hairy patches on the arched, outer petals. The flowers open from early April to May.
**Good Care Guide**
After flowering, or in autumn, plant the rhizomes about nine inches (23 cm) apart in a south-facing window box containing any good potting compost. Leave the top of each rhizome partially uncovered. Water liberally in dry weather. Remove dead or dying leaves regularly. Replant every third autumn and propagate by dividing the rhizomes at the same time.

### Primula auricula
PRIMULA

The species plant is a hardy perennial from the European Alps. Its greyish-green leaves grow in rosettes on short, erect rhizomes, and umbels of purple or yellow, primrose-like flowers are borne on four- to six-inch-long (10- to 15-cm) stems. The flowers open from March to May. There are numerous cultivated varieties in several colours including blue and deep red.
**Good Care Guide**
In autumn, winter or spring plant in a sunny or partially shaded window box containing a good-quality potting compost. Water liberally in dry weather. Replant every other year when flowering finishes. Propagate by division when replanting or by seed from May to September.

# A bold show of colour

Chimney pots, wooden tubs and terracotta boxes, left, can be effectively used outdoors filled with *Pelargoniums*, *Dianthus* and small hardy shrubs.

A simple display of pansies, top, adds colour to a timber-framed window.

*Hydrangea* and *Calceolaria* make a bright display in a window box downstairs, while standard Bay trees and other foliage plants decorate the balcony of a town house, above.

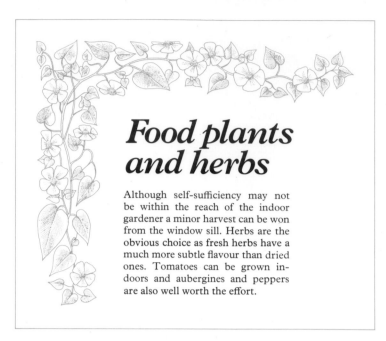

# Food plants and herbs

Although self-sufficiency may not be within the reach of the indoor gardener a minor harvest can be won from the window sill. Herbs are the obvious choice as fresh herbs have a much more subtle flavour than dried ones. Tomatoes can be grown indoors and aubergines and peppers are also well worth the effort.

## *Allium schoenoprasum*
CHIVE

The slender, tubular leaves of this six- to ten-inch-tall (15- to 25-cm) hardy perennial grow in a clump and have a mild onion flavour. Pretty, pinkish-purple flowers open in June and July; they should be removed to encourage leaf growth. Keep chives on a sunny outdoor window sill.

**Good Care Guide**

In March sow seeds in moist seed compost. When the seedlings are large enough to handle, plant two or three in a 3-inch (8-cm) pot containing any reliable potting compost. Keep the soil moist at all times or the leaves will turn brown. Later pot on into 5- or 6-inch (13- or 15-cm) containers. Start cutting when the leaves are about four inches (10 cm) tall. Repot every other year in winter and propagate by division.

## *Capsicum annuum*
RED OR GREEN PEPPER

Although primarily grown for culinary purposes, the two most frequently cultivated forms of *C. annuum*—*C. annuum acuminatum* and *C. annuum grossum*—can also be used as decorative house plants because of their attractive fruit.

**Good Care Guide**

*C. annuum* requires plenty of light, but give it some shade during the hottest weather. Water liberally and when the plant starts flowering, give a weekly liquid feed. Daily spraying is beneficial. To encourage bushiness pinch out the growing tip when the plant reaches six inches (15 cm). Propagate by seed during March at a temperature of 60° to 65°F (16° to 18°C). Pot the seedlings singly in 3-inch (8-cm) pots. Later pot on into 5- or 6-inch (13- or 15-cm) pots.

## *Lycopersicon esculentum*
TOMATO

Nothing is more pleasant than the sweet smell of tomatoes ripening in the sun on a kitchen window sill.

**Good Care Guide**

Although the tomato plant will tolerate a temperature as low as 50°F (10°C), it thrives better when it is considerably warmer. Give it plenty of sunlight and fresh air. Support the plant with canes. In hot weather water every day. Tap the flower clusters daily to help pollination. After the fruit has set, feed weekly with liquid tomato fertilizer. Cut off any yellow leaves and remove side shoots unless lush cultivated varieties are being grown. Propagate by seed at a temperature of 65°F (18°C). Pot seedlings singly into 3-inch (8-cm) pots, then into 6- to 7-inch (15- to 18-cm) pots.

## *Mentha spicata*
MINT, SPEARMINT

In Great Britain, since the third century, the mid-green, oval leaves of this hardy perennial have been used to make a sauce to serve with meat. The plant, which grows two feet (60 cm) tall, bears spikes of small, purple flowers which open in summer and are best pinched out.

**Good Care Guide**

In March or April plant the mint root in a 6-inch (15-cm) pot containing potting compost. Keep it on an outdoor window sill and shade from direct sun. Start cutting, but not too frequently, when the stems are at least three inches (8 cm) tall. Water liberally from spring to autumn but sparingly in winter. Repot every spring. Propagate by cuttings in spring or summer, or by dividing the roots when repotting.

## *Ocimum basilicum*
SWEET BASIL

Basil has shiny, green leaves borne on four-sided stems. Tiny, white flowers open in August and should be removed to encourage leaf growth. Treat the plant as an annual and keep it on the sill of a south-facing window. Sweet Basil reaches a height of two feet (60 cm), but can easily be kept to less than half this size by regular pinching out of the top shoots.

**Good Care Guide**

In March sow seeds in moist seed compost. Germinate at 55°F (13°C). Plant each seedling in a 3-inch (8-cm) pot containing any reliable potting compost. Water liberally. Pot on into a 5-inch (13-cm) container later. Pinch out top shoots to encourage bushiness. Pick the leaves from July onwards.

## *Origanum majorana*
SWEET MARJORAM

Marjoram has a sweet yet spicy flavour. The hairy, somewhat grey-green leaves are borne on reddish stems which can grow one to two feet (30 to 60 cm) tall. In spring and summer it will thrive on a sunny outdoor window sill. Pink or white flowers appear in summer and may be used for flavouring.

**Good Care Guide**
In March sow seeds in moist seed compost. Germinate at 50° to 55°F (10° to 13°C). When the seedlings are large enough to handle, plant each one in a 3-inch (8-cm) pot containing potting compost. Water liberally. Later move into a 5- or 6-inch (13- or 15-cm) container. Start cutting when the stems are about four to six inches (10 to 15 cm) tall. Discard in late autumn.

## *Petroselinum crispum*
PARSLEY

Ribbed stems bear the flat or curly green parsley leaves which are used to flavour or garnish so many dishes. Treated either as an annual or biennial, parsley may be grown in a pot on a sunny or partially shaded window sill. Although it is convenient to keep the plant in the kitchen, it will thrive best outside in a window box or pot.

**Good Care Guide**
From April to June sow the seeds in seed compost and keep moist. When the seedlings are large enough to handle, plant each one in a 3-inch (8-cm) pot containing any reliable potting compost. Keep the soil moist. When well grown, pot on into a 5-inch (13-cm) pot. Pick the parsley regularly to encourage growth. Discard the plant when it loses its vigour.

## *Phaseolus aureus*
MUNG BEAN (BEAN SPROUTS)

Bean sprouts can be grown at home with relative ease and at little cost. Mung beans are used to produce the sprouts. They are indigenous to India and can be purchased from some seedsmen.

**Good Care Guide**
To sprout the beans, soak them overnight in cold water, then put them in a single layer in a shallow container in a place which is completely dark, such as a cupboard. A temperature of 70°F (21°C) is essential. Sprinkle with water several times a day to keep constantly moist. In about seven days they will be two inches (5 cm) long and will be ready to use. A word of caution: do not overgrow them or the flavour will be ruined.

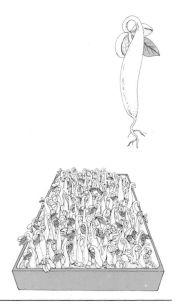

## *Salvia officinalis*
SAGE

Sage is a hardy evergreen shrub which grows two feet (60 cm) tall. The soft, grey-green leaves are used to make stuffings and to flavour cheeses. Attractive, tubular, purple flowers open in summer.

**Good Care Guide**
In March sow seeds in moist seed compost. Germinate in a cool but frost-free room. When the seedlings are large enough to handle, plant each one in a 3-inch (8-cm) pot containing any reliable potting compost and keep on a sunny outdoor window sill. Later pot on into a 5- or 6-inch (13- or 15-cm) pot. Keep the soil moist at all times. Start cutting when the stems are at least six inches (15 cm) tall. Repot every spring. Propagate by cuttings in summer or autumn.

## *Solanum melongena ovigerum*
AUBERGINE, EGGPLANT

Depending on the cultivated variety, this southern Asian vegetable fruit may be round, oval or oblong with a smooth, purple or white skin.

**Good Care Guide**
Keep the plant in full light but shade from the hottest summer sun. In winter the temperature should not fall below 60°F (16°C). Water liberally in summer and apply a liquid fertilizer every two or three weeks. Pinch out the growing tip once the plant reaches six inches (15 cm) and only allow up to three shoots to develop. When each of these shoots bears a young fruit pinch out the tip and any side shoots that appear. Discard the plant after the fruit has matured. Propagate by seed in February or March.

## *Thymus vulgaris*
THYME

Thyme is a hardy, evergreen, shrubby perennial and grows about ten inches (25 cm) tall. Tiny mauve flowers open in June. *T. × citriodorus*, a hybrid, has larger, lemon-scented leaves, which may be put in cold drinks or used to decorate desserts.

**Good Care Guide**
In March or April sow seeds in moist seed compost. Germinate in a cool, frost-free room. Plant each seedling in a 3-inch (8-cm) pot containing any reliable potting compost. Keep on a sunny, outdoor window sill and water liberally. Later pot on into a 5- or 6-inch (13- or 15-cm) container. Start cutting when the stems are at least three inches (8 cm) tall. Repot each spring. Propagate by division when repotting or by cuttings in summer or autumn.

Ceiling-high tomato plants laden with ripe, red fruit thrive in this glass-walled hall and create a pleasant, green passageway through the house.

No kitchen is complete without a herb garden. A terracotta bowl, top, is planted with Mint, Sage, Thyme, Chive, Marjoram and Basil.

*Capsicum annuum*, right, is an attractive plant which produces a cheerful harvest of delicious fruit which successfully grow and ripen indoors.

# Fun plants

It is satisfying to grow plants from the pips and stones of fruits we have eaten, even though we cannot hope they will produce free fruit for us. Avocados with their dark green leaves are among the most popular, although they often grow disappointingly lanky. Lemon, orange, mango, lychee and pomegranate are more attractive and if you have patience a date stone will grow into a sizeable and graceful Palm.

## *Citrus sinensis*
## *Citrus aurantium*
ORANGE TREE

*C. sinensis* is the sweet orange. *C. aurantium* is the sour orange used for making marmalade. A pip from either species will germinate easily, producing a rather bushy tree which can grow to a height of four feet (120 cm) in a large pot. Flowers and fruit rarely develop indoors.

**Good Care Guide**
In March plant the pip in a 3-inch (8-cm) pot containing a reliable potting compost. Germinate at 60°F (16°C). In spring and summer water liberally. Spray in hot weather. Overwinter in a cool but frost-free room and water sparingly. Keep in full light but shade from the strongest summer sun. In March prune if necessary. Pot on or repot every other winter.

## *Ananas comosus (A. sativus)*
PINEAPPLE

Pineapples have arched, strap-shaped, silver-grey leaves with serrated edges. In a warm room a handsome, two- to three-foot-tall (60- to 90-cm) plant may be grown from a pineapple top. The prickly skinned fruit may develop but seldom ripen.

**Good Care Guide**
Cut off the crown of a Pineapple with about half an inch (1 cm) of the fruit. Pare away the disc of fruit then plant the crown in a 3- to 4-inch (8- to 10-cm) pot containing equal quantities of peat and sand, or plain coarse sand, and keep moist. In spring and summer water liberally letting the compost almost dry out between watering. In winter water sparingly and provide a temperature of not less than 60°F (16°C). Repot every March.

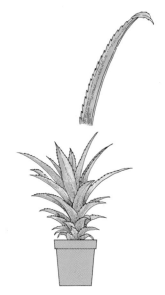

## *Daucus carota*
CARROT

Carrots have lovely, feathery, green leaves which begin to appear soon after the carrot top is planted. Within a month they are well grown.

**Good Care Guide**
Cut the top off a carrot, remove all but the youngest central leaves and plant in a 4-inch (10-cm) pot containing peat, sand or potting compost, which should be kept moist. Alternatively, stand the carrot top on a spiked flower holder and place in a saucer of water. Keep on a partially shaded window sill in a cool room. Another method is to cut off the top three inches (8 cm) of a large carrot. Dig out the core. Make two holes near the top of the shell so formed, thread with string and hang up. Keep the shell almost filled with water. Discard when leaves yellow.

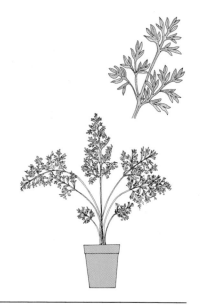

## *Citrus limon*
LEMON

Easy to grow from a pip, the Lemon is an attractive plant with pointed, glossy green leaves. It is slow-growing but may eventually reach a height of four feet (120 cm). Sweet-smelling white flowers and the familiar fruit appear only on large, mature plants and rarely indoors.

**Good Care Guide**
In March plant the pip in a 3-inch (8-cm) pot containing a good-quality potting compost. Germinate at 60°F (16°C). In spring and summer water liberally. Spray in hot weather. Overwinter at 50°F (10°C) and water sparingly. Keep in a well-lit situation. If the plant is to be kept small, cut back hard every other March. Pot on or repot every other year in winter.

## *Ipomoea batatas*
SWEET-POTATO VINE

The Sweet-potato Vine grows from a tuber which, when planted, produces twining stems with heart-shaped, sometimes lobed leaves. The stems grow quickly to a length of about six feet (180 cm) and can be supported or allowed to trail.

**Good Care Guide**
Cut off the sprouted end of a tuber and place in a 6-inch (15-cm) pot containing a good-quality potting compost. Shoots will appear if the plant is kept in a room where the temperature is no lower than 60°F (16°C). In spring and summer water liberally. In winter water sparingly and do not let the temperature fall below 55°F (13°C). Repot in spring. Propagate by cuttings or by detaching, and planting separately, any new tubers which may develop.

## *Litchi chinensis*
LYCHEE

This handsome tree from southern China has glossy, lance-shaped leaves and inconspicuous flowers. But it is for its delicious, oval, strawberry-red, brittle-skinned fruit that it is grown in the tropics. Indoors in a pot it will grow to about three feet (90 cm), but will never flower or fruit.

**Good Care Guide**

In March plant the Lychee stone in a 3-inch (8-cm) pot in any reliable potting compost. Germinate at a temperature of 65°F (18°C). Germination is slow. In spring and summer water liberally. Overwinter at a temperature of 60°F (16°C) and water sparingly. From March to September feed once a month. Keep in good light. Prune every other March. Pot on or repot every spring.

## *Mangifera indica*
MANGO

Mangoes are in season in May. They have large stones, or seeds, which, when planted in pots, produce attractive little trees with lance-shaped green leaves.

**Good Care Guide**

Plant the stone in a 4-inch (10-cm) pot containing any good-quality potting compost. Germinate at a temperature of 70° to 75°F (21° to 24°C), keeping the soil moist. When the seedling is twelve inches (30 cm) tall, pinch out the growing tip to encourage bushiness and later pot on into a 6-inch (15-cm) pot. Keep on a partially shaded window sill. From spring to autumn water liberally and spray regularly. In winter provide a temperature not lower than 60°F (16°C) and keep the soil barely moist.

## *Pastinaca sativa*
PARSNIP

Parsnips have long-stemmed, pale green leaves composed of several large, oval leaflets which are further divided into toothed lobes. They begin to appear soon after the parsnip top is planted and are well developed within a month.

**Good Care Guide**

Cut off the top of the parsnip, remove all but the youngest central leaves and plant it in a 4-inch (10-cm) pot containing peat, sand or potting compost. Water moderately, keeping the soil moist. Place the pot on a partially shaded window sill. Alternatively, put the parsnip top on a spiked flower holder and stand it in a saucer of water. It can also be hollowed out and treated in the same way as a carrot. Discard when the leaves turn yellow.

## *Persea gratissima*
AVOCADO PEAR

A home-grown Avocado tree will not bear fruit. As the tree matures the stem develops into a strong trunk with branches bearing large, dark green leaves. It may reach a height of four feet (120 cm).

**Good Care Guide**

In spring plant the stone, pointed end up, in a 6-inch (15-cm) pot containing any good potting compost. Leave the top half of the stone uncovered. Keep in good light at a temperature of 65°F (18°C). In spring and summer water liberally. Overwinter at 50°F (10°C) and water sparingly. Feed once a month from March to September. Pinch out the growing tip to encourage bushiness. Pot on every spring until the tree is three feet (90 cm) tall, then repot every few years.

## *Phoenix dactylifera*
DATE PALM

This elegant palm from northern Africa can be grown from the stone of an ordinary, commercial date. It has stiff leaves, composed of narrow, somewhat pleated green leaflets. Indoors it may eventually reach a height of about six feet (180 cm).

**Good Care Guide**

Sandpaper the date stone and plant it in spring in a 6-inch (15-cm) pot containing potting compost. Germination in a warm room, about 65°F (18°C), may take three months. In spring and summer water liberally. Overwinter at 50° to 55°F (10° to 13°C) and water sparingly. From May to September feed every two weeks. Keep in good light. Pot on every spring until the palm is about two feet (60 cm) tall, then pot on or repot every few years.

## *Punica granatum*
POMEGRANATE

Although the Pomegranate tree will not flower or fruit in a pot and loses its red-stemmed, shiny, green leaves in winter, it will provide pleasing foliage the rest of the year. It grows to a height of about six feet (180 cm), but can be kept shorter by using small pots and pruning annually.

**Good Care Guide**

Plant several Pomegranate seeds in a 3-inch (8-cm) pot containing any reliable potting compost and place on the sill of a south-facing window. Later select the strongest seedling and pot singly. From late spring to early autumn water liberally. Spray in hot weather. In winter move to a cool but frost-free room and water sparingly. From May to September feed fortnightly. Prune in late winter. Pot on or repot every other April.

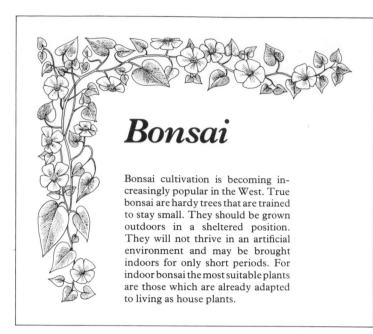

# Bonsai

Bonsai cultivation is becoming increasingly popular in the West. True bonsai are hardy trees that are trained to stay small. They should be grown outdoors in a sheltered position. They will not thrive in an artificial environment and may be brought indoors for only short periods. For indoor bonsai the most suitable plants are those which are already adapted to living as house plants.

## *Acer palmatum*
JAPANESE MAPLE

A deciduous tree from Japan and China, *A. palmatum* has deeply lobed, green leaves which turn orange, red and yellow in autumn. In its natural state it reaches a height of fifteen feet (4.5 m).

**Good Care Guide**
Although this plant thrives best in good light, it will tolerate a shady position. Keep it outdoors at all times, except for short periods in summer when it may be brought indoors. Always keep the soil moist. If possible, in winter plunge the pot into peat or sand to protect the roots from frost. Prune the roots every autumn or winter and repot in bonsai or loam-based compost. In summer trim side shoots and pinch out the growing point. Propagate by seed in autumn.

## *Cryptomeria japonica*
JAPANESE CEDAR

A native of China and Japan, *C. japonica* is an elegant, evergreen conifer which has small, leathery, awl-shaped, rich green leaves. In its natural state it grows to a height of fifty feet (15 m).

**Good Care Guide**
Keep *C. japonica* outdoors in a well-lit or partially shaded position. In summer the plant may be brought indoors for no more than a few days at a time. Keep the compost moist at all times. If possible, in winter plunge the pot into peat or sand to protect the roots from frost. Prune the roots every autumn or winter and repot in bonsai or loam-based compost. In summer trim the side shoots and pinch out the growing point. Propagate by seed in spring or by heel cuttings in late summer.

## *Juniperus chinensis*
CHINESE JUNIPER

This columnar evergreen, which is found in China, Japan and Mongolia, has blue-green juvenile leaves and grey-green adult leaves. In its natural state it reaches a height of twenty feet (6 m).

**Good Care Guide**
*J. chinensis* thrives best if it is kept outdoors in partial shade. It may be brought indoors for short periods in summer after the new growth has appeared. Always keep the compost moist. If possible, in winter the pot should be plunged into sand or peat to protect the roots from frost. Repot every autumn or winter in bonsai or loam-based compost. When repotting, prune the roots. Pinch out the growing point and trim the side shoots in summer. Propagate by cuttings in late summer.

## *Rhododendron simsii* 'Satsuki'
SATSUKI AZALEA

This exquisite cultivated variety has been developed from the species plant, *R. simsii*, which is found in China. It has small, glossy, dark green leaves and deep pink flowers which open in May.

**Good Care Guide**
Keep *R. simsii* 'Satsuki' outdoors in a partially shaded position. The plant may be brought indoors during the flowering period. If possible, in winter plunge the pot into sand or peat to protect the roots from frost. Always keep the compost moist. Every autumn or winter prune the roots and repot in bonsai or loam-based compost. In summer trim the side shoots and pinch out the growing point to maintain a good shape. Propagate by cuttings in summer.

## *Zelkova serrata*
GREY-BARK ELM

A graceful tree from China, Japan and Korea, *Z. serrata* has slender, pointed green leaves which turn bronze or red in autumn.

**Good Care Guide**
This tree should be kept outdoors in a sheltered, well-lit position. In summer it may be brought indoors, but only for a few days at a time. Keep the compost moist at all times. If possible, in winter plunge the pot into peat or sand to protect the roots from frost. Every autumn or winter repot in bonsai compost or any good-quality loam-based compost. At repotting time, prune the roots. In summer trim the side shoots and pinch out the growing point to maintain the trained shape of the tree. Propagate by seed in autumn.

The fascinating art of bonsai is
exemplified in this beautiful apricot
tree. Although only eleven inches
(28 cm) high, it is twelve years old
and has all the characteristics of a
fully grown tree.

144

# Caring for your plants

Michael Rochford, first of the Rochford nurserymen, is reported by Mea Allen in *Tom's Weeds* as saying that to grow perfect *Adiantum* they must have "the right amount of heat, light, moisture and air required to give size, freshness and lasting properties". The same advice would hold good for any plant, and has the virtue of simplicity. Unfortunately, however, there is no simple formula by which the right amounts can be worked out to ensure instant success in indoor gardening. Complete confidence in handling plants comes only with experience, but it comes more quickly with a realization of the difficulties facing a plant that is confined to a pot indoors.

The light may be too poor, the air too dry, and, in heated rooms, too warm. And it is often forgotten that a plant needs rest, just as we do, and that it must be allowed its dormant period. The hardest lesson to learn is not to overwater, but it must be learned, for the plant is unable to thank us for our good intentions or to warn us of the dire results that will otherwise follow. And always use good-quality compost never garden soil (although in this book we have used the word soil as a synonym for compost).

Looking after indoor plants, however, means far more than just keeping them alive, there is the pleasure of caring for them as well. One of the most obvious ways of becoming involved is by propagating them. The ways of doing so are many, some easy, some difficult, but all satisfying. Growing cacti, training bonsai and making miniature gardens are ways of turning indoor gardening into a hobby. And when you have grown plants to be proud of there is the challenge of displaying them to their best advantage.

# The living plant

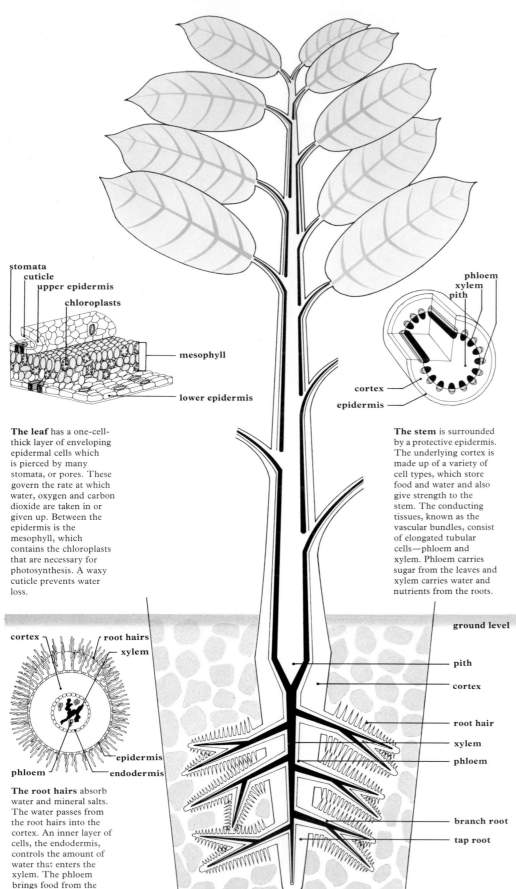

**stomata**
**cuticle**
**upper epidermis**
**chloroplasts**

**mesophyll**

**lower epidermis**

**phloem**
**xylem**
**pith**

**cortex**
**epidermis**

**The leaf** has a one-cell-thick layer of enveloping epidermal cells which is pierced by many stomata, or pores. These govern the rate at which water, oxygen and carbon dioxide are taken in or given up. Between the epidermis is the mesophyll, which contains the chloroplasts that are necessary for photosynthesis. A waxy cuticle prevents water loss.

**The stem** is surrounded by a protective epidermis. The underlying cortex is made up of a variety of cell types, which store food and water and also give strength to the stem. The conducting tissues, known as the vascular bundles, consist of elongated tubular cells—phloem and xylem. Phloem carries sugar from the leaves and xylem carries water and nutrients from the roots.

**cortex** **root hairs**
**xylem**

**epidermis**
**endodermis**
**phloem**

**The root hairs** absorb water and mineral salts. The water passes from the root hairs into the cortex. An inner layer of cells, the endodermis, controls the amount of water that enters the xylem. The phloem brings food from the leaves.

**ground level**

**pith**

**cortex**

**root hair**

**xylem**

**phloem**

**branch root**

**tap root**

The vital needs of a plant are very much like our own—light, water, air, food and warmth. The relative importance of each of these needs differs widely between different plants, but within a particular species the requirements remain the same whether the plant is growing free in its native mountain forest in China or is a captive in an apartment in Park Lane or Park Avenue, or in the front room of 47 Railway Terrace.

The plant's requirements are the same but its environment is totally changed. A plant in a pot in a house is in an entirely artificial situation, and although it is remarkable how well many plants can adapt, there are limits. Beyond those limits you must take over from Nature the full responsibility for satisfying the plant's needs. Understanding the basic facts about the way in which plants live and grow will make more sense of everything you read about looking after them. At least it will make you regard with a healthy scepticism all the old wives' tales you hear.

To manufacture the carbohydrates and proteins which a plant needs to live and grow requires raw materials. Mineral salts such as nitrogen, sulphur, phosphorus, magnesium, potassium and calcium are taken up from the soil through the plant's fine root hairs. The water taken up is a source of hydrogen. Carbon dioxide and oxygen are absorbed from the atmosphere through the minute pores, or stomata, of the leaves.

Light is essential to turn these raw materials into food. In daylight, light energy from the sun is absorbed by chlorophyll, the green pigment in the plant cells. The light energy is used to split the water into hydrogen and oxygen molecules. The hydrogen combines with the carbon dioxide, absorbed from the atmosphere, to form a sugar compound. This whole process is called photosynthesis.

The sugar is used as food by the plant. It is converted into energy to drive all the plant's

**Roots, stems and leaves** are three major functional organs of all plants. The roots anchor the plant in the soil and absorb both water and mineral salts. They also store a certain amount of food. The stem conducts water and mineral salts from the roots. The stem also distributes sugar, which has been manufactured in the leaves, to other plant tissues that require it for growth, or it stores it for future use. The stem also holds the foliage up towards the light, which is necessary for the process of photosynthesis, the primary function of the leaves. A secondary function is that of transpiration, during which excess water is returned to the atmosphere.

vital processes and to make it grow. The conversion into energy takes place by a breaking down of the sugar with the oxygen absorbed by the leaves in a process known as respiration. This process, unlike photosynthesis, takes place day and night.

The various elements taken up through the plant's roots have differing roles. They help in the process of photosynthesis, the production of carbohydrates and protein, in the development of flowers, leaves, roots and seeds and in the maintenance of the plant's general good health.

Where then does a human fit in a house plant's life? The most obvious responsibility is in providing adequate light for photosynthesis to take place. This does not necessarily mean direct sunlight—it is the energy that light produces that is vital, and even artificial light may suffice. "Adequate" light will mean approximately the level of light natural to that particular plant in its own surroundings —whether it is forest shade or desert sun. A plant may tolerate lower levels of light, but this should not be traded on too far, for while a plant deprived of its normal ration of light may not die, it certainly will not flourish.

Plants are more sensitive to the level of light than humans are. However bright a room may seem to you, it is always darker indoors than it is out of doors and it is always much darker than you imagine.

As well as a certain level of light the house plant must also be given the appropriate level of temperature. These levels cover a wide range; some house plants will survive a little frost, while others suffer if the temperature falls below 70°F (21°C). But each species has a level of warmth at which it will grow—as distinct from the level at which it will live— and below which it cannot grow.

A plant needs different temperatures during its growing and dormant periods. In its natural state this is regulated by the sun. (The world's flora has not yet adapted to the erosion of the seasons brought about by central heating.) A plant may also need to be drier and exposed to less light during its period of dormancy. Since a plant needs to rest as well as to grow, the onus for providing the conditions for rest falls on the owner.

The owner's responsibility for providing water is total and tediously recurrent. It is the main chore you take on when deciding to

share your home with plants. If the prospect appalls you it is far better for you to buy a picture. Plants are dependent on the water you give them for the supply of hydrogen for photosynthesis and for dissolving the minerals in the soil or compost to be taken up by the roots. The plant also relies on you not to give it too much water, for waterlogged soil does not hold the air without which the root hairs cannot function and will die.

The plant is almost as dependent on you for nutrients as it is for water, although it does have some reserve in the soil or compost in which it is planted that will cushion your neglect. In a garden it could send out more roots in search of nutrients, but in a pot it cannot do this. Feeding with fertilizer has to be carried out during the growing season. Also, as the plant grows and the roots crowd the pot it will have to be moved to a larger pot with a greater reservoir of nutrients.

Fortunately, you don't have to breathe for your plant. It will take in the vital oxygen and carbon dioxide on its own, but it may help if you keep both sides of the leaves, but particularly the undersides, free of dust and grease that would clog the stomata.

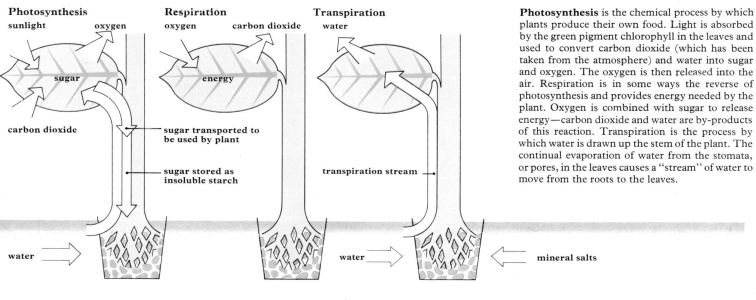

**Photosynthesis**
sunlight    oxygen
sugar
carbon dioxide

**Respiration**
oxygen    carbon dioxide
energy

sugar transported to be used by plant

sugar stored as insoluble starch

**Transpiration**
water

transpiration stream

water          mineral salts

**Photosynthesis** is the chemical process by which plants produce their own food. Light is absorbed by the green pigment chlorophyll in the leaves and used to convert carbon dioxide (which has been taken from the atmosphere) and water into sugar and oxygen. The oxygen is then released into the air. Respiration is in some ways the reverse of photosynthesis and provides energy needed by the plant. Oxygen is combined with sugar to release energy—carbon dioxide and water are by-products of this reaction. Transpiration is the process by which water is drawn up the stem of the plant. The continual evaporation of water from the stomata, or pores, in the leaves causes a "stream" of water to move from the roots to the leaves.

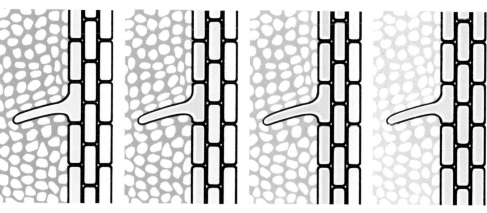

**Osmosis** is the process by which water passes into the root hairs. This involves the movement of water through a semi-permeable membrane from a solution of low concentration to one of high concentration. Osmosis continues until the solutions on either side of the membrane are of equal strength. The loss of water by transpiration through the stomata of the leaves ensures that sap has a higher concentration of mineral salts than soil water. Water is therefore always being drawn into the root hairs. If, however, the solution in the soil is more concentrated than the sap, water leaves the roots and the plant becomes dehydrated. This is the reason why most plants will not grow in a salty soil.

# Temperature and humidity

No plant is a native of a house. A surprising number of house plants, however, are natives of the tropics. But labelling them tropical plants does not mean that they can be lumped together and treated in the same way. Within the tropical zone are not only the steaming jungles of our imaginations but also deserts, which are very dry and very hot, and mountain forests, which are very wet but fairly cool. From these cool, mountain forest regions come many of our house evergreens. It is comparatively easy to provide them with the temperatures they need. Their problem in a house is not insufficient warmth, but the lack of the humidity of their homelands.

House plants are generally divided into three groups, according to the temperature required for growth. Plants which like it cool, such as *Aspidistra*, *Fatsia japonica* (False Castor-oil Plant) and × *Fatshedera lizei* (Fat-headed Lizzie), require a growing temperature of between 45° and 55°F (7° and 13°C). Obviously in a house this temperature will be exceeded for the sake of the occupants if not the plants. Plants which like it warmer belong to a more delicate group. The temperature for them should not fall much below 55°F (13°C), and should not go much higher than 65°F (18°C). Among such plants are *Begonia*, *Coleus*, *Dizygotheca elegantissima* (False Aralia), *Saintpaulia ionantha* (African Violet) and *Sansevieria trifasciata* (Mother-in-law's Tongue). The tenderest group of plants needs a temperature that does not fall much below 65°F (18°C) and goes up to 75°F (24°C). Plants in this group include *Aglaonema commutatum* (Chinese Evergreen), *Allamanda cathartica* (Common Allamanda) and *Mimosa pudica* (Sensitive Plant).

These three divisions are made only to provide guidelines and they should not be interpreted too rigidly. There are whole sets of different rules for cacti and other succulents, which are accustomed to great day and night contrasts in temperature and are not at all worried by dryness in the air. There are even plants—for example some *Philodendron* and *Monstera*—which will equally tolerate cool, temperate and warm situations. With all plants, too, there are other factors to take into consideration besides a simple reading on a

### Room temperatures
It is wise to check the temperature and humidity, which will vary from room to room, before you finally select a position for your plant. Even within the same room there may be a temperature range of more than twenty degrees, from near a radiator to behind a badly insulated window. Soil temperature is as important as air temperature. Extremely hot spots, above radiators and fires, for example, are harmful, not only because the hot air dries out the leaves of the plant but because the roots can also become too warm. Plants from the warmth of the tropics, however, may suffer very badly with cold feet. Although fluctuations of temperature can have grave consequences, a lower night-time temperature, compared to that of the daytime, is desirable.

A window sill may be many degrees colder than the rest of the room.

Cold draughts from ill-fitting doors will cause many plants to drop their leaves.

In a dark room high temperatures make plants grow lank, spindly and weak.

Window boxes and tubs are suitable for hardy plants that require lower temperatures.

A window sill can be scorchingly hot in the sun but icy cold at night.

A *Saintpaulia* placed on a wooden shelf above a radiator will benefit from bottom heat.

Plants that need a fair amount of warmth can stand near a radiator, but never directly above it.

The cooler the room the drier the soil should be because water loss due to evaporation is low.

thermometer. How even is the temperature? How moist or dry are the soil and the air? How light is the room?

A house plant is happier with a fairly constant though cooler temperature than with one that is high and low at different times of the day. While wide fluctuations in temperature are detrimental to the plant's well-being, it will probably benefit from being slightly cooler at night. In fact, even with central heating, few houses have constant temperatures, and the pattern of heating is decided by the family's needs and not by the plant's. In a centrally heated house which is programmed there may be a period of warmth in the morning until the family goes out, to be followed by a cold period until they return at

the end of the afternoon. This is succeeded by a hot and probably fuggy few hours until everyone goes to bed.

Poor plants, but it is totally impractical to pander to them altogether! If we did, depending on which plants we were slaves to, we would have a house which was uncomfortably cold or one with temperatures and fuel bills which were insufferably high. All that we can do is to buy the plants most likely to succeed in our living conditions and then do our best to minimize the extremes of temperature to which our plants are subjected. It is important to remember that cold draughts from doors and windows can be just as dangerous as the direct heat from radiators or fires.

The warmer the room, the more moist the air should be. This is a major hurdle to overcome when successfully growing house plants. Modern methods of heating a house usually result in air that is very dry. It is often too dry for humans, let alone for house plants accustomed to the humid conditions that accompany two or three hundred inches (5,000 to 7,500 mm) of rain a year. This is a problem not of watering—which, with care, can be solved—but of air humidity, which is more difficult to control.

There are a number of ways, of varying effectiveness, of surrounding a plant with air that is more moist than that of the rest of the room. A simple method is to spray the plant with water each day, using a fine mist spray. Although this is better than nothing, the effect does not last long. A better method is to stand a single plant in a shallow dish which has a layer of pebbles at the bottom. It is important to pour just enough water into the dish so that the pebbles are not completely covered. If the pot itself stands in water the soil may become waterlogged, and the plant will eventually die. The water in the dish

**A humidifier and a hygrometer** are invaluable. Relative humidity can be determined using the hygrometer and the humidifier will keep the entire room more humid.

evaporates, making the air around the plant a little more moist than it would otherwise have been. To accommodate a group of plants use this pebbles-in-water method on a tray or at the bottom of a trough. The air around a group of plants will stay more moist than it will around an isolated plant.

A more elaborate and more effective method is to put potted plants in a box and bury them to about two-thirds of the pots' depth in damp peat. This keeps the soil in the pots moist but not waterlogged, insulates the soil against sudden changes of temperature and produces a more moist microclimate than pebbles ever do. The best alternative is an automatic electric humidifier.

Fluctuations of temperature and humidity are tolerated by only a few, very hardy plants.

Never leave plants on window sills at night trapped between cold glass and the curtains.

The continuous air current from a fan causes water to evaporate quickly and leaves to wilt.

The high humidity in a kitchen is excellent for growing many indoor ferns.

**A humid microclimate** can be created in several ways. A single plant can stand on a platform of pebbles or on an upturned pot above a reservoir of water. A more effective method is to accommodate groups of plants in a box containing damp peat. The peat keeps the compost moist but not waterlogged, and insulates the compost against sudden temperature changes. Spraying has an immediate but short-lived effect, and is a repetitive and tedious job on extremely hot days.

# The need for light

Whereas a human being is directly dependent on light for only one of his senses—sight—a green plant depends on light for its very life. Without light it cannot live and with too little light it will not absorb enough energy to enable it to grow. It must then concentrate on trying to keep alive, and before long it will probably die.

How much light is too little and how much light is enough for your plant? Even with the use of artificial light you cannot hope to reproduce the light conditions which prevail in the plant's native haunts. There is never as much natural light indoors as there is out of doors, even in a greenhouse where the walls and ceilings are made of glass.

We tend to think of rooms in terms of "light rooms" and "dark rooms". The human eye is notoriously unreliable in judging variations of light within a room, although these variations are considerable. There is strong direct light at a window and good but indirect light up to five or six feet (150 to 180 cm) from it; the rest of the room is in shade. White walls, which are excellent reflectors, give a brighter, more even light than dark walls.

It would be possible to site plants rather less haphazardly by using a light meter to plot the rapidly diminishing intensity of light as you move away from a window. But for most of us finding a place for a plant that will satisfy (as far as we can) its light needs is pure guess-work. Only time shows whether we have pushed the plant beyond the limits of its tolerance. The signs can be dramatic—such as death—or more subtle; sometimes the plant grows leggy and the leaves stay small, the young leaves grow pale and old leaves turn yellow, variegated leaves turn totally green or flowering plants fail to bloom. If you detect any of these signs early, put the plant in a rather better light, but be careful because too drastic a change can be harmful.

South-facing windows provide most light, and the next in order are east- and west-facing windows. The light from all these windows varies enormously during the day, as the sun travels across the sky. The light from a north-facing window, on the other hand, although less, is steadier. Remember, of course, that in choosing a suitably lit site for a plant the temperature level is also extremely important.

**Light intensity** decreases dramatically over a very short distance within a room that has only a single natural light source. The human eye is notoriously inefficient at judging degrees of darkness, but an electronic light meter, similar to that used by a photographer, will show that only eight feet from a window light intensity may be less than five per cent of that on the window sill. A plant that requires plenty of light cannot, therefore, thrive even a few feet away.

Rooms with south-facing windows are very bright and very hot. In summer only cacti would be able to stand the direct heat on these window sills unless shading is provided by a net curtain. Three feet (90 cm) or so from the window is a good place for many variegated and purple-leaved plants. *Begonia rex* and *Maranta* (Prayer Plant) are exceptions. A variegated plant needs stronger light than a green variety of the same species because the paler parts of the leaves are short of chlorophyll and the green parts have to work harder and need better light for efficient photosynthesis. *Pelargonium* (Geranium) and *Chrysanthemum* are flowering plants for such a bright position, and in winter Daffodil and Hyacinth will be quite happy there.

East-facing windows get the morning sun, which, except in midsummer, is unlikely to scorch plants. A position just away from this window is ideal for shade-loving plants.

Rooms with west-facing windows stay lighter and warmer longer in the evening, thus prolonging the plant's day, but in summer they can become almost as hot as one with a south-facing window. They are suitable for a wide range of house plants which need, or do not object to, good but non-intense light. These include *Peperomia*, *Ficus elastica decora* (Rubber Plant), *Philodendron*, *Monstera deliciosa* (Swiss Cheese Plant) and *Hedera helix* (Common Ivy) for most of the year. In summer *Coleus*, *Impatiens wallerana* (Busy Lizzie), *Crossandra* and many cacti and other succulents will tolerate the direct sunlight.

A gentle light without great fluctuation is provided in rooms with north-facing windows. *Araucaria heterophylla* (Norfolk Island Pine), *Aspidistra*, *Cissus antarctica* (Kangaroo Vine) and *Rhoicissus rhomboidea* (Grape Ivy) —indeed most foliage plants with dark green leaves—do well in such a situation.

Describing rooms by the points of the compass which their windows face highlights a major problem confronting a house plant. It is getting light from only one direction, while out of doors, even in shade, it would receive light from all directions, particularly

**Phototropism**
Light from only one direction will cause a plant to bend towards that light source. If the pot is not turned until the plant has bent over it will become distorted. It is best to mark the pot with a cross so that you know its position and turn the pot a little each day. The plant will then grow upright.

## Growing plants under artificial light

With the use of artificial light you can enliven and transform dull, dark corners, empty fireplaces and basements with plants. Special units can be bought in various shapes and sizes, but it is easy to build your own to fit into any area. Portable units for table-tops are the easiest to use and to make. They consist of a tray, to accommodate the plants, and two supports, which hold a canopy. The canopy eliminates the glare from the fluorescent light tubes, which are set in holders inside it, and directs the light down towards the plants. It is essential that a terrarium be artificially lit, particularly in winter. Large free-standing units with shelves, each fitted with a set of lights, can be used to grow large numbers of plants. Light tubes used for mature plants are usually not suitable for many seedlings as the intensity is too low.

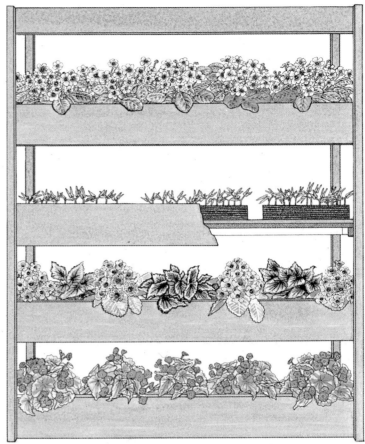

from above. The plant's reaction is to turn towards the light, which is its source of life, and to grow in that direction.

Although your plants will not appreciate constant moving to satisfy your whims there are at times valid reasons for a change. In winter plants may be moved nearer the window to compensate for lower seasonal levels of light and in spring may be moved back.

The quantity as well as the quality of light needed by a plant has to be taken into consideration. Some plants, known as long-day plants, need long periods of light to produce flowers; others, called short-day plants, will grow flower buds only when light is restricted to less than twelve hours.

The many plants which come from the tropics are accustomed to days and nights of almost equal length, and the long nights of northern and southern latitudes may not be to their liking. This problem can be overcome by the use of artificial light to lengthen the short winter days. Lighting may also be necessary to provide a better light than would otherwise be possible indoors to induce plants to flower. Among the plants which particularly respond to artificial lighting in rooms badly provided with natural light are *Saintpaulia ionantha* (African Violet), *Sinningia speciosa* (Gloxinia), *Begonia*, *Columnea microphylla* (Goldfish Vine), *Episcia* and quite

a few of the cacti and other succulents.

An ordinary incandescent light hanging from the ceiling is not very effective as far as plants are concerned except in winter, when they provide valuable additional light for short periods. Spotlights are more decorative than useful, and if they are too close to a plant they can be harmfully hot. Fluorescent tubes provide adequate light fairly inexpensively, without roasting the plants. The colour of the light emitted by the tubes is important. While a "warm white" tube would be used for seedlings, an effective light for growing plants is given by one 40-watt "cool" tube and one 40-watt "daylight" tube. These should be fixed eighteen to thirty inches (45 to 75 cm) above the tops of the plants. The plants will

**Window-sill plants**
usually turn their best face to the outside world. To make them grow upright if they are on a sunless window sill provide a supplement of artificial light by fitting a fluorescent light tube directly above the window sill. The light fitting can be hidden by a pelmet or other facing.

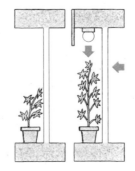

soon indicate whether you have the distance right. If the leaves curl they are too near the light. If the stems start growing lanky the plants are too far away from it.

There are special horticultural tubes, but these give a purplish light which many people dislike. But since plants are not fussy about when they get their extra light, a time switch can be fitted to turn the lighting on and off when you are in bed.

Lighting units are popular among keen indoor gardeners, especially in the United States. A lighting unit consists of a tray to hold the plants, supports for the lights, which can be adjusted to various heights, and a hood over the fluorescent tubes to reflect the light on to the plants and out of the eyes of their owner. Even under these fluorescent lights plants will give off more water than usual and must be watered more often. Bear in mind, too, that in a fluorescent tube the brightest light is at the centre. The intensity of the light it gives diminishes with time and although you may not notice it, the plants will. Tubes will have to be replaced yearly.

Since artificial light is expensive, do not waste daylight. When the days lengthen and the sun rises before you do, always open the curtains before going to bed or you will be unnecessarily depriving your plants of some precious and free daylight.

# Watering and feeding

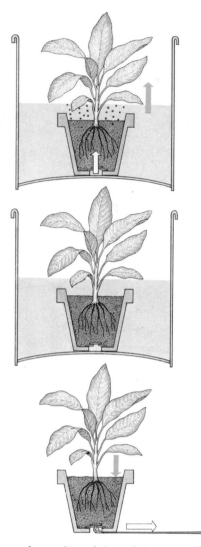

**Thorough wetting** of the soil is achieved by immersing the pot in a bucket of water. Bubbles of air are pushed out as water fills the spaces between the soil particles. When the bubbles stop appearing remove the pot from the water and place it on a board to drain. Fresh, oxygen-rich air, which is as necessary to the roots as water, is then drawn in.

**Water** should be poured into the central vase of some bromeliads in summer, as well as on the compost. Plants that are damaged if water falls on to the leaves, flowers or roots should be watered from the bottom. The pots-in-peat and platform methods of watering also create a suitable humid microclimate. Spraying leaves is a useful way to revive plants that have wilted.

Nature—in the form of the sun—takes a major hand in providing warmth and light for a plant even if it is confined to a house. But giving the plant the water it needs—not too little and not too much—is entirely your responsibility.

Most people overwater "to be on the safe side". In fact it is not safe but full of danger. To understand why this is so, you must understand the basic happenings inside the pot. The pot contains roots and soil, or compost, and also air and water which together make up about half the bulk of the "soil". The more water there is between the solid particles of the soil the less room there is for air, and without oxygen the root hairs cannot take up the water and mineral salts needed by the plant. If the soil is always saturated with water the root hairs, deprived of air, will rot, and consequently the plant will die.

Avoid watering a little and often, for the little could be too little—wetting only the surface of the soil—or the often too often—leading to a waterlogged, airless soil. The rhythm of watering should be to allow the soil to become fairly dry and then to wet it thoroughly.

Nothing could be simpler, but for the fact that a plant gives no unmistakable early warning that it is thirsty. Leaves will wilt when the plant is dangerously short of water —thin leaves do so long before thick fleshy leaves—but it is dangerous to wait for that sign, since rescue may come too late.

The wisest course is to take a look at the plants regularly—once a week in cool, wet weather and daily on the hottest days. If the surface of the soil looks dry, feel below the surface with your fingers. With practice this is a fairly reliable method, and far less time-wasting than using a moisture meter. If the soil is dry all the way through then water thoroughly.

Plants will need more water when they are putting out new leaves or when they are coming into bud. In cold weather far less watering is needed and the soil can be allowed to become almost dry.

The most thorough wetting is achieved by immersing the pot in a bucket of water. Bubbles rise as the water soaks into the spaces between the soil and pushes out the air. When the bubbles stop remove the pot from the water and put it somewhere to drain. As the water drains out new air is sucked back in, and even more is gradually drawn in as the water is used up by the plant or evaporates.

When immersion watering is not convenient, a watering-can with a narrow spout can be used instead. There should be an inch (2 cm) of space between the top of the soil and the rim of the pot, more in pots 6 inches (15 cm) and over, and to begin with that space should be filled with water. Stop watering when water runs through the drainage hole in the bottom of the pot. Do not leave the pot standing in water in its dish; empty the surplus almost immediately or aeration will be impeded.

Whenever possible use tepid water for all watering to avoid harmful lowering of the soil temperature. In hard water areas the lime content of tap water makes the water alkaline. Degrees of acidity and alkalinity are measured as a pH value—a pH of 7 is neutral, below 7 is acid and above 7 is alkaline. The pH is easily determined by using a simple paper indicator with a colour scale. Most house plants, but especially *Rhododendron simsii* (Indian Azalea) and *Camellia*, require acidity in the soil. Lime-hating house plants can be watered with distilled water or water collected when defrosting the refrigerator. Sadly, air pollution in urban areas has made rain water (a readily available and free source of soft water) lethal to most house plants.

You can produce your own soft water by treating tap water with peat. Pack peat into a linen bag, a sock or a stocking, put it in a bucket and pour the water over it. Leave the peat in the water overnight. The water is then ready for use.

Plants growing in plastic pots need less frequent watering than those in the traditional porous clay pots because there is no evaporation through the sides. How often you have to

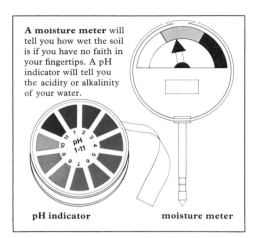

**pH indicator**    **moisture meter**

water also depends on the type of compost in which the plant is growing. A compost of peat and coarse sand dries out far more quickly than a loamy soil compost and once dry it is also harder to wet again without total immersion.

Frequency of watering will be greatly reduced by sinking the pot in damp peat inside a larger container. The plant is watered in the normal way and any surplus runs into the peat. Occasionally, take the plant from the outer pot to see whether you are giving the plant too little water, in which case the peat will be dry, or too much, when the peat will be sodden.

All these watering rules apply to most house plants, but the requirements of cacti and other succulents and of some bromeliads are quite different. Cacti and other succulents which are kept cool during winter will usually not need watering during the resting period, which lasts from the beginning of October to the beginning of March. In a dry, heated room they may have to be watered once a month. During the summer, weekly or even more frequent watering may be necessary, especially if the pots are very small.

Some bromeliads take up moisture from the reservoir of water in the "vase", the rosette of leaves in the centre of the plant. During the summer this should always be kept full of water—clean rain water if possible.

As well as water, plants need nutrients. Watering and fertilizing are intimately connected because the root hairs of the plants take up the nutrients in solution. House plants are as likely to be as overfed as they are overwatered, although with less disastrous results.

Gross feeding of those house plants which are cultivated for their flowers encourages the growth of leaves at the expense of the flowers. On the other hand, some feeding is necessary. Since the plants are contained in pots the roots cannot go in search of new nutrients.

There is probably enough reserve in the soil to last for six months after you have bought the plant—longer if you bought it in early winter. Little if any feeding will be needed for most plants for up to six months after repotting because new reserves will have been provided by extra compost. Fast-growing plants, however, will need feeding three months after repotting. No feeding is done while the plant is resting, usually from October to April.

During the remaining part of the year weekly feeding, although often recommended, should be carried out only during periods of luxuriant growth. Feeding every two or three weeks in the rest of the growing season is adequate. Never feed a sickly plant, it is having a struggle to absorb the nutrients already available. Never use larger amounts or feed more frequently than the manufacturers of proprietary mixtures recommend—preferably considerably less.

Fertilizers can be given as a pill, a powder or a liquid. The nutrients in pills and powders take two or three weeks to become available to the plant. Solutions are taken up more quickly. Whichever method you use always make sure that the soil is already moist before application otherwise the delicate roots may be damaged. Foliar feeds—that is, chemicals dissolved in water and sprayed on the leaves —act faster because they are immediately absorbed by the leaves.

**Feeding your plant**

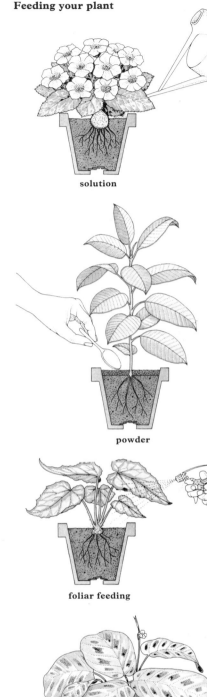

**solution**

**powder**

**foliar feeding**

**nutrient pill**

Nutrient pills placed in the pot, or a nutrient powder dug into the surface soil, take two to three weeks before they are available to the plants. Solutions act more quickly and foliar feeds sprayed on to the leaves are absorbed almost immediately.

**Soil may shrink away** from the sides of the pot after the dryness of winter. Water will then simply pour out of the drainage hole. Hard-packed soil causes water to remain on the surface. Both problems can be remedied by placing the pot in water and giving it a thorough soaking. Then push the soil back down the sides of the pot or loosen it with a knitting needle.

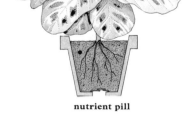

# Soils, composts and hydroponics

In the garden a plant grows in soil, which we manure, fertilize and cultivate. Indoors, the nutrients in a small potful of soil are quickly exhausted, and the open, quick-draining structure of the soil disappears. Unsterilized garden soil is also likely to contain all kinds of pests and diseases.

For the artificial conditions in which house plants grow it is, therefore, best to use artificially concocted "soil". To avoid misunder-standing, the medium in which house plants grow is usually called compost rather than soil. But this is liable to create another confusion. It is not the compost which gardeners make in a compost heap—although well-made garden compost can be used in it.

House plant compost may also contain soil, although soil in this context is usually described as loam. A perfectly good compost can be made without any soil at all—hence the basic division into loam-based and loam-less or all-peat composts.

From the 1930s through the 1950s most house plants were grown in a loam-based compost in a clay pot. Those you buy today are most likely to be planted in peat in a plastic pot and even the compost may be plastic. The reason for the change is simple; loam, like many other things, is not what it used to be. The ideal loam was produced by

---

**LOAM-BASED COMPOSTS**

In the 1930s the John Innes Institute in England developed the basic formulae for balanced potting composts. Although these mixtures are available commercially you can make your own.

**The basic John Innes Potting Compost** is made up from these materials, which must be measured by bulk and mixed thoroughly:
  7 parts damp, sterilized loam
  3 parts damp, granulated peat
  1 part coarse sand

**The John Innes Base** is made by adding fertilizers, measured by weight, to the compost according to the following formula:
  2 parts hoof and horn meal, or dried blood
  2 parts superphosphate
  1 part potassium sulphate

The fertilizer base along with other materials is added to the compost in varying strengths and the resulting mixtures are numbered one to three:

**John Innes Potting Compost No 1:**
4 oz (113 gm) base
¾ oz (21 gm) ground chalk or ground limestone
70 lb (32 kg) compost

Young plants in small pots up to 4 inches (10 cm): *Asparagus*, *Peperomia* and *Vallota*.

**John Innes Potting Compost No 2:**
8 oz (226 gm) base
½ oz (14 gm) chalk
70 lb (32 kg) compost

Mature plants.

**John Innes Potting Compost No 3:**
Treble the amounts of fertilizer and chalk
12 oz (340 gm) base
2½ oz (71 gm) chalk
70 lb (32 kg) compost

Plants in pots of 8 inches (20 cm) and larger: *Allamanda*, *Dieffenbachia* and *Faucaria*.

**LOAMLESS COMPOST**

There are many proprietary loamless composts, known by different names in different countries.

The bulk ingredients are usually peat with or without coarse river sand. (The salt in sea sand is harmful.) For most house plants loamless composts can be substituted for loam-based composts.

*Asparagus, Blechnum, Coleus, Columnea, Cordyline, Erica, Hoya, Philodendron* and *Syngonium*.

**SPECIAL COMPOSTS**

Some plants need, or flourish in, special composts:

*Begonia, Hoya:*
4 parts loam
4 parts peat
3 parts leaf mould
2 parts coarse sand
  or
2 parts leaf mould
1 part coarse sand

*Cacti and other succulents:*
1 part loam
1 part peat
1 part coarse sand
Or add to John Innes Potting Compost No 1
1 part coarse sand

*Ferns (Adiantum, Asplenium, Cyrtomium, Nephrolepis, Platycerium, Pteris):*
4 parts loam
4 parts peat
4 parts leaf mould
1 part coarse sand
1 part granulated charcoal

*Ananas, Cryptanthus, Guzmania, Tillandsia, Vriesea:*
For young plants:
1 part sedge peat
1 part leaf mould
1 part pine needles
For mature plants:
1 part peat
1 part osmunda fibre (the matted roots of the Royal Fern, *Osmunda regalis*)
1 part coarse sand

If you are keen enough, or if you treasure particular plants, you can make up composts more adjusted to their needs than the standard loam-based or loamless composts.

*Aglaonema, Monstera, Philodendron, Scindapsus, Spathiphyllum, Syngonium:*
(the fleshy roots of these may rot unless there is a very open compost):
2 parts loam
1½ parts leaf mould (or peat)
¾ part dried manure
As you pot mix a sprinkling of superphosphate into the compost.

*Dizygotheca, Eucalyptus, × Fatshedera lizei, Fatsia, Hedera:*
4 parts loam
3 parts leaf mould
1½ parts dried manure
1 part peat
As you pot mix a sprinkling of superphosphate into the compost.

*Dieffenbachia, Caladium:*
can be grown in equal parts of:
loam
peat
leaf mould
coarse sand

*Ficus:*
4 parts loam
2 parts leaf mould
1 part peat
2 parts dried manure
1 part coarse sand
As you pot mix a good sprinkling of superphosphate into the compost.

*Cissus, Rhoicissus, Tetrastigma:*
4 parts leaf mould
2 parts manure
1 part peat
2 parts coarse sand
As you pot mix a good sprinkling of superphosphate into the compost.

*Peperomia, Piper:*
2 parts loam
1 part leaf mould
1 part peat
1 part coarse sand

*Palms (Chamaedorea, Howea, Phoenix) and Pilea:*
4 parts loam
3 parts leaf mould
1½ parts manure
1 part peat
2 parts sand

stacking turfs and letting them rot down for a year or more. This was the basis for the famous John Innes composts devised in the 1930s. But such loam is now scarce and that which is available is too variable in quality to be depended on for good results. If they are made with good materials John Innes composts are invaluable. They can still be bought, or they are fairly simply made, if you can get good loam.

Loamless composts are usually a mixture of peat and coarse sand. Because neither peat nor sand contains many plant nutrients a wide range of fertilizers has to be added to create a balanced growing medium. There is much to be said in favour of loamless composts, largely because they drain better and are less likely to become waterlogged than soil composts. So that this advantage is not lost, peat-based composts should not be firmed too tightly in the pot. The danger is that they may dry out too quickly, especially in porous clay pots, and with peat it is better to use plastic pots. If peat is allowed to dry out it is not easy to get wet again. To avoid this you either (wisely) do not let it dry out, or ensure against your possible neglect by buying a soilless compost containing a wetting agent that makes the peat readily absorb water.

You can forget all about composts and soils if you grow your house plants hydroponically. By this method the minerals which the plant normally obtains from the soil are fed directly to the roots in a carefully formulated solution of mineral salts in water.

That soil is not necessary for growth will have been seen by anybody who has grown a hyacinth in a special bulb vase. The bulb sits in the bowl of the glass and puts its roots down into the water below. In this method, however, only plain water is used, with the addition of a little charcoal to prevent it going sour. For food the growing plant draws on reserves within the bulb itself. In hydroponic gardening the plant food is dissolved in the water and drawn up through the roots.

**A bulb vase** is often used to grow a hyacinth. The bulb sits on the neck of the vase and white roots grow down into distilled water, to which charcoal is added to stop the water from turning sour. No feeding is necessary as the hyacinth lives off the reserves in the bulb.

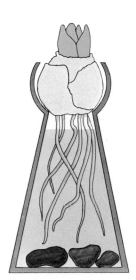

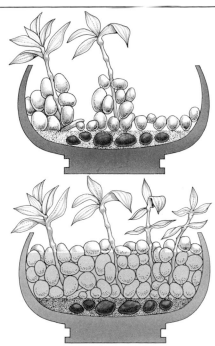

The simplest hydroponic method is to first place a layer of charcoal then a thin layer of sand in the bottom of a bowl. Then "plant" cuttings by anchoring each with pebbles. Add the nutrient solution.

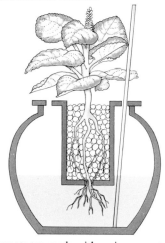

Hydropots are made with an inner container that holds an inert aggregate to support the plant. The nutrient solution is in the outer container.

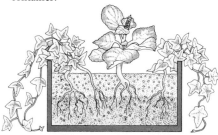

Groups of plants can be grown in a large box that contains an inert aggregate. The nutrient solution half fills the box. When the level drops distilled water is added.

## Soilless culture

Since plants cannot just float on the water, some way of anchoring their roots has to be devised. The first method is simple and requires no more equipment than pebbles, a little sand, charcoal and a watertight container. The choice of the container is limited only by your imagination and good taste. Put a few pieces of charcoal at the bottom of a bowl, for example, and cover them with a shallow layer of sand. Place a layer of pebbles on top of this.

If you use plants which have been growing in soil wash the soil off the roots, but you can use cuttings of plants with a fair chance of success. Anchor each rooted plant or cutting with a few pebbles and then build up the pebbles around the stems of the plants up to the rim of the bowl. Fill the bowl with water in which fertilizer has been dissolved, to just below the rim. Add plain water when necessary to keep up the level of the solution in the bowl, but once a month top up with mineral solution instead.

There are good and reasonably priced proprietary fertilizers available for this purpose and it is pointless to make up your own. Follow the instructions on the packet carefully because if you make the solution stronger than is recommended you will harm, not benefit, the plant. *Hedera helix* (Common Ivy), *Rhoicissus rhomboidea* (Grape Ivy), *Chlorophytum elatum* (Spider Plant), *Plectranthus*, *Coleus* and *Tradescantia* can all be grown effectively in this way.

In Europe and in the United States special hydropots, seldom seen in Britain, are in common use. A hydropot consists of a cylindrical or spherical pot of glass or plastic which holds the nutrient solution. Inside it is another pot containing the plant in an inert aggregate, some coarse sand and gravel (which is heavy, but provides better anchorage for large plants) or lightweight vermiculite. The roots grow through the hole in the bottom of the pot into the solution, which is maintained at a level only a little above the base of the pot.

Growing a number of plants together in a hydroponic box is more effective. It is worth buying a box specially made for this purpose. While it is perfectly easy to make a rough and ready box for use in the greenhouse, to make one which is also an attractive piece of furniture requires more skill. Basically it is a watertight box filled with aggregate. The plants are planted in this and the roots pass down into the nutrient solution below, which is maintained at a level half-way up the container. To make up for evaporation the aggregate is watered with distilled water; in hot weather this will have to be done frequently. Once a month the nutrient solution is drained off through the plugged outlet and replaced with a freshly made nutrient solution. Once again use proprietary fertilizers.

# Potting and repotting

A plant which is not confined in a pot spreads its roots in search of food and water. In a pot the roots reach out towards the sides and then turn around and around, twisting among themselves. Eventually the pot is crowded with roots and emptied of the nutrients the plant needs to grow. At this stage, but preferably some time before, it has to be repotted.

Strictly speaking the operation is called "repotting" if the plant is put in a pot of the same size in order to give it new compost, but not more room for its roots (plants fare better as house plants if the roots are given what seems to be remarkably limited space). "Potting on" is the name given to moving a plant to a larger pot to provide both additional nourishment and more space for roots which are in danger of becoming potbound—in this state the plant's growth will be stunted.

Unfortunately, the visible signs that a plant is becoming potbound appear only when the damage has been done. The evidence that demands immediate action is when roots appear through the drainage hole of the pot, leaves wilt soon after watering (because there is not enough compost left to hold water), new leaves stay small and old leaves turn yellow and fall off because the limited nutrients are concentrated on the growing tip of a plant.

As you gain confidence you will find the courage to take the plant out of its pot at least each spring to look at the roots. Do this a few days after the plant has been watered. Turn the plant and pot upside down, with one hand on the surface of the compost and the fingers around the base of the stem—a useful precaution against everything ending up on the floor. Tap the rim of the pot against a table or draining-board and the soil ball should come away.

The root system you then see exposed will differ depending on whether the pot is clay or plastic. In a clay pot water travels through the compost to the porous sides of the pot and the roots follow the path of the water, and only later fill the compost in the centre of the pot. In impermeable plastic pots the roots travel downwards and then spread outwards. If the roots are obviously not crowded put the pot back over the soil ball, turn the plant the right way up, give the pot a sharp tap on the table top to settle the compost back into place and no harm will have been done.

If the white tips of roots are showing all around the soil ball then the plant is ready to be potted on. This should be done in spring when the roots are active and able to grow quickly into the new compost. The extra nourishment available helps the plant to recover from the shock of the change.

The additional compost needed for a larger pot must be the same type as that in which the plant has been growing. Do not mix a loam-based and a loamless compost, since watering and feeding requirements are quite different.

A plant may need repotting two or three times in its life—obviously you cannot carry on over the years putting it in increasingly larger pots. Avoid large jumps in pot sizes (they are measured across the diameter at the top). A plant in a 3½-inch (9-cm) pot could be moved to a 4½-inch (11-cm) pot, but it would be a fiddling operation, unless a potting stick is used, and a 5-inch (13-cm) pot would be more sensible. But in the larger pots, above 7 inches (18 cm), move up one inch (2 cm) at a time, because the volume of new compost is so much greater.

If possible replant in a similar type of pot, because growing and watering conditions are different in clay and plastic pots, and you may get as confused as the plant adjusting to the change. If you have to change from a clay to a plastic pot you would be well advised to use a more free-draining compost.

Water the plants four or five days before they are to be potted on. Before you begin replanting, all pots which have been previously used must be thoroughly cleaned. New clay pots should be soaked in water for twenty-four hours beforehand. Spread news-paper over the whole surface on which you will be working to catch the inevitable mess as you fill the pots. To save labour do as many plants as you can at the same time.

Make the pots ready to receive the plants by covering the drainage holes of clay pots with a piece or pieces of broken crock. This is not necessary with plastic pots, which have several smaller drainage holes, or with any type of pot destined for a capillary tray. Have enough compost ready before you begin and make sure that it is moist but not sodden. Put a layer of compost at the bottom of the pot. This should be deep enough to bring the soil ball of the plant to no higher than half an inch (1 cm) from the rim of a 5½-inch (14-cm) pot and one and a half to two inches (3 to 5 cm) from the rims of larger pots. This space provides adequate room for watering.

Turn out the plant from its old pot, as already described. Centre the soil ball on the bed of compost, and check that it is the right height. If it is not, gently lift out the soil ball and add to or remove some of the layer of compost. It is vital that after replanting the

**A potbound plant** often has roots growing through the drainage hole in the pot.

level of compost on the stem should be the same as it was before or a little bit below. When you are satisfied that you have got it right start filling the gap around the edges of the pot with compost, pressing it down with your fingers, firmly but not savagely. Press only at the sides of the pot, not at the centre.

There is an alternative method of replanting, which takes a little longer but involves less handling of a plant while pressing in the compost, and therefore less danger of damage to fragile leaves and roots. After putting the layer of compost at the bottom of the larger pot remove the plant from its old pot and lay it gently on the table. Put the smaller pot in the centre of the larger pot, adjusting its depth to find the correct final soil level. Then fill the gap between the two pots with firmly pressed down compost. Remove the small pot, leaving a hole to receive the soil ball of the plant. Press down the compost at the sides of the pot, adding more if needed.

When the potting operation has been completed fill the pot to the brim with water, keep in a cool, shady place and spray the leaves lightly each day. It will soon be ready to go back to its familiar quarters.

Until the roots have grown strongly into the new compost the plant will need watering less frequently than in the old pot. If the replanting has taken place in the spring, it will not need any fertilizer until growth is under way in the following year.

Repotting—without removing to a larger pot—involves carefully teasing some of the old compost from the roots and planting in new compost. Inevitably the plant receives a setback for a time. To avoid this, plants, especially those in large pots, can be left undisturbed except for removing the top inch or two (2 or 5 cm) of soil and replacing it with fresh compost. This method, known as top dressing, should be used when plants have grown too big for potting on.

**Inspect the plant's roots every spring.** If few are visible replace the plant in its pot. If roots are showing all around the soil ball, pot on. Before using a new clay pot soak it well in water.

**Cover the drainage hole of a clay pot** with broken crocks. If you are using a container with no drainage hole, line it with a deep layer of crocks.

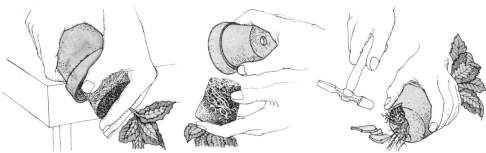

**To remove a plant from its pot** put one hand on the surface of the soil then turn the pot upside-down. Tap the rim of the pot against a table—the soil ball will come away cleanly. If the roots are poking through the drainage hole this method will damage them, so the pot will have to be broken.

**Before repotting a plant**, put a layer of compost over the pieces of broken crock in the bottom of the pot. Lower the soil ball into the centre of the pot, then fill the gap around it with compost, pressing it down firmly. Finally, give the potted plant a thorough soaking in a bucket of water.

**Another method of repotting** is to remove the plant from its pot, then lower the old pot into the centre of the new, larger pot, which has a layer of compost in the bottom. Fill the gap between the pots with compost. Remove the small pot, leaving a hole for the soil ball.

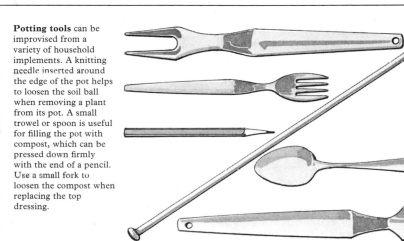

**Potting tools** can be improvised from a variety of household implements. A knitting needle inserted around the edge of the pot helps to loosen the soil ball when removing a plant from its pot. A small trowel or spoon is useful for filling the pot with compost, which can be pressed down firmly with the end of a pencil. Use a small fork to loosen the compost when replacing the top dressing.

# Pruning and training

**Root pruning** is not difficult. Remove the plant from its pot and then, using a very sharp knife, shave away about one inch (2 cm) of the root ball. Replace the plant in the pot and pack it with new compost.

We provide a plant with light, warmth, nutrients and water for its own good and sometimes we have to discipline it, by training and pruning, to make it more attractive and amenable to our life style.

In the wild, some of the most popular house plants grow to an enormous size. It may be hard to imagine, for example, that the tidy and well-behaved specimen in your jardinière, such as the small, elegant *Araucaria heterophylla* (Norfolk Island Pine) grows to two hundred feet (60 m) in its natural habitat.

The conditions in which a house plant lives inhibit growth and keep the plant manageable. You also control growth by regulating the amount of nutrients available.

Pruning does not discourage growth. When the top shoot of most plants is cut even more

new growth replaces it; in this way the plant grows bushier and stays shapely instead of growing lanky or straggly. When roots are pruned there is vigorous new growth of the root hairs, through which the plant takes up its nutrients. Constant renewal of root hairs ensures that the plant is capable of absorbing the nutrients that are available in the restricted space of the pot. The plant stays healthy, but it also stays small.

Root pruning is a major operation from the plant's point of view, but from the owner's it is not difficult to perform. The time to carry it out is in spring when growth is active. The only tool needed is a good-sized, sharp kitchen or butcher's knife.

Having watered the plant a few days earlier, knock it out of the pot. Stand the root ball on a table and evenly shave away roots and compost all the way around, keeping to the original pot shape. Do not be too drastic. Cutting away an inch from around a plant in a 6-inch (15-cm) or larger pot is adequate. Clean the pot and replace the plant in it. Pack it around with new compost and water it.

The plant will recover from post-operative shock more quickly if for a week or two it is kept out of direct sunlight and put under a plastic bag. Use a frame of looped wires to keep the bag from touching the leaves, which may otherwise become mouldy.

Before long the new roots will be reaching out into the new compost. How long it will be before the pot becomes choked with roots again will depend on the natural growth rate of the plant and its age (the younger the stronger). But root pruning can probably be carried out two or three times before the plant becomes too big for the operation.

Pruning above ground is done to keep the plant an attractive shape. It should be regarded as something to be done regularly, gently leading the plant in the way you want it to grow, rather than as drastic corrective action after it has gone astray.

If climbing or vining plants get out of hand they can be cut back with secateurs and will still survive the treatment. On the other hand, plants which grow from rosettes, such as succulents, ferns and *Spathiphyllum wallisii* (Peace Lily), should be left alone except for the removal of dead, dying or diseased leaves.

The gentlest form of pruning is "stopping", which consists of pinching out the growing part of a plant to induce it to put out new shoots. In due course these new shoots may also be stopped, making the plant bushy instead of tall and lanky. Self-branching ivies

### Hard-wood pruning

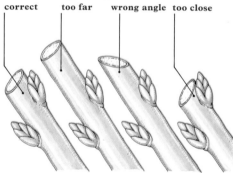

correct    too far    wrong angle    too close

Pruning cuts should not be too close to, too far from or at the wrong angle to the bud. The drawings above show the correct cut compared to three examples of incorrect pruning.

### Stopping

This is a gentle form of pruning. The growing part of the plant is pinched out to make it put out new shoots. The new shoots can themselves be stopped to make the plant even bushier. Although some plants are self-branching, many will become very straggly and lanky if they are not stopped regularly.

produce some side shoots without being stopped, but stopping will encourage even more shoots to grow. *Tradescantia*, for example, must be pinched out regularly if it is not to become straggly.

Hard-wood pruning involves cutting back hard into the old part of the stems. It is the most drastic form of pruning and should be avoided if possible because a hard-pruned house plant can look a sorry object for up to six months afterwards. But if a plant has been neglected—and is of a kind that can be pruned—it has to be done. This kind of pruning forces the dormant eye buds under the bark of the stem into action, to put out new growth. This is severe treatment and it is better to cut back two or three stems at a time rather than the whole plant. Shrubby *Begonia*, *Nerium oleander* (Oleander), the larger *Kalanchoe* and

*Beloperone guttata* (Shrimp Plant) quickly grow straggly and have to be pruned hard.

Soft-wood pruning—cutting away new growth—results in two or more shoots growing where one grew before. It encourages the production of more flowers on such plants as *Fuchsia* and *Hydrangea*, which flower on the same year's growth. Cutting these back at the end of the flowering season will encourage new shoots, which will produce the following year's flowers. In other plants, for example *Bougainvillea*, cutting back new wood means losing the following year's flowers, which appear on year-old wood.

Understanding what happens to a plant after pruning and close observation of your own plants are the best guides to the art of pruning. Think why before you cut and then act without trepidation.

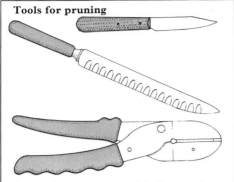

**Tools for pruning**

A pair of secateurs, a small knife and a large kitchen knife is adequate equipment for pruning house plants. It is important that they are all sharp.

## Training and support

Many house plants need some form of support and training to show off to best advantage the shapeliness achieved by pruning. The basic materials employed include canes, wire or plastic netting and raffia or string for tying the plants. The supports should be as unobtrusive as possible when the plant is well grown, although they may not be hidden while the plant is young. Plants with aerial roots appreciate being able to push the roots into a moss stick, which is made by covering a strong stick

with moss, bound on with twine or soft wire. Alternatively you can use a moss column, which is a tube of wire netting stuffed with damp moss. *Hedera helix* (Common Ivy) is attractive climbing up a cane ladder or hanging from a bowl. *Stephanotis floribunda* (Madagascar Jasmine), the traditional Mother's Day plant, is often trained around a hoop. Whatever support you choose—and let your imagination run free—remember to tie the plant to it loosely.

# Propagation/two plants from one

Human beings can only reproduce themselves sexually, but while many plants can do that they can also, with a little help from human friends, multiply in numerous other imaginative ways.

The sexual method of plant propagation is by seed. But vegetative, or asexual, alternatives are widely used, both in Nature and by horticulturists. Bits of stem, root or leaf can create a copy of the original plant—as remarkable as if a piece of your big toe could grow into another you.

Some plants are reproductively more versatile than others. *Achimenes longiflora* (Hot-water Plant), for example, can be grown from seed, from stem cuttings, from leaf cuttings and from the scales rubbed off the rhizome. By nicking the veins on a *Begonia rex* leaf and putting it on sand or compost, new plants will grow. *Tolmiea menziesii* (Pick-a-back Plant) grows a little plantlet on its leaves.

Simple division is the most obvious way of multiplying many large house plants. Offsets,

runners and suckers are other straightforward sources of new plants. The range of plants from which cuttings can be taken is vast, but persuading the cuttings to root requires care and attention.

Bulbs and corms replace themselves by producing new bulbs and corms. These can be removed from the shrivelled parent and replanted. The scales on certain bulbs, mainly lilies, can be broken off and planted to produce new plants.

Most house plants are more difficult to grow from seed than are vegetables and garden annuals and perennials. The main problem is providing the necessary heat, light and humidity. A seed also takes longer than a cutting to grow into an attractive-looking plant. On the other hand, raising plants from seed is very satisfying.

Included in the entries in the catalogue section is the most common method of propagating each plant. In the pages which follow there are descriptions of how the operations can be carried out.

**Layering a Spider Plant**

The *Chlorophytum elatum* (Spider Plant) almost begs to be propagated, since it puts out long flowering stems from which hang young plants with incipient roots. These young plants will rapidly establish themselves if they are pinned down with a wire loop into a pot full of compost. When they are growing well cut the runner. Layer only a few runners from each plant in this way, leaving the rest to hang gracefully, for they are the most attractive part of the plant.

---

Many plants can be divided, but there are also many which cannot be divided under any circumstances. Those which cannot be divided include many climbing or trailing plants, single-stemmed plants, as well as those with leaves which arise on a single stem or from a rosette, for example *Dracaena* and some small palms, and certain succulents such as *Crassula*.

Plants which can be divided include those which send up a tuft or clump of green shoots from the soil and plants which send up two or three distinct clumps of foliage side by side.

The division of a plant by splitting it in half is a brutal business and only strong-growing plants can usually tolerate it. However, by separating the healthiest parts of a dying plant it may be possible to save it. Evergreen foliage plants are best divided in spring when growth is active, while flowering plants should not be divided until after they have bloomed and new leaves are growing.

Before you begin to divide a plant, have everything prepared—clean plant pots, compost and a sharp knife. Spread newspaper over your work surface to contain the mess.

To divide plants that grow in clumps you have to cut through their roots. Use a very sharp knife, although you may need a small saw to get through some root balls, especially those of large ferns. Generally it is best to cut both foliage and roots of such plants into half. They are more likely to re-establish themselves quickly that way. If they are split up into little pieces they not only look absurd, but may easily die.

Deal with only one plant at a time and repot the divided halves as fast as you can. Water each plant well and keep it in a shaded position until it perks up properly. A fine spraying of the leaves helps the plant revive but do

not rewater until the soil begins to dry out.

Large leaves often flop over after a plant has been divided. Put a few canes in the soil around the edge of the pot to hold up a "cat's cradle" of string that will support the leaves and place a large plastic bag over the plant.

Plants which produce suckers are easy to propagate, but the miniature copy should be of a reasonable size. Knock the plant and soil out of the pot, as if repotting, and disentangle the roots of the young plant from the roots of the mother plant.

Plants that grow offsets on runners are also easy to deal with, but the offsets must be a good size and have, therefore, grown a flourishing root system of their own. Just cut the runners, pot the young plants and repot the old.

A very old *Clivia miniata* (Kaffir Lily) can be one of the most difficult plants to divide. But if you do not divide it the plant deteriorates. Fortunately, once you have got it out of the pot you will see the way in which it can be divided. It spreads by offsets and in removing them from the main root system some of the brittle roots will inevitably be damaged. In retaliation the parent plant may not flower the following year. Therefore, if you have several Kaffir Lilies do not divide them all in the same year.

**Plants usually increased by division or offsets**
*Adiantum* spp, *Aechmea fasciata*, *Agapanthus campanulatus*, *Aglaonema commutatum*, *Asparagus* spp, *Aspidistra elatior*, *Billbergia nutans*, *Calanthe vestita*, *Calathea insignis*, *Clivia miniata*, *Cryptanthus* spp, *Episcia* spp, *Fittonia* spp, *Guzmania lingulata*, *Kohleria eriantha*, *Lycaste deppei*, *Maranta* spp, *Nandina domestica*, *Noeregelia carolinae*, *Nidularium innocentii*, *Ophiopogon* spp, *Oplismenus, hirtellus*, *Pellionia pulchra* and *Spathiphyllum wallisii*.

**Taking an offset from an Urn Plant**

Cut down the flower spike of *Aechmea fasciata* (Urn Plant) when it begins to wither. The old plant will also have started dying, but as it does so it puts out a young plant—or sometimes several—alongside it. If the old plant were merely cut down the young one would grow, but it is an architectural-looking plant and would look oddly off-centre in the pot. It is better to knock the whole plant out of the pot, cut away the old shoot from the thick, woody root and replant the root with the young shoot. If there is more than one offset, the surplus can be potted as cuttings.

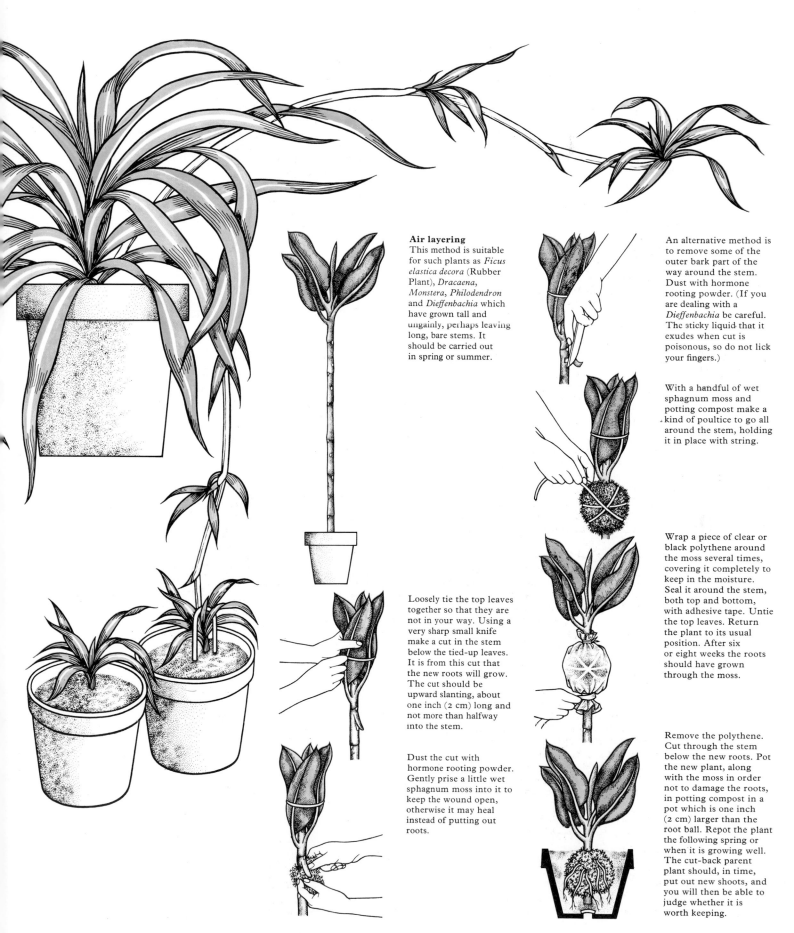

**Air layering**
This method is suitable for such plants as *Ficus elastica decora* (Rubber Plant), *Dracaena*, *Monstera*, *Philodendron* and *Dieffenbachia* which have grown tall and ungainly, perhaps leaving long, bare stems. It should be carried out in spring or summer.

Loosely tie the top leaves together so that they are not in your way. Using a very sharp small knife make a cut in the stem below the tied-up leaves. It is from this cut that the new roots will grow. The cut should be upward slanting, about one inch (2 cm) long and not more than halfway into the stem.

Dust the cut with hormone rooting powder. Gently prise a little wet sphagnum moss into it to keep the wound open, otherwise it may heal instead of putting out roots.

An alternative method is to remove some of the outer bark part of the way around the stem. Dust with hormone rooting powder. (If you are dealing with a *Dieffenbachia* be careful. The sticky liquid that it exudes when cut is poisonous, so do not lick your fingers.)

With a handful of wet sphagnum moss and potting compost make a kind of poultice to go all around the stem, holding it in place with string.

Wrap a piece of clear or black polythene around the moss several times, covering it completely to keep in the moisture. Seal it around the stem, both top and bottom, with adhesive tape. Untie the top leaves. Return the plant to its usual position. After six or eight weeks the roots should have grown through the moss.

Remove the polythene. Cut through the stem below the new roots. Pot the new plant, along with the moss in order not to damage the roots, in potting compost in a pot which is one inch (2 cm) larger than the root ball. Repot the plant the following spring or when it is growing well. The cut-back parent plant should, in time, put out new shoots, and you will then be able to judge whether it is worth keeping.

# Propagation/stem cuttings

Many of the house plants you buy have been raised from cuttings, and there is no reason why you should not increase the number of plants you have in the same way. With some plants this method is ridiculously easy, but with others it is almost impossible. Usually, soft-wood cuttings will be taken from the young growth of the same year.

A glass of water is all that is needed to make the cuttings of such plants as *Hedera helix* (Common Ivy), *Tradescantia* and *Impatiens wallerana* (Busy Lizzie) take root.

Cuttings which have been rooted in water, however, always suffer a severe setback when they are transferred to soil and not all manage to adjust to a new medium and a different way of absorbing oxygen through the roots. Rooting a cutting in compost is, therefore, the better method. The cutting is prepared in the same way for planting in compost as for rooting in water, but before planting, if the plant is difficult to propagate, dip the end in hormone rooting powder. Cuttings which "bleed" heavily can be cauterized with a match or candle flame.

Fill a small pot with a moist mixed peat and sand compost. Put your finger or a pencil into the compost to make a hole for the cutting and push it in. Firm the soil around it. To begin with, keep the pot in shade so that the leaves do not wilt to death in sunlight. A fine spraying of the leaves each day will help to prevent wilting, too.

There is also a greater chance of success if each pot is enclosed in a clear plastic bag. This provides a miniature greenhouse for the cutting, giving it the humid atmosphere it needs. Some kind of wire framework must be devised to keep the plastic away from the leaves, however. They may become mouldy if the plastic touches them.

If a number of cuttings are to be planted at one time it is simpler not to pot them separately but to plant them together in a clear plastic box with a lid. (The kind used for keeping salads fresh is suitable.) Using a heated skewer, make some drainage holes in the bottom of the box before filling it with compost.

Every cutting you plant will not take root, and you will avoid a lot of unnecessary disappointment by not expecting them all to. There are, however, both simple, and fairly cheap, as well as sophisticated and expensive, aids to take much of the hit-and-miss element out of propagation. Their purpose is to create the best possible conditions for that part of

**Stem cuttings** of *Tradescantia* root easily in a glass or jar of water. Choose a growing tip which is about four inches (10 cm) long and cut it off cleanly just below a joint in the stem. Remove the leaves from the lower part of the stem.

Place the stems in water. Within ten days roots will begin to appear. When the roots are strong enough, but before they grow coarse, plant the cuttings in small pots containing any good-quality potting compost. Cuttings may suffer when they are moved from water into compost. Rooting in compost is, therefore, a better method for some plants. The cuttings are treated in exactly the same way, but if they are difficult to propagate it is often necessary to dip the ends of the stems in a hormone rooting powder.

When several small cuttings are to be rooted in compost it is best to use a clear plastic box with a lid. Burn drainage holes in the bottom of the box.

**Propagating case**
A thermostatically controlled heated propagating case provides the humid, warm conditions that increase the rate of rooting and the number of successful cuttings.

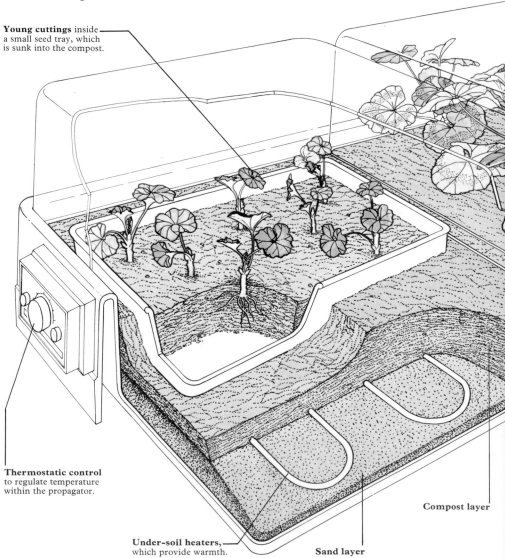

**Young cuttings** inside a small seed tray, which is sunk into the compost.

**Thermostatic control** to regulate temperature within the propagator.

**Under-soil heaters,** which provide warmth.

**Sand layer**

**Compost layer**

the cutting which is in the soil to grow roots before the rest of it above ground dies of thirst. This entails providing a warm soil and a humid and somewhat cooler atmosphere above ground to prevent wilting of the leaves. A heated propagator supplies both these conditions.

A propagator can be little more than a covered box with a small paraffin lamp under it, but an electric propagator is preferable. The electric heating element may either be outside the container—a kind of hotplate— or embedded in the compost like an immersion heater. The most foolproof are those which are controlled by a thermostat. If enthusiasm for house plants is not sufficient reason for buying a propagator, then the cost could be justified by raising plants from seed in them for the garden.

A mist propagation unit is a fine piece of equipment for the houseplant enthusiast who has everything else, including a greenhouse to put it in. Mist propagation is common commercial practice, but is not extensively used by amateurs, probably because the equipment, controlled automatically by electronic devices, is not cheap. It intermittently sprays a mist over the cuttings and seedlings —just enough to keep the surface of the leaves slightly moist without drenching the plants or the soil. The compost in which the cuttings are planted has to be heated, to between 70° and 75°F (21° and 24°C), usually by soil-warming cables. The mist and the warmth together provide the ideal environment. It ensures a greater proportion of success in raising plants from both cuttings and seed, and it virtually looks after the cuttings itself.

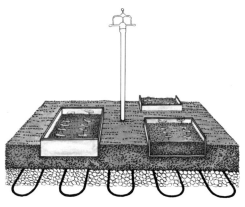

**A mist propagator unit** automatically maintains a constant film of water on the cuttings and under-soil heaters maintain a soil temperature of between 70° and 75°F (21° and 24°C).

**Perspex cover,** which allows the cuttings light but at the same time keeps the atmosphere warm and humid.

**Older cuttings,** which were planted directly into the compost.

**Propagating cacti and other succulents**
Cacti and other succulents are easy to propagate from cuttings. Cacti cuttings are best taken from late spring to August, but other succulents tend to root best in early spring or late summer.

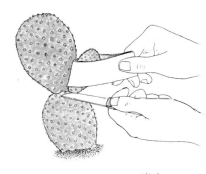

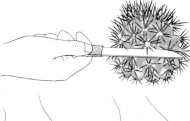

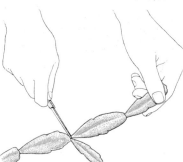

How the cutting is taken depends on the form in which the cactus grows. Use a sharp knife or razor blade and protect your hands from the spines by holding the cutting with a loop of folded paper. The severed end must dry out for a day or two before it is planted.

Plant the cutting in a small plastic pot filled with a compost of one part peat and one part coarse sand. The compost should be moist, but not too wet or the cutting may rot. Push the cutting in about half an inch (1 cm). Place the pot in a propagator at a temperature of 70°F (21°C). Do not water for about ten days.

Cuttings of other succulents can be taken from the terminal shoot of the plant or from side shoots, but choose a ripe shoot rather than the young, soft side shoots. Cut cleanly and let the cutting dry out a little before planting in a compost of one part moist peat and two parts coarse sand. The cutting can then be rooted in a propagator at a temperature of 70°F (21°C). Some succulents produce offsets, and if these are found to have roots when removed, they can be potted immediately; they do not have to be rooted in the propagator.

# Propagation/leaf cuttings

The idea of making new plants from the leaves of old plants is curiously fascinating. *Begonia rex*, *Sansevieria trifasciata* (Mother-in-law's Tongue) and *Saintpaulia ionantha* (African Violet) can be propagated by using only the leaves. Plants such as *Smithiantha zebrina* (Temple Bells) and *Ficus benjamina* (Weeping Fig) need the leaf and all its stem.

## Leaf cuttings in water

*Saintpaulia* leaf cuttings will often take root in water. Pour water into a shallow jar until it is two-thirds full. Add a few pieces of charcoal to keep the water sweet. Cover the jar with aluminium foil and hold it in place with a rubber band. Pierce several holes in the foil.

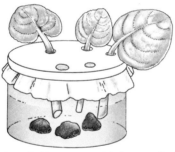

Using a sharp knife or a razor blade, cut off a few *Saintpaulia* leaves along with about two inches (5 cm) of stem. Push the stems of the cuttings through the holes in the foil into the water.

In about a month roots will begin to form. They will be followed by small plantlets.

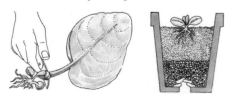

When these little plants are large enough to handle, sever them from the old leaf and pot them.

## Leaf cuttings in compost

*Saintpaulia* leaf cuttings in compost do not suffer from being moved from one medium to another.

Put a layer of compost with a two-inch (5-cm) layer of sand on top in a shallow pot. Dip the ends of the cuttings in a rooting hormone powder.

Make several holes in the sand with a pencil and push the cuttings in. Water liberally.

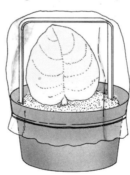

Cover the pot with a clear plastic bag for two weeks. This maintains a humid environment. Support the plastic bag with a wire frame to keep it away from the leaves.

Plantlets will form at the base of the leaves. When they are large enough to handle sever and pot them.

## Cuttings from pieces of leaf

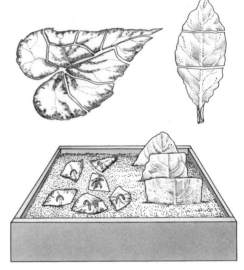

*Begonia rex* and *Streptocarpus × hybridus* (Cape Primrose) leaves can be cut into small pieces and used as cuttings. The one-inch-square (2-cm) *Begonia* piece should be laid flat on damp sand, while the three-inch-long (8-cm) *Streptocarpus* pieces should be pushed vertically into the sand for about one-third of their length. They are then treated in the same way as are whole-leaf cuttings of *Begonia*.

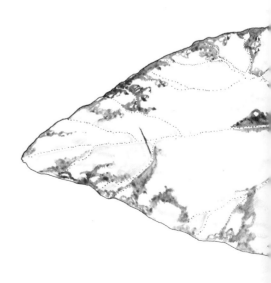

## Whole-leaf cuttings

The simplest way to propagate *Begonia rex* is to use one whole leaf. With a sharp knife or razor blade cut through the thick veins on the underside of the leaf below the point where they join other veins. Then lay the leaf face upwards on damp sand. Peg it down with loops of wire so that the leaf is in close contact with the sand. Plantlets will grow where the cuts have been made if there is enough moisture and warmth. These conditions can be met by using a heated propagator in which the temperature can be kept at about 70°F (21°C). When the plantlets appear, gradually lower the temperature to harden them off. When they have two or three good leaves they are ready to be put into individual pots, but they must still be kept in a humid environment for about three weeks.

## Leaf cuttings of Mother-in-law's Tongue

*Sansevieria trifasciata* (Mother-in-law's Tongue) can be propagated by leaf cuttings as well as by division. During spring or summer cut a healthy leaf away from the crown.

Cutting across the leaf slice it into two-inch (5-cm) pieces. As you cut make a little snip in the edge which was nearest to the soil because each piece must be planted with that end down.

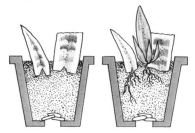

Push a few cuttings into a pot containing any good proprietary potting compost. After about six weeks a new young plant will develop from each cutting.

Curiously, leaf cuttings will only produce plants with green mottled leaves, even when they are taken from a variegated plant.

# Propagation/seeds

Sowing seed is the most difficult way to propagate a house plant. The actual sowing is simple enough; the difficulty is that the seeds, many of which are of tropical origin, are reluctant to grow without a high level of warmth and humidity. This is not easy to provide unless you have a greenhouse and a propagator. It is feasible to use a heated propagator indoors. You must, however, put it under a light unit as soon as the seeds have germinated, because the ordinary light in a room, except perhaps next to the window, is inadequate for growing sturdy seedlings.

Some plants are easier to raise from seed than others. They include herbs and such plants as *Primula* and *Sinningia speciosa* (Gloxinia), which are grown for their flowers. You can start them off in a warm cupboard,

**Sowing seeds**

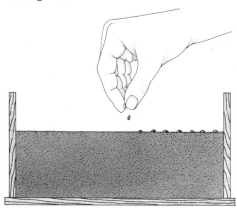

Fill a shallow box to within one inch (2 cm) of the top with a good-quality seed compost. Scatter the seeds thinly from between your finger and thumb.

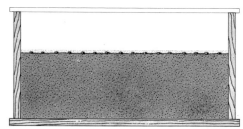

Cover the seeds with a thin layer of compost. Water well. Place a piece of glass on top of the box and put it in a warm, dark place.

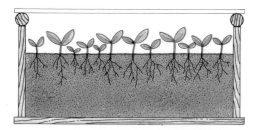

When the seedlings emerge, move the box into the light and lift the glass for ventilation. Pot the seedlings singly when large enough to handle.

but as soon as they germinate they must be moved to a warm place in good light. An ideal site would be a window sill with a radiator underneath it.

To sow seeds, fill a box or pot, to within one inch (2 cm) of the top, with any good proprietary seed compost. Sow the seeds thinly from between your finger and thumb; if you try to scatter them straight from the packet they are liable to come out in a sudden rush. Cover the seeds with a very thin layer of compost or, even better, with sand. Do not bury small seeds deeply—they need air.

Put the pot or box in one inch (2 cm) of water in a bowl or in the kitchen sink and let the compost soak it up. Take the pot or box out when the surface of the compost has darkened and glistens. Let it drain thoroughly for about two hours. Cover the pot or box with a piece of glass, or make a tent over it with a clear plastic bag. Transfer it to a warm cupboard. If there is heavy condensation on the glass wipe the underside of it each morning. To deal with condensation inside a plastic bag, remove the bag, turn it inside out and then put it back over the pot.

As soon as the seedlings have emerged and straightened themselves, move the box into a good light; but not direct sunlight otherwise the seedlings will be cooked! Raise the glass or plastic bag a little during part of the day for ventilation. If the seedlings become crowded thin them. In order not to disturb the roots of those seedlings which are to be left, carefully snip out the weaklings at soil level with a pair of small scissors.

When the seedlings are large enough to handle pot each one in a small pot which contains seed compost. Before long the plant will need potting on, and a potting compost is then used. Gradually harden off the plants to accustom them to the temperatures in which they will eventually grow, but avoid any sudden changes.

Using a heated propagator greatly increases the range of plants that can be grown from seed. A lot of laborious work can be saved, too, if the seeds are planted in Jiffy strips of compressed peat instead of in loose compost. When the time comes for potting on the seedlings, the strip can be separated into individual sections and each put straight into a pot, with the minimum of disturbance to the roots. This method is particularly suitable for large seeds which can be spaced out to avoid thinning.

An extremely high rate of germination, even with difficult seeds, is reached in a mist propagator in a greenhouse. Fill plastic pots with a very loose compost composed of half peat and half vermiculite or coarse sand. Sow the seed very thinly because more are expected to grow. Put the pots on the sand base of the mist unit and turn on the mister. After that the seeds can almost be left to themselves until they have grown large enough for pricking out.

House-plant owners are justifiably proud if they manage to keep the beautiful specimens they buy alive and flourishing. There is more elementary enjoyment to be derived from persuading fruit pips, stones and seeds to bring forth, homespun rather than exquisite though some of the results may be.

Avocado is an almost inevitable choice and is almost equally inevitably disappointing; the seed or stone either does not root or grows into a long naked stick supporting a few withered leaves. The seed must be mature if it is to root. All shop-bought fruit have mature seeds, but not all of them have embryos, so plant several at once as an insurance.

When the plant is approximately eighteen inches (45 cm) high, pinch out the growing

## Plants from pips and stones

**An avocado seed** can be rooted if the base is allowed to sit in water. Push three small sticks into the seed so that it can be supported on the rim of a wine glass or similar container. After about eight weeks the thick white roots will begin to break through. As the single shoot develops, transfer the seed to a pot containing any good-quality potting compost.

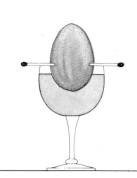

**Orange, lemon and grapefruit pips** are easy to germinate. Put several large seeds into 3-inch (8-cm) pots containing any good potting compost. Keep them at a temperature of 60°F (16°C). After the seedlings appear, within a few weeks, pull out the weak ones and leave the sturdiest.

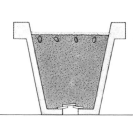

**A date stone** should be sandpapered lengthwise, to make it easier for moisture to penetrate, before you plant it in a fine, moist potting compost. Ideally, for quick germination, the stone should be kept at a temperature of 75°F (24°C). If the stone is kept in a temperature of about 65°F (18°C) or less it may take three months to germinate.

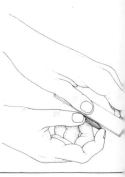

tip to encourage bushiness. If the leaves turn brown around their edges it means the air is too dry and you must spray the leaves regularly. Too dry or too wet compost may also be the cause.

Orange, lemon and grapefruit pips are easily grown. They will grow into bushy shrubs, not unattractive, but unlikely to flower and even less likely to fruit. If you want fruit and flowers then you will have to buy the specially cultivated small species.

Apple and pear pips and plum stones are also easy to grow, but their youthful charm soon evaporates. When it does, do not banish or promote the young plants to the garden because seeds do not grow true to type. To grow a Cox apple, for example, you have to plant a grafted Cox tree.

Peanuts, chestnuts and coffee beans (all of them, naturally, unroasted) will grow. The coffee plant, with evergreen, dark, glossy leaves, is most attractive. In the plantations it grows more than twelve feet (3.5 m) tall, but indoors it fortunately rarely exceeds two feet (60 cm). It will be several years before it begins to produce any fragrant white flowers.

In spring sow two or three coffee beans in a pot of damp sand and put it in a propagator at a temperature of between 75° and 80°F (24° and 27°C). Transplant the seedlings into ordinary potting compost and repot singly after a few months into a rich compost. Seed of the dwarf variety *Coffea arabica* 'Nana' can sometimes be bought from seedsmen.

Date stones produce palms, although you will have to contain yourself in patience

while they do. The early leaves are smooth-edged and two years go by before even the first palm-like leaves appear. *Phoenix dactylifera* is the palm that produces the dates of North Africa and Arabia, and there it grows fifty feet (15 m) tall. There is no danger of that in your home. It is, however, easier to grow than *Phoenix roebelinii* from India.

There are seeds of many exotic fruits which are worth planting; lychees, for example, produce charming little plants. Indeed, if anything is sowable, sow it. If it grows and you do not like it you can always put it on the compost heap, and if it does not grow it has cost you nothing.

The main cause of failure is overwatering. The compost in which the seed is sown should be moist and not sodden. Moisture and warmth together will start the seed germinating, but at that stage it has not got a voracious thirst, and it quickly has its fill of the water it needs. It is only when a plant has put out a mass of leaves that it starts to lap up water.

Among the plants which might be grown from seed using either ingenious improvisation or conventional equipment are: *Achimenes longiflora, Araucaria heterophylla, Asparagus* spp, *Begonia* spp, *Browallia speciosa, Celosia argentea, Coleus blumei, Crassula argentea, Cyclamen persicum, Eucalyptus globulus, Fuchsia* spp, *Impatiens wallerana, Jacaranda mimosifolia, Kalanchoe blossfeldiana, Mimosa pudica, Peperomia* spp, *Primula* spp, *Saintpaulia ionantha, Senecio cruentus, Sinningia speciosa, Solanum capsicastrum* and *Streptocarpus × hybridus.*

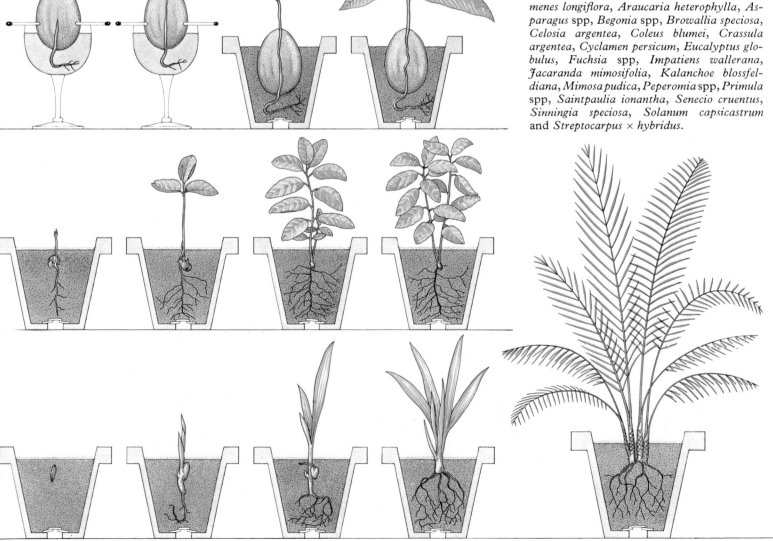

# The right container

A fine plant deserves a fine pot, but all too often it does not get one. Having spent a lot of money on attractive plants you may be tempted to skimp on containers. But this is a false economy, for the effect will be ruined and you will never enjoy your plants to the full.

Admittedly, beautiful containers are not easy to find, and many are abysmally tawdry and ugly. There are, however, simple, honest designs among the larger lightweight plastic containers. They tend to be more attractive in bold colours—orange, scarlet, white and black—rather than in muddy greens and browns. These large containers, intended to hold groups of plants or one large one, are items of furniture and must be chosen to fit the room as well as to suit the plant. Wooden boxes or troughs which have been painted or have a matt polyurethane varnish finish are excellent, but wood is very heavy, especially when the compost is wet. Glass fibre is tough, light and expensive, and is a favourite material for fake antique containers which can often be uncannily convincing.

It is among the smaller plastic containers that vulgarity and bad taste are hardest to avoid. If you cannot find satisfactory designs consider using glazed or unglazed pottery instead. Again it is best to keep to simple shapes, because the purpose of the container is to set off the plant. Some people have the knack of making collections of dissimilar pots look attractive, but most of us can achieve more satisfying results by buying containers which go together well—not boring and the same, but compatible in texture, shape, colour and style.

When you start indoor gardening it is practical from time to time to buy containers that catch your eye even if you have no plants to put in them. Choose various sizes, for your plants will grow and will need larger containers. From the beginning adopt the system of growing your plants in a pot inside a container packed with damp peat. The growing plant will benefit and so will you, for you will be able to change containers if you wish while rearranging the grouping of your plants without having to repot them.

The kind of container you choose will be governed by where it is to be placed—on the floor, at window-sill or table level, or hanging at or above eye level. The floor is the place for a container of bold, simple design; it is more likely to contain a large, tall plant which reaches eye level, and that is what you tend to look at rather than the floor. At window-sill level you will see both the plant and container together and then the blending of the two is important. The container for hanging plants will usually be the pot in which they are growing. You will see it at or above eye level, but ideally you should not see it at all, only luxuriant growth of leaves and flowers. As this will not be achieved when the plant is young, choose a holder that is pleasantly innocuous when empty and most practical for satisfying the plant's needs at all times.

**When a hanging potted plant** is stood inside a container, surround it with damp peat for extra moisture.

**When planting a hanging container** fitted with a drip tray, plastic sheeting is unnecessary.

**A hanging basket** filled with damp compost becomes heavy, so make sure it is suspended from a strong chain and hook. For convenience when watering, fix a pulley to a basket placed high up on a wall.

### How to plant a hanging wire basket

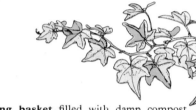

Line the basket first with moss and then with plastic sheeting. For good drainage, put broken crocks and charcoal in the bottom of the lined basket.

Put a layer of compost over the charcoal. Then bed trailing plants around the edge of the basket, mounding compost around the roots of each one.

Press the compost firmly around the trailing plants. Fill the rest of the basket with compost, then bed upright plants in the centre. Water the compost.

## Hanging baskets

A hanging plant has a hard life indoors, stuck up amid the rising heat, fumes and cigarette smoke. It will also probably be far too dry (in contrast to most overwet house plants) because it is so much trouble to water. All hanging baskets—and that means all hanging containers whether made of wire, clay or plastic—dry out very quickly. For much of the year they will need more frequent feeding, because the extra water that is required washes the nutrients out of the soil more quickly. To make these chores less difficult hang an indoor basket at eye level, near a wall so that you do not bump into it, or, if it is to hang high, fix it with a pulley.

A wire basket can be used out of doors—on balconies or on porches—but for use indoors, if possible, buy a special hanging pot with a saucer attached. The saucer will reduce the danger of drips and will also cut down the need for watering by acting as a reservoir for the plant.

Not all plants are suitable for indoor hanging baskets. For variegated foliage you can group *Chlorophytum elatum* (Spider Plant), *Zebrina pendula* (Wandering Jew) and *Tradescantia* and let them fight it out among themselves. Try *Schlumbergera truncata* (Christmas Cactus) or *Aporocactus flagelliformis*, the "rats' tails" of which hang over the edge of the basket. Suitable flowering plants include *Plectranthus oertendahlii* (Prostrate Coleus), *Campanula isophylla* (Bell Flower) and *Hoya carnosa* (Wax Plant). The more demanding *Columnea microphylla* (Goldfish Vine), the most beautiful and long-lasting hanging plant, would be criminal to grow in any other way but alone.

On balconies you can grow Ivies, trailing varieties of *Fuchsia*, *Browallia*, ivy-leaved and zonal *Pelargonium*, hanging *Begonia* and *Achimenes longiflora* (Hot-water Plant).

# Window boxes

Window boxes outside the house are neither indoor nor outdoor gardening. This kind of cultivation combines something of both. Below the surface of the soil the plant has to put up with indoor gardening conditions—restricted space and a reliance on its owner for food and, probably, water. Above ground it is in the great outdoors, with such benefits as better light and refreshing showers of rain and also such hazards as gales and frost. A small window box remarkably extends the scope of indoor gardening and makes it possible to grow many hardy plants which do not thrive in the house.

Window boxes are, in a sense, an unselfish form of gardening because the plants will always turn their backs on the room behind them and put on the best show for the neighbours. One consolation is that window-box gardening is contagious—one brilliant display in a street will often bring out a rash of colour at other house windows.

On the other hand, window boxes can be a hazard to neighbouring flat dwellers or passers-by because of dripping water or even falling boxes. Standing the box on a galvanized or plastic tray prevents drips. But the other danger is far more serious. So the first unbreakable rule is that a window box must be absolutely secure. If you live where a window box could conceivably fall on anyone then employ a builder to fix proper supports and see that you are covered by your insurance policy if they fail.

Window boxes can be bought in endless designs and many materials. Asbestos, cement and terracotta are heavy while glass fibre and plastic are light—but by far the best of all are those made of wood. Making one of wood is a fairly simple job, but be sure to treat it with a preservative otherwise the wood will quickly rot. Do not, however, use creosote, which is deadly to plants.

Although window boxes can be planted with small shrubs and perennial flowering plants, for many people the attraction of a window box is change—to provide a brave show of colour with bulbs in spring and in summer with such long-flowering plants as *Fuchsia* and *Pelargonium* (Geranium), with perhaps a few variegated *Hedera helix* (Common Ivy) as a permanent feature to soften the hard outlines of the box.

The boxes can also be planted with annuals to blaze with colour in summer—*Antirrhinum* (Snapdragon), *Dianthus* (Pinks), *Godetia grandiflora* and *Viola* (Pansy), although if you include them all you will end up with a floral knickerbocker glory. Restraint is needed even in colour, and far better effects are to be achieved with one bright colour and plenty of green foliage.

Bulbs are usually planted straight into the compost in the window box. Larger plants can be left in pots and buried in the compost. Then if any die or if you get bored with them, they can easily be replaced.

Magnificent boxes can be made up of a mixture of the long-flowering ivy-leaved *Pelargonium* and the scented-leaved *Pelargonium*—scents to choose from include apple, balsam, peppermint, lemon and orange. Even when the leaves die the smell lingers.

Another excellent use for a window box is to grow herbs. Try thyme, sage (but keep renewing it with a young plant), marjoram, chives and basil. There are so many mints that they can well have a box of their own. Lettuce for the family and strawberries for whoever gets to them first are other possibilities for window boxes.

A window box can be used, too, for a miniature garden or for bonsai trees, as long as its contents are sheltered from wind.

## Planting a window box

Place a layer of crocks or pebbles in the bottom of the box to act as a reservoir for excess water. Add a layer of charcoal to keep the water sweet followed by a layer of turf.

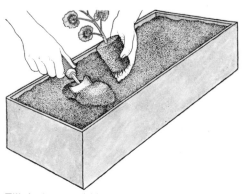

Fill the box to within two inches (5 cm) of the top with any good potting compost. Plants can be planted directly into the box. Water the compost thoroughly.

If you wish to replace plants successively throughout the year then it is best to leave them in their pots. Small pots may need to stand on blocks of wood or bricks.

When choosing plants to fill a window box it is best to decide on those which provide a brave show of colour. Long-flowering *Pelargonium* and *Fuchsia* are particularly suitable.

A window box with a difference can be built by making the front of chicken wire. The wire is lined with moss to keep the compost and plants in. Plants can then be planted through the wire.

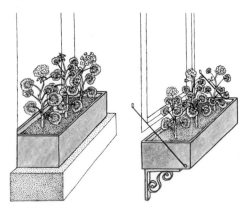

Fixing a window box on a wide, flat window sill is simple; but if the box obstructs opening the window then it will have to be mounted on brackets below the sill and secured with wire.

## A wooden window box

Although you can buy a window box which is made of terracotta, fibreglass, plastic or wood, there is no guarantee that it will be the correct size for your window sill. It is fairly easy, however, to construct a wooden box of the right size and the basic principles are outlined below. The materials that you will require are a length of 9 × 1 in (23 × 2 cm) timber to make the sides and the base of the box. Battens can be fixed to the bottom to raise the box off the sill. Brass screws, which do not rust, should be used for all joints which are likely to become damp.

All wood should be treated with a proprietary wood preserver. A final coat of polyurethane varnish will waterproof the box.

Another method of waterproofing the box, and preventing water dripping into the street, is to line it with plastic sheeting.

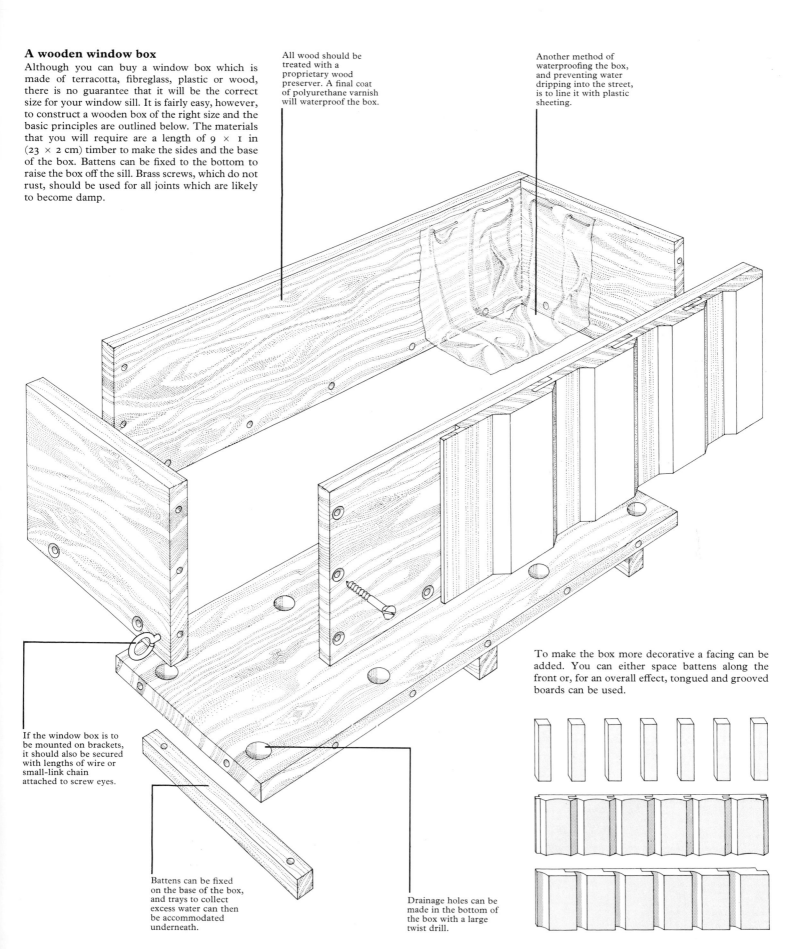

If the window box is to be mounted on brackets, it should also be secured with lengths of wire or small-link chain attached to screw eyes.

Battens can be fixed on the base of the box, and trays to collect excess water can then be accommodated underneath.

Drainage holes can be made in the bottom of the box with a large twist drill.

To make the box more decorative a facing can be added. You can either space battens along the front or, for an overall effect, tongued and grooved boards can be used.

# Plant furniture

The ways of displaying house plants are almost inexhaustible. One of the most effective is to use them in harness with furniture—either with existing fixtures, such as book-cases, or with specially constructed pieces of furniture, such as room dividers. In addition there are many large containers which rank as furniture in their own right.

A reasonably competent handyman can make many attractive items himself as long as his ambitions do not outrun his skill and he has a reasonable selection of tools. Natural wood is one of the best materials to use and, with cane and pottery, appears to have a natural affinity with plants.

One simple room divider that reaches from floor to ceiling requires little expertise to build. It only needs a lot of long bamboo canes and some patience. Vertical canes, three to four inches (8 to 10 cm) apart, are wired to horizontal canes. The highest horizontal cane should be about twelve inches (30 cm) from the ceiling. The others are spaced at twenty-four- to thirty-inch (60- to 75-cm) intervals. For extra strength wire alternate vertical canes on opposite sides of the horizontal canes, or, for even greater firmness and attractiveness, wire the up-right canes in pairs on opposite sides of the horizontal canes. Fix the divider to battens at floor and ceiling. Obviously such a structure would not be suitable for a room in which children are liable to play football, but it would perfectly well support many climbing or trailing plants and even a rampant *Philodendron oxycardium* (Parlour Ivy).

A similarly constructed bamboo screen can be placed against a wall as a variation on the more usual trellis. It is always advisable, if practicable, to paint the wall behind a climbing plant with a waterproof paint so that you can mist-spray the foliage and clean the dust off the canes at the same time without damage. If the wall is papered, use a piece of rush matting as a background for the plants, both emphasizing the display and protecting the wall.

A simple bank of shelves filled with trailing plants instead of books makes an effective room divider. It can extend from floor to ceiling or be only waist high. The top of a low divider might sensibly be made as a trough, to be filled with damp peat in which pots of plants could be contrastingly grouped.

All furniture which is designed to display plants should enhance the plants rather than distract attention from them. Simplicity and clean lines are therefore needed, especially with wooden floor containers. Treat all wood that comes into contact with damp compost with a preservative, but it must not be one that is creosote-based or the plants may suffer. Polyurethane is safe, but wait a few days after painting the box with it before putting in the compost. Put large boxes on castors, so that you can move them easily as plants and damp compost are surprisingly heavy.

**The box** on the left is planted with *Anthurium scherzerianum* (Flamingo Flower), *Howea forsteriana* (Kentia Palm), *Plectranthus oertendahlii* (Prostrate Coleus), *Sansevieria trifasciata* 'Laurentii' (Mother-in-law's Tongue), *Saintpaulia ionantha* (African Violet), *Tradescantia fluminensis* (Speedy Jenny)—all plants which prefer temperate shade. Instructions for constructing the box are given right.

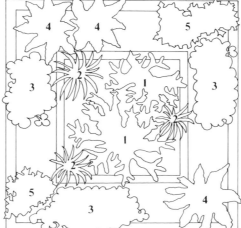

**Plants** suitable for the planter in cool partial shade are:
1. *Araucaria heterophylla* (Norfolk Island Pine)
2. *Chlorophytum elatum* 'Variegatum' (Spider Plant)
3. *Saxifraga sarmentosa* (Mother of Thousands)
4. *Adiantum capillus-veneris* (Maidenhair Fern)
5. *Hedera helix* (Common Ivy)

**Plants** suitable for the planter in warm partial shade include:
1. *Aglaonema pictum* (Chinese Evergreen)
2. *Ficus benjamina* (Weeping Fig)
3. *Campelia zanonia*
4. *Codiaeum variegatum pictum* (Croton)
5. *Peperomia argyreia* (Watermelon Peperomia)
6. *Hemigraphis colorata* (Red Ivy)

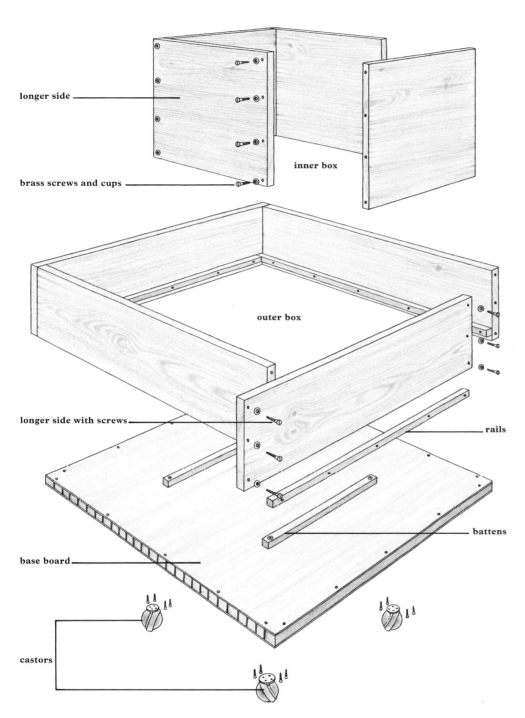

longer side

brass screws and cups

inner box

outer box

longer side with screws

rails

battens

base board

castors

Groups of plants can be used in a wide variety of ways to produce interesting and attractive displays. Group plants in containers which stand on the floor, table or window sill, as well as in hanging baskets and on wall fixtures.

A wall fixture with plants standing on several small shelves produces a dramatic cascading effect.

A wooden box with a central trellis is an ideal room divider. Different climbers can be grown on either side of the trellis to create a screen of living shades of green.

One idea for a wooden planter is shown above, but the dimensions can be changed to suit any room.
**Materials required are:** 5 ft 6 in (165 cm) of 9 × ¾ in (23 by 2 cm) and 3 ft 6 in (105 cm) of 12 × 1 in (30 by 2 cm) planed timber for sides of boxes.
A 3-ft-square (90-cm) sheet of marine or exterior-quality ply ¾ in (2 cm) thick for baseboard. 1½ in (3 cm) No. 10 brass screws and brass cups. Urea-resin glue.
16 ft (4.8 m) of 1-in-square (2-cm) wood for rails and battens.
1. Cut the timber for the sides of the boxes.
Two sides at 2 ft 9 in (83 cm).
Two sides at 2 ft 9 in (83 cm) minus twice the thickness of the timber.

Two sides at 1 ft 9 in (53 cm).
Two sides at 1 ft 9 in (53 cm) minus twice the thickness of the timber.
2. Cut the rails to length and screw them on to the outer box, 1 in (2 cm) from the bottom.
3. Drill screw holes on the longer sides of each box.
4. Apply glue to joints and screw them together. Wipe off excess glue.
5. Put the large box on the base board and trace under the rails. Cut the board and glue and screw it on to the rails.
6. Screw battens on to the base board to hold the inner box in position.
7. Screw castors under wall of the inner box.
8. Coat boxes with a proprietary wood preservative and then varnish with polyurethane.

# Plants without pots

Not all indoor plants have to be grown in pots filled with compost; some will grow on branches of trees or on tree trunks as they do in nature. These are epiphytes, which grow not on the ground but in the air, anchored to another plant, usually a tree. Epiphytes do not live off their host tree, as the parasitic Mistletoe does, but merely live on it. They have evolved in this way primarily to take advantage of light. When growing an epiphyte in your home you can simulate its natural surroundings by planting it on the branch of an oak or apple tree.

The most common epiphyte house plants are among the bromeliads. These include *Aechmea fulgens* (Coral Berry) and *Vriesea splendens* (Flaming Sword). (Of course not all Bromeliads are epiphytic; the Pineapple and the popular *Billbergia nutans* [Angel's Tears], for example, grow on the ground.) When a bromeliad has flowered the rosette dies and the offsets it has put out are nourished by the decaying leaves of the parent. At least that is what happens in its natural habitat in the forest. When domesticated, the bromeliad has the old rosette removed after the offsets are established and have been potted to grow as replacements.

Bromeliads grow best in crevices of a tree trunk or in the fork of a branch. It is often necessary to chisel away some bark or wood to provide a suitable perch for the plant. Wrap the roots in sphagnum moss mixed

with a little potting compost and tie securely to the wood with plastic-coated wire or nylon fishing line. After the plant has established its roots the main problem is watering. Bromeliad enthusiasts fit up all kinds of ingenious devices for trickle irrigation, but this is easier to do in a conservatory than in a living-room. Careful spraying of the trunk is probably the best solution, but it will have to be done once or even twice a day in summer. In any event in summer the vases of some bromeliads should be kept filled with water, preferably rain water or water from the defrosting of a refrigerator.

Your choice of plants is not restricted to bromeliads. Other good tree-growers are epiphytic orchids, and such cacti as *Epiphyllum × ackermanii* (Orchid Cactus) and hybrids, *Aporocactus flagelliformis* (Rat's-tail Cactus) and *Schlumbergera truncata* (Christmas Cactus). Another dramatic example is *Platycerium bifurcatum* (Stag's-horn Fern).

Unless you regard the tree only as a showcase for epiphytes it can be made to look less bare with the addition of a kind of ground cover. Some of the best for a small "tree" planting are *Philodendron oxycardium* (Parlour Ivy), philodendron is Greek for "tree lover", the variegated *Scindapsus aureus* (Devil's Ivy), but only when young while the leaves are still small, *Syngonium podophyllum* (African Evergreen) and some of the smaller leaved ivies with aerial roots.

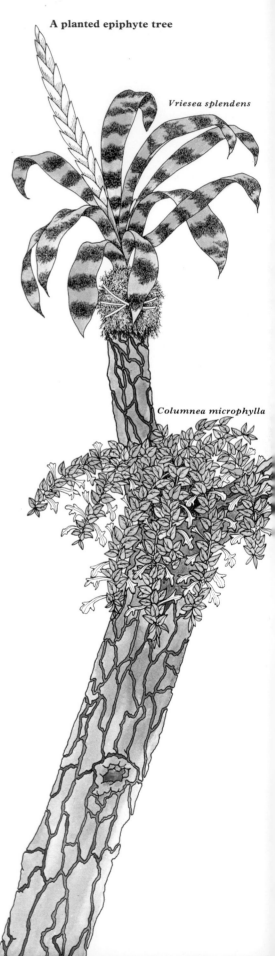

**A planted epiphyte tree**

*Vriesea splendens*

*Columnea microphylla*

## Making an epiphyte tree

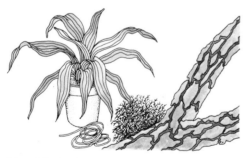

Materials for the construction of an epiphyte tree include the branch to which the plants are to be attached, a length of plastic-coated wire and sphagnum moss mixed with a little potting compost.

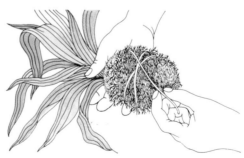

Take the epiphytic plant out of its pot and wrap the roots in the mixture of sphagnum moss and potting compost. Secure the sphagnum moss by binding it lightly with the plastic-coated wire.

Attach the plant to the branch with another length of wire. The plant will grow best in a crevice or fork. It may, therefore, be necessary to chisel away some of the bark.

In the wild epiphytes grow along the pathways that rain water takes. Indoors spray regularly or use a trickle irrigation system so that water collects in the crevices where the plants are lodged.

*Aechmea fasciata*

*Platycerium bifurcatum*

*Asplenium nidus*

*Nidularium innocentii*

## Unusual containers

Sometimes "good taste" can be as execrable as bad taste, and frequently more boring. The "decorating" approach to house plants provides endless evidence of this. When tastefully and studiedly arranged in their exquisite containers even living plants may lose their individuality and reflect none of the personality of their owner. When style becomes sterile it is time to introduce the unusual. Since you are growing house plants for enjoyment there is scope for fun.

In choosing unusual containers, however, you may create certain practical problems for yourself. The lack of any drainage in cups, jugs and teapots, for example, demands both skill and discipline to avoid killing plants by overwatering. Some apparent difficulties, on the other hand, can easily be overcome. If you long to use cane or other open-weave baskets for your plants but feel you cannot surround the pots with damp peat because the peat would fall out or dry out quickly then line the baskets with sheets of plastic.

Old chimney pots, decorated Victorian lavatory pans, brass coal scuttles and preserving pans, shiny milk churns and enormous shells are beautiful objects in themselves and beg to be used for house plants. They do not, however, cry out to be used together, for the unusual appeal of one container would defeat that of another.

In some countries epiphytic orchids are reportedly grown in the skulls of sheep; you may find it hard to think of a more macabre hanging basket than that.

# Miniature gardens

An indoor miniature garden can be grown in an old sink, a mixing bowl or on a platter. Few Alpines, the popular miniature plants that come from mountainous areas all over the world, can, however, survive in a heated house. Most miniature indoor gardens are, therefore, usually composed of small, young house plants, which are replaced as they grow large and out of scale.

There are innumerable variations for an indoor miniature garden. The emphasis might be put on flowering plants, including small-growing varieties of *Begonia*, *Campanula isophylla* (Bell Flower) or the inevitable *Saintpaulia ionantha* (African Violet). The orange berries of *Nertera depressa* (Bead Plant) will add colour for many months. Young creepers and trailers, including the variegated *Pellionia pulchra* (Dark Netting), *Zebrina pendula* (Wandering Jew), and the club moss *Selaginella kraussiana* (Spreading Club Moss), make excellent "ground cover"

and also soften the hard edges of the planter.

A striking miniature garden can be created with cacti and other succulents. It is best not to try to mix them with other plants because of the difficulty of reconciling their differing needs. Indeed, for ease of cultivation, cacti may be planted separately from other succulents, although they will look less interesting.

Succulents harmonize better than most plants, except Alpines, with the kind of landscaping popular in miniature gardens. Little piles of pebbles are often used to imitate rocks and "deserts" are created with small areas of sand. This can be taken further, but descends to the absurd when wishing wells, lychgates, bridges and pools made from mirrors are included.

Avoid using large cacti in a miniature garden—they cannot be cut down to size without showing horrible scars. Also, do not mix terrestrial types with epiphytes, which are best grown on branches of trees. The

choice is still wide: *Faucaria tigrina* (Tiger's Jaws), *Gasteria verrucosa*, *Haworthia margaritifera* (Pearl Plant) and *Kalanchoe blossfeldiana* (Tom Thumb) are all suitable for a miniature garden. So is *Lithops lesliei* (Living Stones), which is hard to distinguish from the pebbles amongst which it is often grown. And *Aporocactus flagelliformis* (Rat's-tail Cactus) could trail over the edge of the planter.

For a fairly cool room a particularly charming miniature garden can be made with such small, spring-flowering plants as *Crocus*, dwarf *Narcissus* and *Iris*. Miniature roses are also suitable but only for short periods in summer.

Another idea is to plant a miniature forest, using orange and lemon pips. Acorns and horse chestnuts may also be used, but it is important that these plants overwinter outdoors. To observe closely the growth of great trees in the days of their infancy is both instructive and exciting.

**Planting a miniature garden**

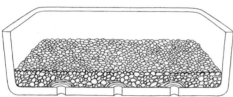

To prepare the container, cover the drainage holes with broken earthenware crocks, then add a one-inch (2-cm) layer of small pebbles or gravel.

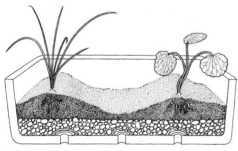

Add a shallow layer of compost. Position the plants, mounding the compost around the base of each one.

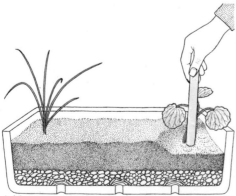

Add more compost, then, using a stick, firm it around the plants. Water, spray and feed according to the plants' requirements.

**A perfect use for an old kitchen sink**

Plants suitable for a miniature garden include *Nertera depressa* (Bead Plant), front, and, from left to right, *Hedera helix* (Common Ivy), *Saxifraga sarmentosa* (Mother of Thousands), *Carex morrowii* 'Variegata' (Japanese Sedge) and *Oxalis deppei* (Lucky Clover). When plants grow out of scale, they should be carefully removed and replaced. Flat pebbles may be used to make a miniature path through the garden.

# The art of bonsai

Hundreds of years ago the Japanese perfected the art of bonsai or tray planting. The inspiration for bonsai came from the cliffs and mountains of China and Japan where, in the crevices of rocks, windswept and undernourished trees stay alive for perhaps a century without ever growing taller than one or two feet (30 or 60 cm).

The aim of the Japanese has always been to make their trees perfect miniature reproductions of majestic trees in their own surroundings. Unlikely as it may seem, by training the tree as it grows and pruning the roots and the shoots, they often achieve this remarkable effect.

True bonsai utilizes trees that should be kept outdoors for most of the year, although they may be brought indoors for short periods. In the West, however, the art of bonsai is now being extended to include tropical plants that can be grown indoors.

The Japanese have five basic styles of

### Traditional bonsai styles

There are five basic bonsai styles. The easiest for the beginner is formal upright, above left. For the informal upright style, above right, the tree is trained to grow with a curved trunk.

For the slanting style, above left, the tree is trained to grow at an angle. The cascade style, above right, is the most difficult to achieve, for the tree looks as if it is cascading down a mountainside.

A tree trained in the semi-cascade style grows upright first and then parallel to the ground.

bonsai training: formal upright (an erect trunk and horizontal branches); informal upright (the tree has a curved trunk); slanting (the tree is trained to look as though the prevailing winds have forced it to grow at an angle); semi-cascade (the trunk extends over the side of the container); and cascade (the tree is trained to look as though it is growing on a mountainside).

Bonsai vary in size. Any plant between eighteen and twenty-two inches (45 and 56 cm) tall is designated "small". Above that bonsai become "large". Those below five inches (13 cm) are "miniature", but although in bonsai small is thought to be beautiful, it is considered that this is taking miniaturization a little too far.

There are several methods of growing bonsai. If you are fortunate you may find a naturally stunted tree high up on a mountain. The Japanese think these natural dwarfs are the finest. Or you can begin by rooting a cutting from a fully grown tree or by buying a young tree from a nursery. In either case bonsai training should not begin until the tree has a good strong stem. An expensive but instant method is to buy a fully trained, beautifully shaped tree. You will, however, have the fullest control over the training of your bonsai if you grow it from seed. The basic training is done in the first four years.

First Year: in autumn sow the seed in a pot containing seed compost. Unless you are growing a tropical plant put the pot outdoors. Keep the soil moist at all times. Transplant the seedling into a 4- or 5-inch (10- or 13-cm) pot containing potting compost.

Second Year: in autumn pot the seedling on into a 6-inch (15-cm) pot. Unless you are growing an upright bonsai, start training the seedling. To obtain a slanting style, insert a cane into the compost at an angle of forty-five degrees, then secure the stem to it. For the cascade and semi-cascade styles, twist a piece of soft wire around the stem. Bend the seedling over until the tip is level with the soil, then attach the end of the wire to a piece of string tied around the pot.

Third Year: in autumn remove the wire from the plant—the stem will now be permanently set at an angle. In winter cut the stem back to about six inches (15 cm) from the base. Side shoots will develop along the stem during the year.

Fourth Year: in October remove the tree from its pot. You will see that some of the roots are thick and others fibrous. Rigorously cut back the thick tap roots. Repot in a 3- to 4-inch (8- to 10-cm) pot. Bearing in mind the final shape that you are aiming at, cut off some side shoots. If necessary trim those which you have decided to keep. To create a gnarled effect, wrap wire around the side shoots and bend them into the desired shape. Attach the end of the wire to a piece of string tied around the pot. The wire may be removed a year or so later.

### Training an informal upright bonsai

When the tree is one year old start training it by inserting a cane into the compost at an angle of forty-five degrees. Using soft wire attach the stem to the support. Make sure the stem lies flat.

In the autumn of the following year remove the cane from the stem, which will now be permanently set at an angle. In winter cut the stem back to four to six inches (10 to 15 cm) from the base.

Remove the tree from its pot in the autumn of the next year. Inspect the roots. Then cut the thick tap roots right back. To give an all-over gnarled effect, twist wire around the side shoots after repotting.

# The art of bonsai

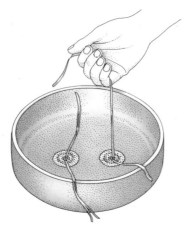

**Using florist's wire,** attach small discs of zinc gauze to cover the drainage holes in the bottom of the bonsai pot. Thread two-foot (60-cm) lengths of raffia or wire through the holes in the gauze.

**Line the bottom of the bowl** with a layer of gravel or small pebbles for good drainage. Then cover with a thicker layer of bonsai compost or any loam-based proprietary potting compost.

**Remove the tree from its old pot.** Using chopsticks tease the compost from around the roots.

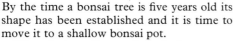

**Cut the thick tap roots right back,** then prune the feathery, fibrous roots by about one-third of their length. For convenience, when pruning the roots, stand the tree on an inverted pot.

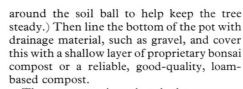

**After pruning the roots,** tie the raffia or wire in the pot around the soil ball. Fill the pot to within half an inch (1 cm) of the rim with more proprietary bonsai or loam-based compost.

**Using a flat-bladed trowel,** smooth the surface of the compost. Water the plant. Thereafter keep the compost moist at all times. In hot weather you may need to water it once or twice a day.

By the time a bonsai tree is five years old its shape has been established and it is time to move it to a shallow bonsai pot.

The choice of container is important. Traditionally, a tree with an upright trunk is planted just off-centre in a rectangular or oval pot, while a tree which has been trained to grow at an angle is planted in the centre of a round or square container.

Before transplanting your bonsai, the container must be prepared. Unless you have chosen the upright style, the tree may need some support; thread lengths of raffia or thin wire through the discs of zinc gauze, which should be placed over the drainage holes in the bottom of the pot. (When the tree has been repotted the raffia or wire is wound

around the soil ball to help keep the tree steady.) Then line the bottom of the pot with drainage material, such as gravel, and cover this with a shallow layer of proprietary bonsai compost or a reliable, good-quality, loam-based compost.

The next step is to knock the tree very carefully out of its pot. Then, using chopsticks or knitting needles, gently tap the soil ball to remove as much compost as possible from around the plant's roots. When the roots become visible, any large tap roots should be cut right back. Fibrous roots should be pruned by about one-third of their length. Keep a bowl of water beside you while you are pruning. Dip the roots in it regularly to keep them moist.

Plant the pruned tree in the bonsai pot, then fill the pot to within half an inch (1 cm) of the rim with more bonsai or loam-based compost. To make the tree look gnarled and ancient, the upper roots may be left above the compost. Thereafter a bonsai tree should be re-potted annually in autumn or winter. In summer trim the side shoots and pinch out the growing point.

The compost should be kept moist at all times—remember that compost in shallow containers dries out quickly. Since the plants are re-potted every year they need no feeding.

It can take from five to fifteen years for a plant to reach bonsai status. How long it will live will depend on the species. The life-span of conventional bonsai can vary from several

**Pinch out the growing point** and trim the side shoots every year in summer. The Satsuki Azalea, right, is a perfect example of a beautifully shaped, well-trained bonsai.

decades to several centuries, but if you grow bonsai trees indoors do not pitch your hopes too high.

Plants suitable for growing indoors include *Abutilon striatum* 'Thompsonii' (Spotted Flowering Maple), *Allamanda cathartica* (Common Allamanda), *Gardenia jasminoides* (Gardenia), *Hibiscus rosa-sinensis* (Rose of China) and *Ixora coccinea* (Flame of the Woods).

The following plants should be grown outdoors, but may be brought indoors for short periods: *Acer palmatum* (Japanese Maple); *Cryptomeria japonica* (Japanese Cedar); *Juniperus chinensis* (Chinese Juniper); *Rhododendron simsii* 'Satsuki' (Satsuki Azalea) and *Zelkova serrata* (Grey-bark Elm).

**Tools**
Only a few tools are needed for bonsai culture—a pair of chopsticks for removing compost from around the plant's roots when repotting; a sharp knife and a pair of scissors for pruning; a small fork and trowel and a flat-bladed trowel for general use.

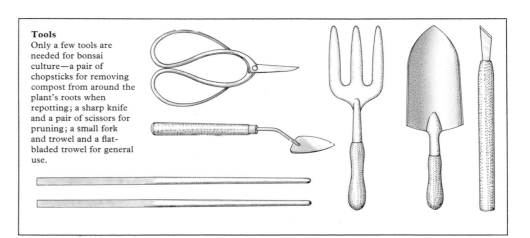

# Bottle gardens

Ships and plants in bottles are perennially fascinating. But whereas ships in bottles derive no benefit from being there, many house plants do. To plants a bottle provides a refuge from an environment in which human comfort is paramount. Although inside the bottle their growth may be even more restricted than it is in a pot, at least the moist, draught-free, unpolluted conditions in which they grow are more to their taste. Of course, plants can also be made to feel very much at home in plant cases and in conservatories, but a bottle garden is the cheapest way of creating a suitable microclimate for them.

In planting a bottle garden patience can make up for lack of skill, and once established bottle gardens take up little of your time. They are usually self-watering, since the water which evaporates from the compost in the bottle and that which is given off by the leaves condenses on the sides of the bottle and runs back into the compost. Watering, the greatest chore in looking after house plants is, therefore, avoided.

Think of bottle gardens and almost inevitably you think of carboys. But many other types of bottles, as well as glass jars, are suitable. Wide-necked containers, such as sweet jars and goldfish bowls, are obviously easier to plant than are narrow-necked flagons or carboys. Coloured bottles should not be used; the plants need all the light they can get.

Only plants which enjoy a humid atmosphere should be chosen for the true—that is, enclosed—bottle garden. Moreover, the plants which are going to share a bottle must all have the same requirements for warmth

and light and should have similar dormant periods. The plants in a bottle should be treated as a community, not as individuals.

Avoid the temptation to overcrowd your bottle. Although you choose slow-growing miniature plants, as you must, you are planting them when they are small—in order to get them in the bottle—and they will grow. Having to replant every year or so is infuriating. While a carboy might take six or more plants, in a small bottle there will be comfortable room for only two. A single plant—especially a fern—can be strikingly effective even in a big bottle. Visualize, too, how tall each plant is likely to grow and choose those which make sense in relation to the height of the container. A plant which has to stoop inside a bottle is a miserable-looking object.

In most cases, and certainly for narrow-necked bottles, it is better to use foliage rather

than flowering plants. Keep flowering plants for containers from which the dying flowers are easily removed; you could live to regret the day you planted an exuberant *Saintpaulia* (African Violet) at the bottom of a carboy.

Certain tools are essential for bottle gardening. They may be bought or can be improvised. To make a spade, take an old spoon, cut off part of the handle, dip it in strong adhesive and ram it into a hollow bamboo cane about two feet (60 cm) long. You can adapt an old kitchen fork in the same way. To make a rammer for firming the soil during planting push a cane into the hole of an empty cotton reel. A piece of wire with a loop at the end is needed for lowering the plants into the bottle. A pair of long tongs can be bought, but two bamboo canes, used like chopsticks, are a good substitute. A piece of cardboard shaped into a funnel is ideal for pouring the compost

**Containers suitable for bottle gardens** vary in size and shape and range from large jars to flagons. Wide-necked bottles are best for flowering plants so that dead petals can be removed.

## Planting a bottle garden

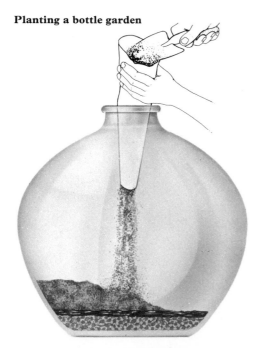

Using a paper funnel, pour a layer of gravel into a clean, dry carboy. Cover the gravel with charcoal chips to keep the compost sweet, then add a layer of dry, all-peat compost.

Using a stick make a hole in the compost. Then, with the wire loop, lower the first plant into the bottle. If the plant is bushy, enclose it in a paper cone before you put it in the bottle.

Use two sticks to push the roots into the hole. Unwrap the plant and remove the paper from the bottle with the sticks. Then carefully straighten the plant.

into the bottle and completes the equipment needed for planting.

Dead leaves and flowers must be removed immediately or mould will quickly develop. To make a simple cutting tool fix a razor blade into a bamboo cane. A cane with a sharp nail projecting from it can then be used for spearing and withdrawing the dead foliage and flowers. Other useful equipment is an artist's brush, fixed to a cane, for cleaning the leaves of the plants, and a piece of sponge attached to a wire for cleaning the inner surface of the bottle.

Before you begin to plant wash out the bottle thoroughly with water and detergent. Then fill it with water containing bleach or disinfectant to kill any possible fungus. Rinse the bottle and let it dry thoroughly.

Planting a carboy or flagon is the trickiest operation in bottle gardening; by comparison planting a wide-necked bottle is child's play. First pour a layer of gravel one to two inches (2 to 5 cm) deep in the bottom of the bottle. Cover this with some charcoal chips. This provides the drainage which is essential in an enclosed container. Now add a layer of compost three to five inches (8 to 13 cm) deep, depending on the size of the bottle and plants. The most suitable compost is an all-peat mix. The compost should be fairly dry so that it does not stick to the sides of the bottle.

You must next decide exactly where the plants are to go. The tallest plants should be in the centre and you must work from the sides of the bottle inwards so that the centre plants are not in the way. Look at the bottle from all angles while planting to make sure

you are achieving the effect you intended; any changes must be made immediately and not days or weeks later.

After planting is finished water the compost, but only enough to make it moist, not sodden. Watering can be done with a spray, first directed all around the sides of the bottle to remove any traces of soil and then over the surface of the compost. Seal the bottle and move it carefully to where it is to stand. Remember that a bottle garden needs light, but it should never be placed in direct sun.

A few days will show whether the compost is too wet or too dry. If there is no condensation on the sides of the bottle in the mornings the compost is too dry and needs more spraying. If there is heavy condensation, rather than a light film, the compost is too wet. Unseal the bottle for a few hours or for a day or two to let it dry out.

### Plants for bottle gardens and terrariums

Foliage plants for narrow-necked containers:
Cool: *Adiantum capillus-veneris*, *Hedera helix* (small-leaved), *Ophiopogon planiscapus*.
Temperate: *Adiantum hispidulum*, *Calathea insignis*, *Calathea makoyana*, *Calathea ornata* (when young), *Maranta leuconeura* 'Kerchoveana', *Pellionia pulchra*, *Pilea muscosa (microphylla)*, *Scirpus cernuus*, *Selaginella kraussiana*.
Warm: *Fittonia argyroneura*, *Peperomia caperata*, *Siderasis fuscata*.
Flowering plants for wide-necked jars:
Cool: *Nertera depressa (granadensis)*, *Oxalis deppei*, *Saxifraga sarmentosa*.
Temperate: *Begonia boweri*, *Plectranthus oertendahlii*, *Saintpaulia ionantha*.
Warm: *Episcia dianthiflora*, *Sonerila margaritacea* 'Argentea'.
Many ferns flourish in closed containers. If the container is small, plant only very young ferns, or choose small and slow-growing varieties.

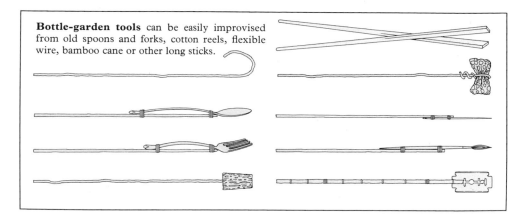

**Bottle-garden tools** can be easily improvised from old spoons and forks, cotton reels, flexible wire, bamboo cane or other long sticks.

When the plant is in position firm the soil around it using the rammer. After adding each new plant look at the bottle from all angles to ensure a balanced arrangement.

When you have finished planting use a mist spray to moisten the compost, then cork the bottle. If there is too much condensation in the bottle remove the cork to allow the moisture to escape.

After several months the growing plants will resemble a miniature tropical garden or forest. As plants grow too large for the bottle replace them, but try to maintain a balanced arrangement.

# Terrariums and plant cases

A glass container in which plants are grown is often referred to as a terrarium, just as a glass container for fish is called an aquarium. Some terrariums are enclosed and need little or no watering. Others are open to the air and need watering occasionally, but far less frequently than pots.

Enclosed plant cases or cabinets, modern versions of the Victorian Wardian cases, are all shapes and sizes and most of them provide more space for plants than even the largest bottles. They give, therefore, greater scope for imagination and ingenuity in planting, but it is best to avoid being carried away by whimsy. A terrarium is a case for plants and not a showcase for a model of a leafy, old-world village or a cactus-strewn sandy surface of the moon.

Most plant cases are made of glass in a framework of metal or wood. A large aquarium tank with a glass cover can be used. There are also cylindrical cases made of plastic. Although some plastics tend to discolour in time, a plastic case may be safer than a glass case if there are young children about.

Planting a case presents none of the problems of planting a narrow-necked bottle. To begin, put a one-inch (2-cm) layer of gravel at the bottom of the case and scatter pieces of charcoal over it. Add a layer of all-peat compost. This layer need not be level; a little undulation, especially in a large case, will add interest to the garden.

A popular arrangement of the plants is to place those that are tall at the back of the case and the smaller ones in front, but the layout will depend on the siting of the case in a room. It must never be put in direct sun.

Post-planting care of enclosed containers is the same as that for carboys, described on pages 180–1. The plants should not be fed, since you do not want to promote rapid growth. When a plant grows too big for the container remove it and replace it with a similar smaller plant, or a different one if you want a change.

**The terrarium** below has been designed with mounds and valleys, pieces of log and a small path to represent a woodland scene. All the plants included in the scene will flourish in the same cool and shady conditions. There are such well-known plants as *Hedera helix* (Common Ivy), *Chlorophytum elatum* 'Variegatum' (Spider Plant), *Adiantum capillusveneris* (Maidenhair Fern) and *Tolmiea menziesii* (Pick-a-back Plant), which provide contrasts in the texture, the shape and the colour of their leaves. There are two grass-like plants, *Acorus gramineus* 'Variegatus' (Myrtle Grass), with green leaves that are striped with white, and *Ophiopogon planiscapus* (Lily Turf), which in the 'Nigrescens' form has arching leaves of purple-black. Colour is provided by the low-growing *Nertera depressa* (*granadensis*) (Bead Plant), which produces very small whitish flowers in April followed by long-lasting bright orange berries.

**A large glass dish cover** that is used to keep cheese moist will provide the humid atmosphere for a number of tropical plants. Those illustrated here are plants that need warmth and shade. Like all those chosen for growing in glass containers they are comparatively dwarf in habit as the common names show—*Begonia boweri* (Miniature Eyelash Begonia), *Chamaedorea elegans* (Dwarf Mountain Palm) and *Pellaea rotundifolia* (Button Fern).

The real interest of the collection is in the contrasting shapes and wide variety of colours of the foliage. Variegated *Sansevieria hahnii* (Dwarf Mother-in-law's Tongue) has dark green leaves banded with yellow. The *Maranta leuconeura* 'Kerchoveana' (Prayer Plant) provides grey, green, chocolate and purple colouring. The waxy leaves of the *Begonia* are emerald green marked with chocolate brown, and those of *Pellionia pulchra* (Dark Netting) are patterned with green.

The dish to go under the cover should be about five inches (13 cm) deep to allow room inside it for a one-inch (2-cm) layer of pebbles and three to four inches (8 to 10 cm) of an all-peat compost.

**Ferns which can be grown under a bell jar** include *Adiantum hispidulum* (Maidenhair Fern), *Asplenium bulbiferum* (Hen and Chicken Fern), *Asplenium nidus* (Bird's-nest Fern) and *Pellaea rotundifolia* (Button Fern).

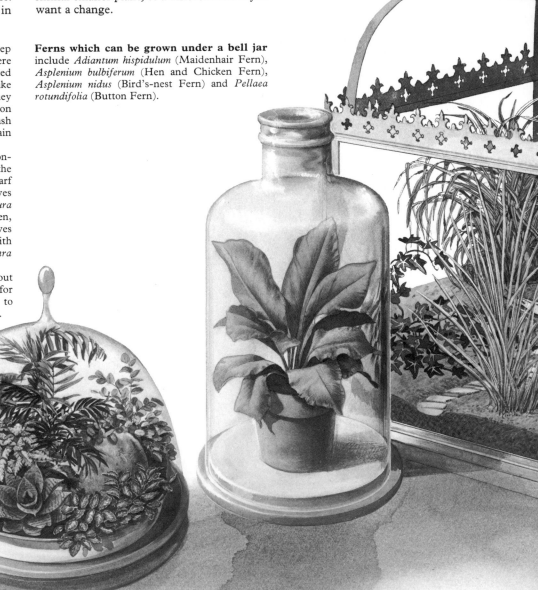

1 Chamaedorea elegans
2 Sansevieria hahnii
3 Maranta leuconeura 'Kerchoveana'
4 Pellaea rotundifolia
5 Begonia boweri
6 Pellionia pulchra
7 Rock

1 Acorus gramineus
  'Variegatus'
2 Chlorophytum elatum
  'Variegatum'
3 Ophiopogon
  planiscapus
4 Adiantum
  capillus-veneris

5 Hedera helix
6 Nertera depressa
  (granadensis)
7 Tolmiea menziesii
8 Oxalis deppei

1 Echeveria gibbiflora
  'Carunculata'
2 Rebutia kupperiana
3 Haworthia
  margaritifera
4 Lithops lesliei
5 Echinocereus
  pectinatus
6 Gasteria verrucosa

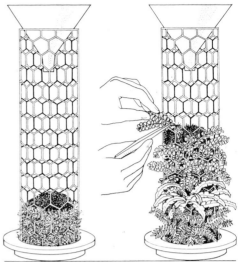

**To grow ferns** under a tall glass dome first make a wire netting column, three inches (8 cm) in diameter and a few inches less in height than the dome, using half-inch (1-cm) mesh netting. Put the column in a shallow, waterproof dish and anchor it with a little cement. When the cement has set thoroughly, line the inside of the column with sphagnum moss to a height of a few inches. Fill the column to that level with an all-peat compost in which a few pieces of charcoal have been mixed and firm it. Carefully poke the roots of the young ferns through the mesh and the moss into the compost. Repeat this process in small stages until the whole column has been lined with moss, filled with compost and planted all the way around. Space the ferns irregularly and do not crowd them. Spray the column with water and place the dome over it. This is, in effect, a bottle garden and the means of establishing the correct level of moisture are exactly the same.

Suitable ferns for growing on a column include *Adiantum hispidulum* (Maidenhair Fern), *Asplenium bulbiferum* (Hen and Chicken Fern), *Asplenium nidus* (Bird's-nest Fern) and *Pellaea rotundifolia* (Button Fern). These will need shade and temperate warmth.

**A large brandy balloon** is a more appropriate glass for plants to live in than for humans to drink from. Such a glass is a particularly suitable container for dwarf cacti and other succulents.

Attractive shapes are provided by the fleshy rosettes of *Echeveria gibbiflora* 'Carunculata' and *Haworthia margaritifera* (Pearl Plant), and by the reddish-brown pebbles of *Lithops lesliei* (well described by its common name of Living Stones). The *Lithops* has yellow flowers in September, but it is the remaining plants in the collection that contribute most of the colour—above all the beautiful red flowers of the ever-popular *Rebutia kupperiana* (Red Crown), which appear in May and June.

Planting is best done in late spring. Put a one-inch (2-cm) layer of gravel or pebbles at the bottom of the glass, and arrange the plants on top of this without crowding them together. Then fill in the spaces between the plants with compost—one part loam, one part peat and one part crushed brick or sharp sand. Do not firm the compost too much. Water well, but then let the compost get quite dry before watering again. In winter the garden must be kept in a cool place and watered little.

# The conservatory

A conservatory can be regarded as a glorified plant case—but modified to make it habitable for human beings as well as for plants. Anyone who has a Victorian-style conservatory is indeed lucky, for it vastly widens the horizons of indoor gardening.

The modern gardener will use the conservatory in a different way from his predecessors of the nineteenth century. Then, one of the conservatory's main functions was to serve as a reservoir of plants that were taken into the house for brief periods—especially when they were in flower—and returned before they died from lack of light or were suffocated by coal and gas fumes. Today, because of the cost of heating, the house in winter is likely to be warmer than the conservatory, but the conservatory still has the advantage of being lighter, and this is of inestimable value. It is also possible to make the atmosphere of the conservatory more humid than would be tolerable in rooms in which you live all day.

The kind of plants you can grow in a conservatory basically depends on how much money you are able, and willing, to spend on heating it from October to May. At one extreme, with no heat, you could treat the conservatory solely as an alpine house. A little heat, however, if only to keep the temperature above freezing point, would increase the usefulness of such a conservatory. It would, for example, provide winter quarters for dormant house plants when they need cooler conditions than those of a heated house. At the other extreme you could provide, at a cost, the hot and humid conditions required by many tropical orchids. But many other plants would not tolerate sharing the conservatory with them, and neither would you.

The best value for money spent on fuel to heat a conservatory is achieved by aiming at a minimum winter temperature of 50°F (10°C) at night and 65°F (18°C) by day—a temperate conservatory. In it can be cultivated those plants which are difficult to grow indoors because they need plenty of light as well as reasonable warmth. Moreover, plants which prefer shade in summer would benefit from a spell in winter in a temperate conservatory where conditions are not so hot and dry as in a living-room.

Heating a temperate conservatory involves balancing cost with convenience. Extending the heating system from the house is often possible, but it has to be adequate to meet the extra demands. Although high temperatures are not aimed at, heat losses through a large expanse of glass are considerable. When installing a heating system in a conservatory it is important to remember that a gentle heat distributed evenly around the perimeter is far better than a fierce heat from a single radiator which you may be tempted to place against the wall adjoining the house to cut down installation costs.

Tubular electrical heaters, which can be bought at a reasonable price, are a simple alternative. Fan heaters are increasingly popular for use in conservatories because they circulate the air as well as warm it and in summer they can be run cold to assist ventilation. It is vital that the electrical wiring in the conservatory is carried out professionally to ensure that it is shockproof.

If the house is piped for natural gas a simple heater can be installed in the conservatory. And there is no need for a flue because the carbon dioxide from natural gas is beneficial rather than harmful to most plants. Paraffin heaters should be avoided, if only because they will make it impossible to grow many plants which are sensitive to the fumes. Whatever the heating system, insist for the sake of the plants and your pocket, that it is thermostatically controlled.

Whereas the problem in winter is keeping the conservatory warm, in summer it will be keeping it cool. Even warmth- and light-loving plants quickly begin to suffer in hot direct sunlight. The conservatory must have windows which open, and open easily so that you cannot make any excuses for not giving your plants ventilation.

Plants need shade as well as ventilation in summer. A great variety of blinds is available for this purpose. To avoid the labour of constantly pulling them down and pulling them back, automatic blinds can easily be installed in an existing conservatory.

Most indoor plants thrive best in a humid atmosphere and this can be more easily achieved in the conservatory than in the house with an electrically operated humidifier. It can, if you wish, be turned off when you are sitting in the conservatory.

Whatever you decide to grow in your conservatory you can choose either of two approaches for displaying them—landscaping or staging. The modern approach is landscaping; you provide a setting which either exactly copies or suggests the natural background of the growing plants. This usually involves starting at floor level and creating banks and hollows in which the plants are grouped. While landscaping can look attractive it has two disadvantages—it greatly reduces the space and restricts the choice of plants to those best calculated to produce the desired effect.

The other alternative, staging, means simply growing the plants in pots and containers on shelves, or staging. This method, now less fashionable than landscaping, offers the opportunity to grow a more mixed collection of plants and most amateur gardeners certainly find it gives them greater scope and interest. For the elderly it also has the considerable attraction of gardening without bending. The burden of daily watering of individual pots can be avoided, too, by fitting the staging with trays filled with sand which is kept constantly moist; the pots placed on them are watered by capillary action.

**A conservatory** widens the horizon for the indoor gardener. Here you can grow plants that require a different temperature or atmosphere from that which prevails in the rest of your home. You can indulge a desire to be surrounded by plants that would be too large for an ordinary room, or you can cultivate fruit and vegetables, many of which are very beautiful.

# The garden room

Conservatories met the needs of the nineteenth-century middle classes, but garden rooms fit in better with twentieth-century life styles. A garden room is a hybrid, conservatory × living-room, which balances the needs of plants and human being. It makes it possible to live outdoors indoors.

To let the plants have as much light as possible, particularly in winter, a garden room should have large sun-facing windows, at best extending from floor to ceiling. These also give the inhabitants the feeling of being in contact with the outside world, but warmer. While there is more light in a garden room than in an ordinary room in the house, there is less light there than in a conservatory because the roof is not made of glass, which would be unpleasantly hot to live under.

Popular components of a garden room are an indoor bed at floor level running the length of a picture window; an enclosed plant wall, often covered with ferns, and a plant window full of colourful foliage or flowers.

A fern wall should be on the north side of the room so that it escapes the direct summer sun that fills much of the room through the south-facing window. A steady gentle northern light can be provided for the ferns by small windows in the roof of the enclosure. The wall may be faced with artificial tufa rock, with built-in pockets in which the ferns are planted. Sliding doors of glass give access for tending the ferns. Behind the glass the essential humid atmosphere can be created, as it never can in a dry, heated room. By trickle irrigation of the tufa wall and the use of a humidifier the ferns can largely be left to themselves.

Although it is possible to fill such a fern case with ferns that need cool, humid conditions or tropical ferns that need very humid heat, temperate ferns are the most popular for garden rooms—as they were for Victorian conservatories. A choice can be made from *Adiantum capillus-veneris* (Maidenhair Fern), *Asplenium bulbiferum* (Hen and Chicken Fern), *Asplenium nidus* (Bird's-nest Fern), *Cyrtomium falcatum* (Holly Fern), *Polystichum acrositichioides* (Christmas Fern) and *Pteris cretica* (Ribbon Fern). *Platycerium bifurcatum* (Stag's-horn Fern) and *Nephrolepis exaltata* (Sword Fern) may be used as hanging ferns and *Selaginella kraussiana* (Spreading Club Moss) makes excellent ground cover. Avoid *Pellaea rotundifolia* (Button Fern), which dislikes such moist conditions. Some bromeliads and other epiphytes may be grown among the rocks or along trunks of trees behind the glass.

An enclosure containing orchids is extremely beautiful. But since orchids need plenty of light the outside wall of the enclosure would have to face the sun and be of glass. Blinds should be provided to give shade in the summer. The choice of orchids will depend on the temperatures that can be maintained in the enclosure. All but one or two of those suggested in the Catalogue of Plants for use as house plants will thrive in winter temperatures between 60° and 65°F (16° and 18°C) by day and 50°F (10°C) by night. In summer, day temperatures should not go much above 75°F (24°C), although this is difficult during hot spells, nor fall below 50°F (10°C) by night. When temperatures are high humidity must also be high. Tubular electrical heaters can be used to boost the heat in the enclosure, if necessary, on winter nights, and a humidifier would provide the humidity on warm days.

Cacti and succulents present the same problem in a garden room as in any other room of the house. But if you like succulents, and if they can be moved elsewhere in winter, they are among the most attractive plants for a garden room. The smaller specimens can make up a plant window, and the larger can be displayed among rocks at floor level.

The bed by the south-facing window is an ideal place for light-loving foliage plants, especially those with variegated leaves, and a succession of plants in flower could be introduced to add a splash of bright colour. Or the bed could be given over entirely to flowering plants—for example, massed bulbs in spring, followed by a collection of *Fuchsia*, *Pelargonium* and *Begonia*, or a mixture of annuals.

If the garden room has sliding windows the bed in summer becomes almost as much a part of outdoors as of indoors and the same bedding plants can be used on both sides of the window. But sun shining through glass can be dangerously hot even when it is tolerable in the open, and some form of shading must be provided.

The wall of the garden room backing on the house is an obvious place for climbing plants. Four of the best are *Jasminum polyanthum* (Jasmine), *Stephanotis floribunda* (Madagascar Jasmine), *Clerodendrum thomsonae* (Bleeding Heart Vine) and *Hoya carnosa* (Wax Plant).

With a garden room like this, and a comfortable chair, who needs the rest of the house, or even a garden?

**Plan for a garden room**

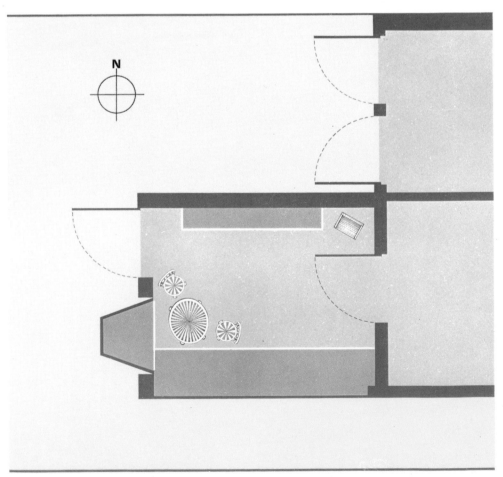

A garden room can be created by building an extension on to your house. Ideally a large window reaching from floor to ceiling and pitched at an angle of fifty degrees to collect as much light as possible should be built on a south-facing wall.

The north side of the building could contain an enclosed plant wall, although skylights above may be required to supply a small amount of extra light. The west or east wall are ideal sites for a plant window to house such plants as orchids.

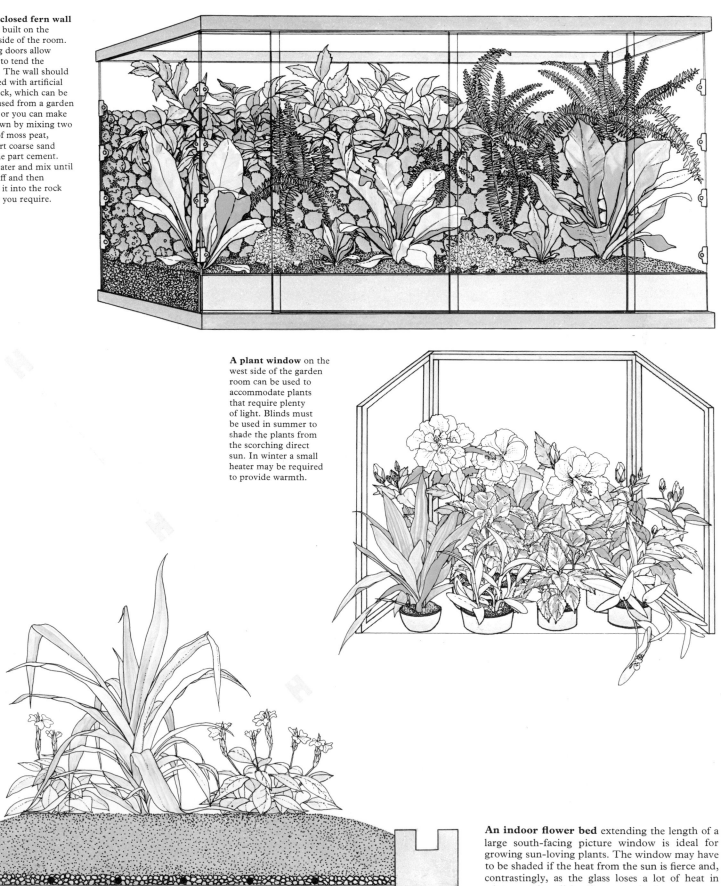

**An enclosed fern wall** can be built on the north side of the room. Sliding doors allow access to tend the plants. The wall should be faced with artificial tufa rock, which can be purchased from a garden centre or you can make your own by mixing two parts of moss peat, one part coarse sand and one part cement. Add water and mix until it is stiff and then mould it into the rock shapes you require.

**A plant window** on the west side of the garden room can be used to accommodate plants that require plenty of light. Blinds must be used in summer to shade the plants from the scorching direct sun. In winter a small heater may be required to provide warmth.

**An indoor flower bed** extending the length of a large south-facing picture window is ideal for growing sun-loving plants. The window may have to be shaded if the heat from the sun is fierce and, contrastingly, as the glass loses a lot of heat in winter, undersoil heating may also be necessary.

# Pests and diseases

Plant pests usually prefer the great outdoors or a cosy greenhouse to the comforts of a home. But do not be lulled into a false sense of security—like burglars they can and do break in.

Many, if not most, pests simply gate-crash, tagging along with the plants you buy. The golden rule, therefore, is to inspect every plant as soon as it crosses your threshold.

If there is any sign of a living thing on the plant or if it appears at all unhealthy keep it by itself. It should remain in isolation until you have got rid of the pest or diagnosed the disease and, if it is curable, dealt with it. Never take the gamble of introducing a doubtful plant into a healthy collection. Pests do not just go away. They multiply and spread.

Even with these precautions your house plants are not immune from attack and you should always be alert, without making too great a performance of it. Get into the habit of really noticing your plants when you water and feed them, or even when you are just admiring them. In this way you will soon detect if anything is wrong. And do not forget that leaves have undersides—greenfly, red spider mites, whitefly, scale insects and mealy bugs never do.

Greenfly are hard to avoid. They multiply prodigiously, so kill them the instant you see any signs of them. Flowering pot plants tend to be the most vulnerable and *Senecio cruentus* (Cineraria) is a classic example of a plant which can be quickly "eaten to death" by greenfly. Derris kills greenfly, but it is also fatal to fish, so before spraying cover or remove fish bowls or tanks. Aerosol sprays, although expensive, are the simplest pesticide weapon, but always spray from at least twelve inches (30 cm) away from a plant or the leaves may turn brown and wither. Cover furniture, curtains and carpets in the vicinity of the plant to avoid spotting. Ideally spray in an unoccupied room and leave the window open as some insecticides are poisonous and foul-smelling. On warm days spray outdoors.

Attacks by other pests are far less common, but they may be harder to cope with. For example, red spider mites are so small that they are hard to detect. The first evidence may be a small greyish or brownish flecking on the surfaces of leaves underneath which the mites are feeding. Red spider mites strike in hot, dry weather, so maintaining humid conditions will help to avoid them. Use a mist sprayer regularly. The cure is to spray with Malathion, but a plant takes a long time to recover from a bad infestation.

The tiny whitefly lays eggs underneath the leaves, and the larvae—whitescales—suck the sap and exude a sticky "honeydew". Liquid derris will kill the flies, but the larvae are difficult to get rid of.

Scale insects cling to the stem and undersides of the leaves and suck the sap. At this stage of their existence they are immobile and almost look like part of the plant. If they are not detected early, getting rid of them is extremely tedious. The only way is to rub them off with a matchstick tipped with cotton wool and soaked in methylated spirit. Be sparing with the amount of methylated spirit you use—leaves are easily damaged by it.

Mealy bugs are a less common house plant pest in Europe than they are in the United States. The bugs, which look like small pieces of cotton wool, are found on stems and on the undersides of leaves in summer. If they are noticed early they are easily disposed of by employing the methylated matchstick method which is used against scale insects. If mealy bugs get a real hold in the crevices of a plant they are almost impossible to eradicate; heavily infested *Saintpaulia ionantha* (African Violet), for example, are often best discarded.

It is unfortunate that the more acceptable the environment is made for plants the more desirable it becomes for pests. There is a greater risk of attack in conservatories and there an even keener watch should be kept, particularly for red spider mites and whitefly. It is possible, however, to buy two insects which will take over the job of controlling these two pests. The parasitic wasp *Encarsia formosa* lays its eggs in whitefly scales; the eggs hatch and the scales die. *Phytoseiulus persimilis* has an enormous appetite for red spider mites. Neither of these natural predators, however, are very effective in the home unless you have many plants and many pests.

Cacti and other succulents are subject to all these pests and have a few particular troubles of their own. Ants are rather partial to making nests in the pots of cacti and other succulents growing in conservatories. Since ants also spread aphids, and sometimes mealy bugs, they should be destroyed with a proprietary ant killer.

If you are watchful for early signs of pest attacks and if you keep your plants healthy you are unlikely to suffer any losses from pests, unless they carry virus diseases. Outward signs that a plant has been attacked by a virus include pale or yellow mottling of leaves and crippling or distorting of shoots or stunting. There is no room for sentiment when faced with such a plant. Burn it.

**Red spider mites** are tiny, almost invisible pests which infest the undersides of leaves and feed on the sap. When infestation is severe the leaves discolour and fall prematurely. If humid conditions are maintained the mites are discouraged. If they are already in residence, spraying with liquid derris or Malathion should effectively destroy them.

**Cyclamen mites** can spell disaster, since safe pesticides do not effectively control them. The affected plant is best destroyed. Often found on African Violets, *Cyclamen* and sometimes on *Pelargonium*, the mites are difficult to spot, but their presence is indicated by the curling of the outer leaves of the plant and the rotting or withering of the shoot tips and flower buds.

**Worms and woodlice** are intruders from outdoors. They attack pot plants put out in summer. Earthworms enter through drainage holes and burrow among the roots, disturbing the soil. This can be prevented by standing the pot on a layer of gravel. Woodlice infest conservatories. They cause slight damage to roots, stems and leaves, particularly of orchids. Spray or dust around the base of the plant with BHC.

**Sciarid-fly maggots,** sometimes called fungus-gnat maggots, feed on the root hairs of young plants, particularly in damp and humid conditions. Watering the compost with a solution of Malathion will destroy them.

**Although ants** are not in themselves harmful, they carry aphids from one plant to another. They may also tunnel in the soil and disturb the plant's roots. Destroy them with ant poison when necessary.

188

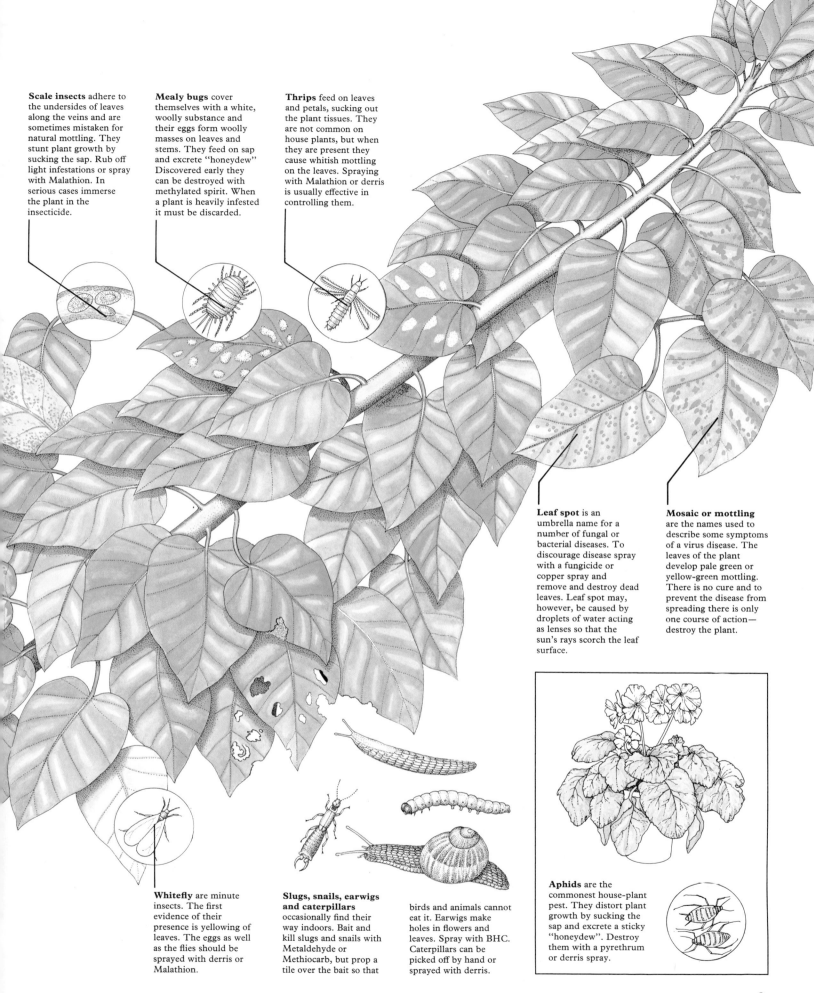

**Scale insects** adhere to the undersides of leaves along the veins and are sometimes mistaken for natural mottling. They stunt plant growth by sucking the sap. Rub off light infestations or spray with Malathion. In serious cases immerse the plant in the insecticide.

**Mealy bugs** cover themselves with a white, woolly substance and their eggs form woolly masses on leaves and stems. They feed on sap and excrete "honeydew" Discovered early they can be destroyed with methylated spirit. When a plant is heavily infested it must be discarded.

**Thrips** feed on leaves and petals, sucking out the plant tissues. They are not common on house plants, but when they are present they cause whitish mottling on the leaves. Spraying with Malathion or derris is usually effective in controlling them.

**Leaf spot** is an umbrella name for a number of fungal or bacterial diseases. To discourage disease spray with a fungicide or copper spray and remove and destroy dead leaves. Leaf spot may, however, be caused by droplets of water acting as lenses so that the sun's rays scorch the leaf surface.

**Mosaic or mottling** are the names used to describe some symptoms of a virus disease. The leaves of the plant develop pale green or yellow-green mottling. There is no cure and to prevent the disease from spreading there is only one course of action— destroy the plant.

**Whitefly** are minute insects. The first evidence of their presence is yellowing of leaves. The eggs as well as the flies should be sprayed with derris or Malathion.

**Slugs, snails, earwigs and caterpillars** occasionally find their way indoors. Bait and kill slugs and snails with Metaldehyde or Methiocarb, but prop a tile over the bait so that birds and animals cannot eat it. Earwigs make holes in flowers and leaves. Spray with BHC. Caterpillars can be picked off by hand or sprayed with derris.

**Aphids** are the commonest house-plant pest. They distort plant growth by sucking the sap and excrete a sticky "honeydew". Destroy them with a pyrethrum or derris spray.

# What went wrong?

**The over-indulged plant**

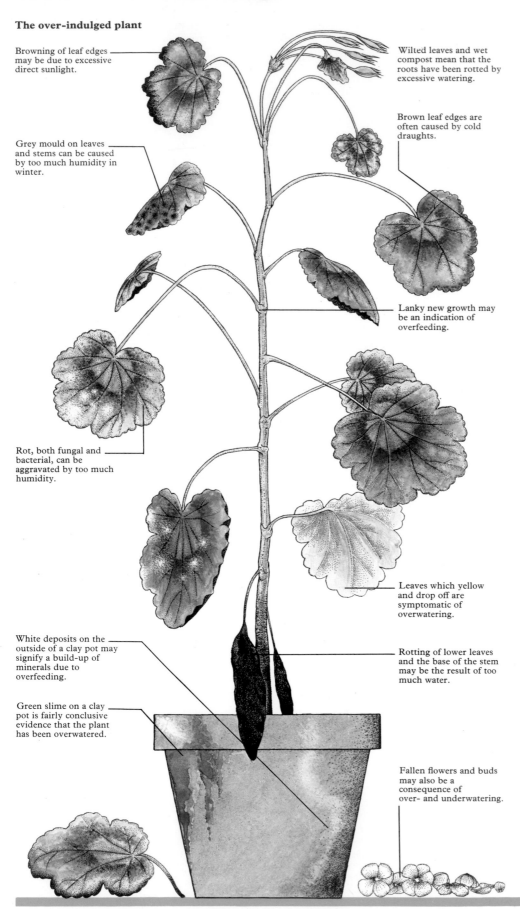

Browning of leaf edges may be due to excessive direct sunlight.

Grey mould on leaves and stems can be caused by too much humidity in winter.

Rot, both fungal and bacterial, can be aggravated by too much humidity.

White deposits on the outside of a clay pot may signify a build-up of minerals due to overfeeding.

Green slime on a clay pot is fairly conclusive evidence that the plant has been overwatered.

Wilted leaves and wet compost mean that the roots have been rotted by excessive watering.

Brown leaf edges are often caused by cold draughts.

Lanky new growth may be an indication of overfeeding.

Leaves which yellow and drop off are symptomatic of overwatering.

Rotting of lower leaves and the base of the stem may be the result of too much water.

Fallen flowers and buds may also be a consequence of over- and underwatering.

Human beings are the main cause of the death of house plants. Nothing is more dangerous than a human being with a watering can, for more house plants die from drowning than from anything else. This is particularly so when plants are dormant and their water needs are at a minimum.

The reason that overwatering causes death is simple. The root hairs, through which water is drawn up into the plant, need oxygen, but if all the spaces between the particles of compost are always filled with water there will be no oxygen and the plant will die. The plant gives many warning signs before it dies, but the same signs may indicate only one of a number of totally different maladies.

If the plant is wilting even when the compost is wet, if several leaves turn yellow and fall, if buds and flowers drop off, if leaves and stems rot at the base then it is always wise to suspect overwatering. The presence of green slime on a clay pot is fairly conclusive evidence of excessive watering. At this stage the odds are that the roots have also begun to rot. It may be too late to save the plant, but it is worth trying. Put it in a warm room and let the compost dry out. This may take some weeks, because with many rotted roots the plant is taking up scarcely any water. Even when the compost seems dry restrain yourself from watering it for another week or ten days, although during that period you can help the plant to recover by spraying the leaves. Then gently turn the plant out of the pot and if new roots have started to grow in place of the rotten ones you can begin to water sparingly. When the plant is again growing healthily the correct cycle of watering can be resumed.

At times too much moisture in the air as well as in the compost creates problems. In winter excessive humidity can provide the right conditions for grey mould to attack leaves and stems. Cut away all affected parts and burn them.

Slight underwatering will slow down the rate of growth and the plant will produce smaller, darker leaves. More serious underwatering will cause the plant to shed some of the older leaves in order to save younger growth. Extreme dryness will often cause a dramatic wilting of all the leaves. As soon as this happens spray the leaves and water the compost and, hopefully, little damage will have been done. Stiff-textured leaves, however, just dry out with nothing more than a few wrinkles. The plant may be dead and mummified, but the leaves remain a dull green colour.

Many plants, especially those of tropical origin, find it hard to tolerate dryness in the atmosphere. Even when pots are plunged in damp peat to make the air around the plant more humid, a mist spray should also be in regular use in warm weather.

Although all plants need water to live, hard

water will kill such lime-hating plants as *Rhododendron simsii* (Indian Azalea) and *Camellia japonica*. Some others merely tolerate lime. They survive, but the leaves may turn yellow even though they do not drop off as they do as a result of overwatering. In these cases use distilled or softened water.

After too much water the greatest bane of a house plant's life is too little light. The warning signs are pale leaves, spindly growth, leaves distorting themselves to get the maximum amount of light, green leaves turning yellow and variegated leaves turning green. Light starvation in the end means death, because the process of photosynthesis cannot be carried out properly. The suffering plant should be moved into better natural light or should be given supplementary artificial lighting.

Too much direct sunlight can also be harmful, especially for plants which in natural conditions grow in some shade. Young leaves are particularly at risk. Excessive sun causes wilting and scorching of the leaves. Roots are killed if the pot stands in baking sun.

All plants hate draughts and continued exposure to them will prove deadly. Even if the plant lives its appearance is ruined by the edges of the leaves turning brown. Frosty draughts around windows are especially dangerous. If leaves are touched by frost spray them with cold—not warm—water and put them in a cool room so that they thaw out slowly. This may save some plants but not those which come from tropical climates.

Just as they can be overwatered or underwatered, so house plants can be overfed or underfed. Overfeeding usually leads to sappy growth which is susceptible to disease. A warning signal of an excessive build-up of minerals in the soil is the appearance of white deposits on the sides of a clay pot. Evidence of underfeeding is given by slow growth, small, poorly coloured flowers and leaves and the early drooping of lower leaves. Lack of nitrogen is the primary cause. Patches of brown, yellow and silver on the leaves indicate the plant's lack of some mineral, for example, calcium, potassium or iron. Fertilizers are needed and foliar feeding is the quickest way of putting right any deficiencies.

**The under-indulged plant**

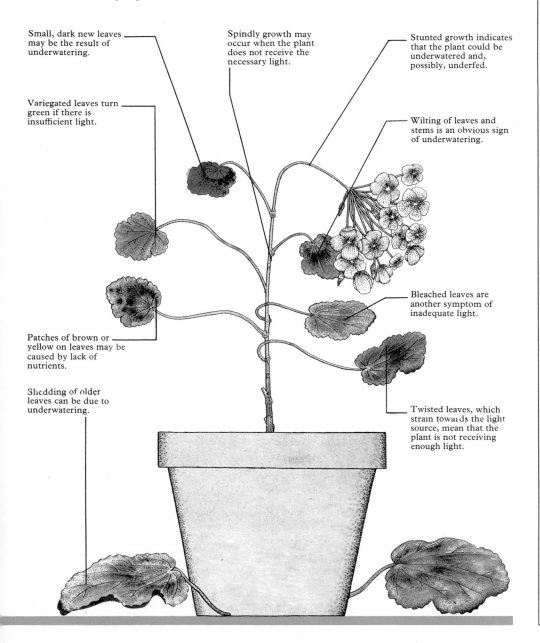

Small, dark new leaves may be the result of underwatering.

Variegated leaves turn green if there is insufficient light.

Patches of brown or yellow on leaves may be caused by lack of nutrients.

Shedding of older leaves can be due to underwatering.

Spindly growth may occur when the plant does not receive the necessary light.

Stunted growth indicates that the plant could be underwatered and, possibly, underfed.

Wilting of leaves and stems is an obvious sign of underwatering.

Bleached leaves are another symptom of inadequate light.

Twisted leaves, which strain towards the light source, mean that the plant is not receiving enough light.

**Leaf cleaning**

There are usually very few stomata on the upper surface of a leaf to be clogged. A layer of dust, however, reduces the light necessary for photosynthesis.

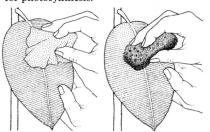

Wipe the dust off large, waxy leaves and then sponge them with cold water to which a few drops of liquid detergent have been added. Do not handle young leaves. Never use beer, milk or vinegar for cleaning leaves, or olive oil or cooking oil to make the leaves glossy. If you want the leaves of your rubber plant to shine, use a harmless proprietary leafshine, which should be applied with a pad of cotton wool.

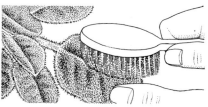

Never wash hairy leaved plants or cacti and other succulents. To get rid of the dust use a soft brush.

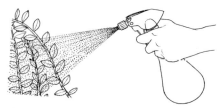

Small-leaved plants can be mist sprayed to remove dust.

# Holiday care

Each year a house plant is subjected to a traumatic experience—its owner goes on holiday. You, who have tended it with loving care all the year, are suddenly not there. In summer the plant is left in a tightly closed, stuffy room, deprived of frequent spraying of its leaves and regular watering of its roots. In winter it is left in a cold and cheerless house. You cannot become housebound because of your plants, but there are things that can be done to mitigate the shock of your absence.

The problems of winter holidays are the easiest to deal with. Before you go away remove plants which are near windows and put them in the centre of the warmest room in the house. Since most plants are dormant at this time of year watering does not present a major problem. Tender plants can be put on top of the refrigerator or the freezer to benefit from the warmth that rises from the back.

In summer if you are only away for a long weekend there are few problems, especially if the plants are in pots within peat-filled containers. Water them just before you leave the house and put them in a part of the room where no direct sunlight will fall on them.

The longer you are away the more tedious are the precautionary measures necessary to keep the plants in good health, but they are worth while if only to avoid the depressing experience of arriving home to a houseful of dying vegetation. A week or more before your

holiday inspect all the plants to see that they are free of pests; if not, take immediate action to get rid of them. Even a few pests will take advantage of the uninterrupted holiday you are offering them and multiply prodigiously. Any plant which still looks unhealthy when you are due to leave should be isolated.

The major problem is how to keep the compost moist. One of the most reliable do-it-yourself methods is to use plastic bags. Water the plants so that the compost is moist but not sodden. Slip each small plant, pot first, into a plastic bag and, trapping as much air as possible in it, seal the open end of the bag with a strong rubber band or adhesive tape. What you have made, in effect, is a temporary bottle garden, and the atmosphere within the bag will remain moist. Put the pots in good light but safely out of the way of any direct sunlight. Make doubly sure the plants are pest free before they go in the bags. Your plants should be safe for up to two weeks.

If the plant is too big to be completely enclosed, put only the pot in a polythene bag and tie the bag around the base of the stem. This will, however, not keep the plant moist for more than one week because, although the bag will cut down evaporation from the pot, moisture will still be lost through the leaves.

Another way to keep the plants watered is by capillary action, and the ways in which this can be done range from the homespun to

the sophisticated. Spread a layer of newspaper or an old blanket on the bottom of the bath and place a row of bricks on top. Put plants which have clay pots on top of the bricks and run water into the bath to the level of the top of the bricks. The plug must be tightly fitting or the water will seep away.

You can buy capillary mats in various sizes which hold one and a half pints of water to the square yard (1 litre to the square metre). Stand the plants on the mat in the kitchen sink, or in the bath if you have many plants, but do not let the matting cover the drain hole. Leave the tap dripping slightly and the plants will be kept watered. A trial run is a good idea to make sure that the tap can be kept dripping, for, by some perversity, even taps which normally cannot be stopped from dripping dry up under these circumstances. There must be good light, but not direct sunlight, in the bathroom or the kitchen or the plants, reaching up for the light, will grow spindly in your absence.

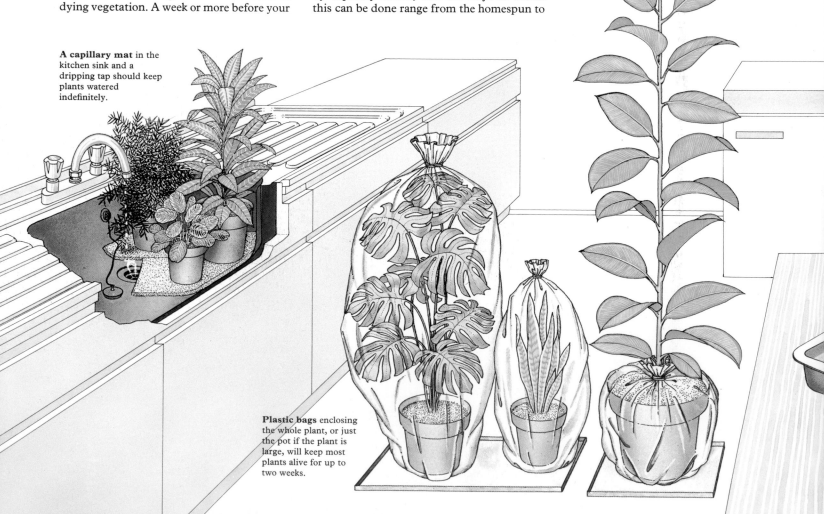

**A capillary mat** in the kitchen sink and a dripping tap should keep plants watered indefinitely.

**Plastic bags** enclosing the whole plant, or just the pot if the plant is large, will keep most plants alive for up to two weeks.

An alternative method, if you only have a few plants, requires a table or worktop, two roasting tins and a piece of capillary matting. Turn one tin upside down and cut a piece of capillary matting to cover it, plus an extra few inches at one end to extend into the second adjoining tin which is full of water. Water the matting and stand the pots on top. Capillary mats work best with plastic pots, so if you use clay pots push a piece of the matting into the pot's drainage hole to act as a wick.

A more permanent capillary system can be set up in a conservatory or garden room. But under glass there are such other problems as shading and ventilation. If you have the whole paraphernalia of automatic blinds and ventilators plus a humidifier, you can lie on your sun-drenched beach without qualms. If not leave the conservatory shaded and some windows open, and trust to luck.

Indoors, any peat-filled containers which are too big to move can be kept quite easily watered. Take a large funnel and plug the neck so that only the smallest hole remains. This will allow a little drip of water to go through. Push the neck of the funnel into the peat among the plants in the centre of the container, and fill the funnel with water at the last moment before you leave.

Friendly neighbours may be willing to keep an eye on your house plants, but if they are novices they may water indiscriminately with the best of misguided intentions. It might help them—unless they are liable to take it as an insult—to attach a card to each pot outlining that plant's special needs. The use of professional plant-sitters has not yet spread to Europe from the United States, but it doubtless will. But even skilled attendants cannot replace you. Whether or not you are on intimate speaking terms with your plants there is no doubt that plants do become accustomed to the kind of treatment given to them by one person and do not enjoy change. Maybe it is a comforting thought that plants grow as devoted to you as you do to them.

**Delicate plants** can be placed on top of a refrigerator or freezer during winter holidays to benefit from the warmth that rises from the cooling mechanism.

**Capillary matting,** used as a wick from a water-filled baking tin, will keep plants moist for as long as the water lasts.

**Line the bottom** of the bath with an old blanket or newspaper and place bricks on top. Fill the bath to just above the level of the top of the bricks and place plants in clay pots on top. Capillary action will do the rest.

193

# The indoor gardening year

## January

Gardening in artificial indoor warmth makes you less the slave of climate than gardening outdoors, and artificial light, too, can in part compensate for long nights and poor daylight. But the natural rhythm of your plants —the periods of growth and rest—must still be respected. This rhythm can be changed only within certain limits. These limits vary from plant to plant and the result is usually growth and flowers "out of season", although often only a few weeks ahead of the normal pattern. An indoor gardening calendar therefore cannot be precise—a warmer, brighter environment will hasten growth, and cooler, darker conditions will delay it.

At the start of the year few house plants are coming into flower; *Chlorophytum elatum* and *Manettia bicolor* produce rather modest blooms. The flowers of *Billbergia nutans*, *Begonia* (*socotrana* hybrids) *Hiemalis*, *Senecio cruentus*, the delicate *Primula malacoides* and *Primula obconica*, the glorious, pendulant *Columnea microphylla* and *Schlumbergera truncata* will still be providing good colour. Among the orchids the white *Calanthe vestita* and *Dendrobium nobile* will begin to flower, and the white *Coelogyne cristata* and the colourful *Vanda tricolor* and *Paphiopedilum insigne* will still be in bloom.

Cacti are resting and need no water. Among other succulents the *Lithops* must not be watered at all, but most other succulents will need water once a month.

Early in the month bring pots and bowls of bulbs into the light, but keep them in a cool position until the flower buds appear. Only then move them into the warmth.

A *Clivia miniata* brought into a warm room will be encouraged to flower earlier. Start a few *Hippeastrum* into growth in a temperature of 60°F (16°C). *Zantedeschia aethiopica*, the white Arum Lily, will need a fair amount of water as growth begins.

You should be moderate in the amount of water that you give most plants in winter, especially if they are dormant and in cool rooms. They survive cold spells far better when the compost is fairly dry.

## February

*Camellia japonica* is beginning to flower, but it is mainly bulbs that bring colour to February. Among them are *Crocus*, *Narcissus*, *Hyacinthus* and *Lachenalia aloides*, with its pendulous yellow and red flowers. The neat *Begonia boweri*, with its small white and shell-pink flowers, joins the other *Begonia* in flower and the popular *Pleione formosana*, with delicate pink and mauve flowers blotched with brick-red and magenta, is a notable addition to the orchids. *Primula malacoides* will be encouraged to continue flowering if given weekly feeds of liquid fertilizer.

It is time to start the resting *Fuchsia* into growth. Cut it back fairly hard, bring it into the warmth and when new growth begins, repot it. Tuberous *Begonia* and *Hibiscus rosa-sinensis*, the Rose of China, can also be started into growth if you can provide a temperature of about 60°F (16°C).

There is little propagation to be done, but cuttings of *Saintpaulia ionantha* can be rooted in a warm room with a temperature not lower than 60°F (16°C). At the same time sow seed of *Jacaranda mimosifolia* and of *Browallia speciosa*, if you want it to flower in summer (further sowing can be made in succession to give flowers into the autumn).

A heated propagator will be needed for sowing the seeds of *Impatiens wallerana* 'Holstii' (orange, red and white versions of Busy Lizzie).

Remove dead flowers of *Rhododendron simsii* (Indian Azalea) that were in bloom at Christmas, lightly prune the branches and water less. When *Schlumbergera truncata*, the Christmas Cactus, has finished flowering keep it dry for a few weeks. Prune *Bougainvillea* by cutting back the strong branches by a third and removing any remaining weak or thin straggling stems.

## March

Some dramatic flowers come into bloom in March. *Clivia miniata* begins its period of flowering with clusters of ten or more orange-red flowers. There is *Zantedeschia aethiopica*, the white Arum Lily, and, if conditions have been warm enough, the large white flowers of *Hymenocallis calathina* (but if it has been cool it may be as late as July before this plant is in bloom). Against all this flamboyant display the primrose-yellow flowers of *Jasminum mesnyi* seem very restrained. There are two excellent orchids. *Lycaste deppei* showy and spicily perfumed; flowers at various times throughout the year, but is at its best this month and next. *Cymbidium* × Rosanna 'Pinkie' may be bearing from ten to forty blooms on long, pendulous stalks.

Not all the month can be spent admiring your plants, for there is plenty of work to be done. Start *Campanula isophylla* into growth by giving it more water and warmth. Pot *Gloriosa rothschildiana* using a 6-inch (15-cm) pot for each tuber. Pot the tubers of *Achimenes longiflora* and *Sinningia speciosa* (Gloxinia). Plant the bulbs of *Zephyranthes grandiflora* and the rhizomes of *Smithiantha zebrina*. Plant or repot the beautiful Blue African Lily, *Agapanthus campanulatus*, and *Plumbago capensis*, and repot *Adiantum capillus-veneris*, the delicate Maidenhair Fern.

Take cuttings of *Passiflora caerulea*, using young shoots with a heel, and of *Campanula isophylla*, taking basal shoots. Large plants of *Streptocarpus* can be divided into separate crowns when they are repotted.

Seeds to be sown include *Begonia semperflorens*, *Capsicum annuum*, *Thunbergia alata*, *Asclepias curassavica* and *Grevillea robusta* (which will make reasonable-sized plants in less than two years).

Look at all your ferns and remove the decaying fronds. When the leaves of *Cyclamen persicum* turn yellow stop watering and let the corm dry out before you put the pot in the dark.

# April

There are few new plants coming into flower this month. The most showy is *Acacia armata*, the Kangaroo Thorn, its fluffy yellow flowers standing out against dark foliage. Pale blue flowers start appearing on the climber *Plumbago capensis*, and will continue for months. *Peperomia caperata* will be starting its long flowering period if you have been able to provide the warmth it requires.

The resting period for cacti draws to a close early this month or early in May. When you restart the summer pattern of watering, do it gradually, giving the plants only a little water at first.

The propagating season is getting under way. Cuttings of *Saintpaulia ionantha* can now be rooted without using a heated propagator, and it is also a good time to root cuttings of *Impatiens wallerana* 'Holstii'. *Hydrangea* cuttings root easily; use the non-flowering shoots. *Aphelandra squarrosa* basal-shoot cuttings need a temperature of 65°F (18°C) to root. Divide *Aspidistra elatior*.

Seeds of *Senecio cruentus* (Cineraria) sown now will produce flowers in winter, and seeds of *Freesia* will produce flowers in about six months. Seeds of cacti need a temperature of 75°F (24°C). *Fatsia japonica* can be raised from seed as well as from basal cuttings, and now is the time to sow them.

*Clivia miniata*, which has finished flowering, and *Agapanthus campanulatus* can be repotted, but do this only when they are really overcrowded, for they flower better when somewhat potbound. *Rechsteineria cardinalis* and *Rechsteineria leucotricha* should also be repotted.

Prune *Ardisia crispa* to keep it an attractive shape and pinch *Hedera helix* to make it branch. Move *Rhododendron simsii* (Indian Azalea) to a cool and shady room.

April is also the best time to plant hanging baskets.

Before the onset of summer inspect all indoor plants to see that they are free of pests and diseases. Take immediate action with any affected plants and put them in quarantine until they are pest free. Wash the grime of winter off waxy leaved plants. Clean windows, especially in towns; it is surprising how much light is excluded by dirt.

# May

May brings many flowers that will last through the summer and even into the autumn. Among them is the brilliantly coloured *Pelargonium × domesticum*, the Regal Pelargonium. There are also *Pelargonium crispum*, with a scent reminiscent of balm, and *Pelargonium tomentosum*, which smells of peppermint, and the ubiquitous *Calceolaria × herbeohybrida*. Some of the *Begonia coccinea*, the pink *Begonia serratipetala* and *Begonia semperflorens*, with cultivated varieties that range from white to dark crimson, will flower through until autumn if they are in warm conditions.

There are many more. The showy Albany Bottlebrush, *Callistemon speciosus*, the fragrant myrtle, *Myrtus communis* 'Microphylla', *Solanum capsicastrum*, *Sparmannia africana*, the fragrant *Hoya bella* and *Hoya carnosa*, the long-lasting *Spathiphyllum wallisii*, *Stephanotis floribunda*, which continues until early autumn, and *Streptocarpus × hybridus*, which flowers until October or later.

Some orchids are coming to the end of their flowering seasons, but the very fragrant and long-lasting *Epidendrum prismatocarpum* is just beginning to flower.

Cuttings can be taken of *Abutilon*, *Coleus*, *Hoya bella* and *Hoya carnosa* and *Hydrangea*. Cuttings of zonal *Pelargonium* taken now will provide a show of colour in late summer and autumn. Repot *Vallota speciosa* and remove and plant the offsets.

Two of the most colourful foliage plants can be propagated this month. Take leaf cuttings of *Begonia rex*. Remove the basal shoots (with a heel) which have grown from cut-back plants of *Euphorbia pulcherrima* (Poinsettia) when they are about three inches (8 cm) long. Root them in a heated propagator. Sow seed of *Primula obconica* and *Eucalyptus globulus*, the Blue Gum Tree from Tasmania, at the end of the month.

Stop watering *Nerine flexuosa* when the leaves turn yellow and do not water it again until growth begins towards the end of summer. This is the month to repot *Schlumbergera truncata*, but only every other year. Remove tips from the shoots of *Solanum capsicastrum*, the Winter Cherry, to make it bushier in shape.

# June

June is another month rich in flowers, and many of them are long-lasting. The most showy are the tuberous *Begonia* and these will continue flowering until September. So will the brilliant vermilion *Fuchsia triphylla* and the white, waxy and perfumed *Gardenia jasminoides*. To add to the list of plants that need to be raised in warmth is the curious but striking *Clerodendrum thomsonae*.

Plants now in flower which have been raised in cool conditions are *Thunbergia alata*, *Bougainvillea* and *Agapanthus companulatus*, with great heads of blue flowers. Other plants which have begun to flower and will continue for several months are *Asclepias curassavica*, with dense clusters of orange flowers, *Bouvardia × domestica*, with delicate flowers of white, pink or red, and also *Nerium oleander*, with pink and red periwinkle-like flowers.

Exotic bulbs or tubers in flower are *Canna × hybrida*, with orchid-like flowers in orange, yellow, pink and red, *Gloriosa rothschildiana*, the climbing Glory Lily, *Haemanthus multiflorus*, *Vallotta speciosa*, the Scarborough Lily, and *Zephyranthes grandiflora*.

There is a lot of propagating that can be done now. This month and next are the best for rooting cuttings of Regal Pelargonium, although they can be taken almost all year. *Erica* can be propagated by cuttings of side shoots, as can *Stephanotis floribunda*, but for the *Stephanotis* a temperature of 85°F (29°C) will be needed.

Sow seeds of *Calceolaria*, *Primula malacoides* and *Senecio cruentus* (Cineraria) to flower next spring. Transplant the seedlings of *Primula obconica* which were sown last month. After the foliage of *Lachenalia aloides* has died down keep the pots dry until repotting in September.

As the weather gets hotter and the atmosphere drier use your mist spray constantly to keep a humid atmosphere around all plants. If you have a humidifier in the conservatory keep it working, and see that the plants are shaded and well ventilated. This tedious and essential regime will probably have to continue into September.

# The indoor gardening year

## July

The most dramatic flowering plants in July are *Lilium longiflorum*, the Easter Lily, pure white and deliciously fragrant, the scarlet *Rechsteineria cardinalis* and coral-red *Rechsteineria leucotricha*. There is also the showy climber *Allamanda cathartica*, with yellow, trumpet-shaped flowers. *Browallia speciosa*, violet blue, and *Achimenes longiflora*, the colours of which range through pink, scarlet, violet and purple to yellow, will flower profusely this month. The grassy *Ophiopogon jaburan* will be producing its white clusters of flowers and *Beloperone guttata* its shrimp-like flowers, which continue into September. The sprawling *Mimosa pudica*, the Sensitive Plant, which cringes when touched, is in bloom, but the flowers are modest as you might expect.

Two superb bulbs can be potted now: *Amaryllis belladonna* and *Nerine flexuosa*, which should not be watered, however, until growth begins.

It is worth while taking cuttings of some zonal *Pelargonium* early in the month to produce flowers in winter. Cut the shoots with about six leaves just below a node, provide a warm, well-lit position. Remove any premature flower shoots in autumn.

*Browallia speciosa* is in bloom, but seed can be sown to produce flowers in winter. Transplant the seedlings of *Primula malacoides* which were sown last month.

Just as in hot weather horses sweat, gentlemen perspire and ladies glow, so plants transpire heavily. See that they have all the water and protection from the sun they need. Make sure they are taken care of when you go on holiday; for advice on ways of looking after them, see pages 192 and 193.

## August

Although many of the plants which came into flower in the last two months are still making a fine show, there are a few newcomers. The most splendid is an orchid, *Odontoglossum grande*, which makes a good pot plant for the house. The flowers—yellow blotched with brown and white blotched with red—can be up to six inches (15 cm) long. Flowering continues until November. The shrub *Jacobinea carnea* is bearing pink flowers and the violet flowers among the grass-like foliage of *Liriope muscari* may be followed by berries. The trailing *Campanula isophylla*, with a profusion of starry white or blue flowers, is particularly effective in a hanging basket.

Looking forward to winter flowers, start potting *Narcissus* this month, and continue next month as well. Pot *Veltheimia viridifolia* and repot every other year; pot *Zantedeschia aethiopica* and repot yearly.

Take cuttings of *Hydrangea* and *Euphorbia pulcherrima* (Poinsettia). Side shoots of tuberous *Begonia* root well this month and fibrous rooted *Begonia* can be propagated from base shoots. Transplant *Calceolaria × herbeohybrida* seedlings into pots.

Sow the seeds of *Eucalyptus globulus*, which makes an interesting house plant when it is young. Never allow the young plants to get dry. Seed of *Cyclamen persicum* sown now will flower in about fifteen months.

Stop watering *Hippeastrum* and let the bulb dry out, and when the leaves of *Gloriosa rothschildiana* start to yellow dry it off and keep dry until March. *Callistemon speciosus* should be cut back to just below the flower clusters when flowering has finished.

## September

This month there are few plants which come into flower, so two are most welcome. *Nerine flexuosa* will be producing its pink or white blooms, ten or more in a cluster, and only then will the leaves appear. The pink flowers of the lustrous silvery leaved *Begonia metallica* also open.

Be sure to buy bulbs in good time for planting, which begins in earnest late this month and can continue for many weeks. Most bulbs have to be put in a cool, dark place after planting and the length of time they have to be kept there varies with the species. 'Paper White' Narcissus must be in the dark for at least three weeks and will flower in about seven weeks. Roman Hyacinth, unless precooled, will need five weeks in the dark and up to four weeks in the light.

Other bulbs need longer in the dark; allow ten to twelve weeks for Hyacinth, twelve to thirteen weeks for Daffodil, and up to fifteen weeks for Tulip. When leaves begin to show move the plant to a cool, light room for a few days and then into the warmth—about 65°F (18°C) during the day and not lower than 55°F (13°C) at night.

Root cuttings of *Fuchsia* and *Coleus* in a propagator. Cuttings of *Hedera helix* (Common Ivy) can be taken most of the year, but autumn is the best time.

Bring *Rhododendron simsii* (Indian Azalea) back into good light. Keep *Camellia* moist to avoid bud drop. Other plants are into their dormant period. Dry off *Achimenes longiflora* ready for repotting the tubers in March, and also dry off *Rechsteineria cardinalis*. Give *Clivia miniata* scarcely any water until January and keep *Agapanthus campanulatus* almost dry until March. Reduce the amount of water given to cacti and succulents in preparation for their winter rest. Among the orchids *Dendrobium nobile* will be resting until winter and *Lycaste deppei* until spring.

# October

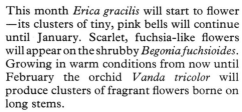

This month *Erica gracilis* will start to flower —its clusters of tiny, pink bells will continue until January. Scarlet, fuchsia-like flowers will appear on the shrubby *Begonia fuchsioides*. Growing in warm conditions from now until February the orchid *Vanda tricolor* will produce clusters of fragrant flowers borne on long stems.

Begin to heat the cool conservatory earlier or later in the month depending on the latitude and the vagaries of the year's weather. The aim should be to maintain a night temperature of about 50°F (10°C).

Cacti grown in a conservatory with little or no heat will probably not need any water from the beginning of the month until April. In the warmer, drier atmosphere of the house they may need water once a month. Other succulents, too, must have some water during the winter—once a month or so.

When *Fuchsia* finish flowering give them less water. As *Vallota speciosa* goes out of flower apply a little liquid fertilizer once every two weeks until the leaves die down.

# November

If you have managed to keep your *Cyclamen persicum* alive since last year it is likely to be the most showy pot plant coming into flower. There is another magnificent *Columnea* starting to bloom—the scarlet and yellow flowers of *Columnea microphylla*, which are borne on long, hanging stems among coppery leaves. Clusters of white flowers appear on the vigorous evergreen climber *Jasminum polyanthum* and will continue until April. The orchid *Calanthe vestita* bears spikes of twenty or more blooms, but the leaves will by now have turned yellow and fallen off. The most vivid colour is that of fruit, not flowers, carried by *Capsicum annuum*—yellow, red, orange, green and violet. All this makes it almost worth while having November.

By now you should have adjusted to the winter pattern of watering, giving less to all those plants which are no longer in growth. The cooler the room the less water they should have. Plants in warm, dry rooms will need careful watering, not so much as to encourage growth but enough to prevent dying from drought.

Give more water to *Rhododendron simsii* (Indian Azalea) when the flower buds begin to swell. *Aphelandra*, about to come into flower, will benefit from a liquid fertilizer; above all keep it out of draughts, which it loathes. Keep *Begonia rex* just moist, in as good a light as the month allows, and maintain a temperature of at least 55°F (13°C).

This is not a time for propagation, but in a warm conservatory prune back the exuberantly growing *Allamanda cathartica*, removing more than half of the year's growth.

# December

Two beautiful *Primula*, which make excellent house or cool conservatory plants, come into flower in December. *Primula malacoides* has flowers of white, red and lilac, according to their cultivated variety, and the flowers of *Primula obconica* range from pink to purple and have a pungent scent. Unfortunately, the plant has hairy leaves to which some people are extremely allergic. Both species will continue flowering for several months. The pendulous flowers, yellow shading to red and green, of *Lachenalia aloides* also appear now.

Since house plants are obvious Christmas gifts you will probably receive during your lifetime your quota of *Rhododendron simsii* (Indian Azalea), *Euphorbia pulcherrima* (Poinsettia), *Cyclamen persicum* and *Saintpaulia ionantha* (African Violet). However delighted you may be to receive them, regard them with some suspicion until you have inspected them for pests and diseases. But when you have decided that they are fit to join your collection treat them with extra loving care, for their winter journeying from cosy nursery to cold shop and then to you will have done them no good whatsoever.

*Rhododendron simsii* (Indian Azalea) (which would make better gifts a few weeks later when in bud but not in full flower) are the most tricky. They must be kept moist, not wet, and not too hot; watering them with hard water is one way to kill them. *Cyclamen persicum* needs an even temperature of about 55°F (13°C) and a slightly humid atmosphere. When watering try to avoid watering the centre of the leaf cluster. *Erica* must not be allowed to dry out (which it quickly does in a small pot) or it will die. *Euphorbia pulcherrima* (Poinsettia) needs a temperature of about 65°F (18°C), which falls only a little at night. *Saintpaulia ionantha* needs light and a humid atmosphere. *Senecio cruentus* (Cineraria) will go on flowering only if it is cool, not more than 60°F (16°C) by day and a little cooler at night.

The large leaves of such plants as *Ficus*, *Dracaena*, Croton and palms get dirty in winter. Clean them up for Christmas.

# Glossary and metric conversions

**Acid medium.** A growing medium that is lacking in lime and has a pH content below 6.5.

**Aerial root.** A root that grows above ground on the stems of such plants as *Monstera deliciosa* (Swiss Cheese Plant).

**Aggregate.** A material such as coarse sand, gravel, small pebbles or vermiculite that is used to grow plants hydroponically.

**Air layering.** Also known as Chinese layering. A way of propagating single-stem plants that have grown too tall and leggy. For example *Ficus elastica decora* (Rubber Plant) and *Dracaena deremensis* (Dragon Plant).

**Alkaline medium.** A growing medium containing lime and having a pH value above 7.5.

**All-peat compost.** A loamless growing medium composed of peat, fertilizers, and, sometimes, sterile sand.

**Annual.** A plant that lives for only one year.

**Areole.** A small, hairy, cushion-like swelling found on cacti which often bears sharp spines and barbed hairs known as glochids.

**Axil.** The angle between the upper side of a leaf and the stem.

**Basal offset.** A shoot, growing from the base of a plant, that puts out roots and forms a new plant.

**BHC.** A persistent organochloride insecticide that is toxic to many beneficial insects as well. It should be used with discretion.

**Bonemeal.** A fertilizer made from crushed bones.

**Bonsai.** The Japanese art, based on an ancient Chinese technique, of dwarfing trees by root and stem pruning and planting in a small, restricting container.

**Bract.** A modified leaf, often highly coloured, found on such plants as *Euphorbia pulcherrima* (Poinsettia) and *Euphorbia milii* (Crown of Thorns).

**Bromeliad.** A member of the *Bromeliaceae* family. There are sixty genera with about fourteen hundred species. New World natives, they are either epiphytic (using a tree branch for support) or terrestrial. The leaves of many species form watertight funnels at the base for holding water.

**Bulb.** An underground bud, composed of scale leaves or fleshy leaf bases, that stores food and protects the next season's embryo shoot and flowers.

**Bulbil.** A tiny immature bulb that forms on a stem above ground.

**Bulblet.** A small bulb that forms at the base of a larger mature bulb.

**Calyx.** A ring of modified leaves that protects the flower bud. It can be composed of separate petal-like organs (sepals) or fused into a cup or tube.

**Capillary action.** The upward rise of liquid in confined areas, such as fine tubes or spaces between soil particles.

**Carboy.** A large glass bottle made for storing liquids.

**Celsius.** Centigrade scale of measuring temperature. The first centigrade thermometer was constructed in 1742 by Anders Celsius.

**Chlorophyll.** The green pigment found in the leaves and stems of plants which is necessary for photosynthesis.

**Corm.** A swollen underground stem base that acts as a storage organ.

**Crown.** The junction between the root and the stem of a plant.

**Cultivated variety.** Sometimes abbreviated to cultivar. A mutant form of a species or a plant of hybrid origin maintained in cultivation.

**Derris.** A safe insecticide manufactured from the Derris root. The poisonous ingredient in it is rotatone. It is considered safe because if sprayed in the evening it loses its toxicity by the next morning. It will, however, poison fish, so keep it away from aquaria and ponds.

**Dormant period.** The resting period of the plant, when it requires a lower temperature, less or no water and no feeding.

**Dorsal petal.** The upright, petal-like sepal at the back of some orchid flowers.

**Epidermis.** The outer layer of a plant's tissues which forms a protective skin.

**Epiphyte.** Non-parasitic plant that grows above ground on another plant. Epiphytes evolved originally in response to the need for light. Bromeliads and orchids are examples of epiphytes.

**Fern column.** A column made from wire netting which is lined with sphagnum moss, filled with compost and used for growing ferns.

**Fibrous roots.** The slender, often wiry, usually much branched, lateral roots of a plant.

**Floret.** A single flower in a tightly packed flower head.

**Flower spike.** A flower head composed of a straight central stem with flowers growing directly from it.

**Foliar feed.** Fertilizer that is sprayed on to the leaves of a plant for rapid assimilation.

**Fungicide.** A fungus-destroying chemical.

**Genus.** A botanical category containing a group of plants of closely related species.

**Germination.** The sprouting of a seed or spore.

**Glochid.** A barbed hair found on cacti areoles.

**Grey mould.** A fungal disease that may attack plants that have been kept in excessively damp or humid conditions, particularly if the plants have been bruised or damaged in any way.

**Growing shoot.** The leading shoot on a stem which extends its length.

**Hardening off.** Gradual process of acclimatizing plants to colder conditions.

**Hard-wood pruning.** The cutting back of woody stems.

**Hardy.** In temperate countries this term describes a plant that can withstand frost.

**Heel.** The base of a cutting that includes a little of the harder growth of the stem from which the cutting was taken.

**Hormone rooting powder.** An organic compound that speeds up the formation of roots in cuttings.

**Humidifier.** A device for increasing or maintaining humidity.

**Hybrid.** A plant produced as a result of crossing different species or distinct forms within a species.

**Hydroponics.** Method of growing plants without the use of soil. The plants are fed with mineral nutrients in solution.

**Hydropot.** A special pot used in hydroponic culture.

**Hygrometer.** An instrument for measuring the relative humidity of the air.

**Jiffy strip.** A strip of compressed peat blocks in which seeds are planted.

**John Innes composts.** Seed and potting composts developed at the John Innes Institute (formerly the John Innes Horticultural Institution, London).

**Lateral shoot.** A side shoot growing from the leading stem of a plant.

**Leaf-bud cutting.** The cutting includes a leaf, a leaf bud and a piece of the stem cut from the parent plant.

**Leaf cutting.** Whole leaves or pieces of a leaf used as cuttings. When inserted into the compost plantlets develop at the base or from nicks made in the main veins.

**Leaflet.** The leaf-like lobe or division of a compound leaf.

**Leaf spot.** The name for a number of fungal or bacterial diseases that cause discoloured patches on leaves.

**Lime-free compost.** See Alkaline medium.

**Loam-based compost.** A compost based on a mixture of sand, clay particles and humus.

**Loamless compost/mixture.** See All-peat compost.

**Long-day plant.** A plant that for a certain period requires more than twelve hours of daylight to induce flowering.

**Malathion.** A synthetic insecticide effective against most plant pests. Unfortunately it is foul-smelling, but it has the virtue of being non-persistent.

**Metaldehyde.** A chemical that is mixed with bait and used, in pellet form, to kill slugs. It is, however, dangerous to pets and wildlife and should be kept covered.

**Methiocarb.** A chemical that is used, in pellet form, to kill slugs. (See also Metaldehyde.)

**Microclimate.** The environment directly surrounding a plant. It may be warmer, cooler, drier or more humid than the rest of the room.

**Mineral salts.** Inorganic substances that are required by the plant for many vital processes.

**Mist propagation.** A method of providing ideal conditions for propagation, which involves the use of an electronically controlled sprinkler and a soil heating unit.

**Moisture meter.** An instrument that indicates whether the compost is wet, moist or dry.

**Neutral medium.** A growing medium that has a pH value between 6.5 and 7.5—neither too acid nor too alkaline. (See pH value.)

**Node.** A joint in the plant stem from which leaves, buds and side shoots arise.

**Nutrient pill.** A pill containing inorganic fertilizer which when placed in compost gradually dissolves as the plant is watered.

**Offset.** A young plant that appears naturally on the parent plant. It is easily detached and provides a simple method of propagation.

**Offshoot.** A branch or side shoot.

**Osmosis.** The process by which water passes across a membrane, from the soil into the roots of a plant, for example.

**Osmunda fibre.** The matted roots of *Osmund regalis* (Royal Fern), used in potting compost, particularly for epiphytic orchids.

**Perennial.** A plant that lives for more than two years, flowering and seeding annually.

**pH indicator.** Paper or liquid that is used to measure the acidity or alkalinity of compost or water.

**Photosynthesis.** The light-requiring process by which plants manufacture their food.

**Phototropism.** The response that makes stems and leaves of plants grow towards a light source.

**pH value.** The degree of acidity or alkalinity in compost or water. Below pH 6.5 is acid, above pH 7.5 is alkaline.

**Phyllode.** A flattened stalk that resembles and performs the same function as a leaf.

**Pinching out.** See Stopping.

**Pinnule.** An individual leaflet.

**Plant case.** An enclosed glass case in which a plant may be grown when the environment in the room does not meet its requirements.

**Plantlet.** A small plant that may appear on the stems or runners of the parent.

**Potbound.** The condition of a pot plant when its roots are overcrowded.

**Potting on.** Transplanting a pot plant from one pot to a larger one.

**Propagating case.** A heated box in which seeds are germinated and cuttings are rooted.

**Pruning.** The controlled cutting back of a plant to keep it in good shape, to promote bushy growth and flowering and to maintain it at a manageable size.

**Pseudobulb.** A bulb-like swelling formed from one or more joints of an orchid stem.

**Pyrethrum.** An organic insecticide produced from the flower heads of several species of *Pyrethrum* (Chrysanthemum). It is non-persistent.

**Respiration.** The process by which the plant produces energy.

**Rhizome.** The name given to a creeping stem that grows underground or on the surface of the soil. It acts as a storage organ.

**Root ball.** The total mass of roots that is exposed when the plant is taken out of its pot.

**Root hair.** Fine hairs that grow in a zone near the tips of most roots of a plant and through which water and dissolved mineral salts are absorbed.

**Runner.** Long shoot sent out by certain plants to propagate themselves. The runner roots when it comes into contact with moist soil and a new plant then grows.

**Sepal.** One of the modified leaves that form the ring or cup around the outside of the petals of a flower. (See Calyx.)

**Setting.** The swelling of the ovary of a flower after fertilization and usually observed as a very small fruit or seed pod.

**Short-day plant.** A plant that requires less than twelve hours of daylight per day, for a given period, to induce it to flower.

**Shrub.** A branched perennial that has persistent woody stems, mainly arising from near ground level.

**Soft-wood pruning.** The cutting back of new, non-woody growth.

**Soil ball.** The soil that surrounds and contains the roots of a plant. In house plants this usually means all of the compost and roots in the pot.

**Spadix.** A fleshy flower spike with small flowers embedded in little pits. It is usually surrounded by a modified bract called a spathe. The Arum Lily provides a good example.

**Spathe.** A modified bract that surrounds a spadix or flower spike.

**Species plant.** An original wild species, as distinct from a variety or cultivated variety.

**Sphagnum moss.** An umbrella name for all bog mosses of the genus *Sphagnum*, which are spongy and can hold a lot of water.

**Spore.** A single reproductive cell produced by fungi, mosses and ferns.

**Stamen.** The male reproductive organ of a flower.

**Standard.** A plant that has been pruned to produce a long, bare stem with a head of branches.

**Stem cutting.** A piece of the stem used for propagation.

**Stem-tip cutting.** A cutting taken from the tip of a young stem.

**Stigma.** The tip of the female reproductive organ (pistil) of a flower.

**Stomate (stomata).** A pore in the epidermis of a leaf through which gases and water vapour can pass in and out.

**Stopping.** The pinching out of the growing tip of a stem to promote bushy growth.

**Stove plant.** An old-fashioned name for a hothouse plant.

**Succulent.** Plants that have developed fleshy stems or leaves in order to store water. Cacti are the classic example.

**Sucker.** A shoot that arises from an underground stem or root.

**Tap root.** The main root of a plant.

**Terrarium.** A glass plant case with an environment best suited to plants that need a humid, clean atmosphere.

**Terrestrial.** Growing on the ground. A term applied to such plants as bromeliads and orchids, which are usually epiphytic.

**Transpiration.** The loss of water through the pores in a leaf caused by evaporation.

**Trifoliate.** A leaf made up of three separate leaflets.

**Tuber.** Natural swelling of an underground root or stem which acts as a storage organ.

**Umbel.** A flower cluster (inflorescence) where all the individual flower stalks arise from the same point at the top of the primary stem.

**Variegated.** A term used to describe leaves and petals that are marked or decorated with contrasting colours as the result of mutation or virus.

**Vermiculite.** An inert aggregate used in hydroponics which is derived from superheating the natural mineral mica.

**Wardian case.** The original plant case or terrarium developed by Dr Nathaniel Ward in the 1830s and used to transport plants on long sea journeys.

## Metric conversions

All metric equivalents in this book are approximate.

**Weight:** 1 ounce = 28.35 grams. For convenience it has been rounded up to 30 grams.

**Volume:** 1 pint = 568 millilitres. For convenience it has been rounded down to 500 millilitres.

**Temperature:** 32°F = 0°C. To convert Fahrenheit into centigrade: subtract 32, multiply by 5, divide by 9. The conversions used in this book are made to the nearest round figure.

**Length:** 1 inch = 2.54 centimetres. For convenience it has been rounded down to 2 centimetres and 2 inches to 5 centimetres.

## Botanical names

Common names are easy to spell and pronounce but can lead to confusion when dealing with plants. *Echinocactus grusonii*, for example, is one man's Golden Barrel but another man's Mother-in-law's Chair. And a Coral Berry may be two totally different plants, *Aechmea fulgens* or *Ardisia crispa*. To eliminate confusion all plants have been given at least two internationally agreed names in Latin form and mainly derived from Latin and Greek. The first name gives the genus to which the plant belongs—each genus embraces all plants that have the same botanical characteristics, although they may not necessarily look alike. The second name indicates the species to which the plant belongs, and all plants within the species will be recognizably alike.

There may, however, be some variation between plants within the species, for example in the colour of flowers or foliage. Any difference is indicated by a third name, that of the variety. (Correctly, the word "variety" refers to distinct, true-breeding populations of plants in the wild, whereas the term cultivated variety [cultivar] is used for mutations and hybrids maintained in cultivation.)

# Index

# Acknowledgements

The publishers gratefully acknowledge the assistance of the following individuals and organizations:
A.E. Bicknell; Casa Pupo, 17 Sloane Street, London SW1; Clifton Nurseries, Clifton Villas, London W9; Cucina, 8 England's Lane, London NW3; M.C. Howell-Jones; Stuart Low & Co. (Enfield) Ltd, Park View Nursery, Theobalds Park Road, Enfield, Middlesex; Elizabeth Mugridge; The New Neal Street Shop, 23 Neal Street, London WC2; The House of Rochford, Turnford Hall Nurseries, Turnford, Broxbourne, Hertfordshire; The Royal Horticultural Society; Selwyn Davidson, Florist, 31 Berwick Street, London W1.

**Indexer:** Susan Wilson.

**Photographers and archives:**
Archiv Gerstenberg **8–9**, **11**, **15** *top*; Arkitekter Sven Backstrom, Leif Reinius, A.B. Stockholm **15** *bottom*; Eli Beintema **130**, **135** *bottom*; Michael Boys **23**, **114** *top and bottom*, **115**; Mary Evans Picture Library *front cover bottom right*, *back cover bottom left*, **14**, **16–17** *centre*, **17** *top left*, **17** *top right*, **17** *bottom left*, **17** *bottom right*; Foster Associates (Architects and Engineers for Willis Faber & Dumas Ltd: photo Jocelyne van den Bossche) **33**; Mansell Collection **13**, **14–15**; Radio Times Hulton Picture Library **16** *top left, centre left, bottom left*, **17** *centre*; The House of Rochford **12**; Shostal Associates **126–127**; Harry Smith Collection **126** *bottom*, **127**; Snark **10**; Peter Wrigley **32**, **118**; ZEFA **131**, **135** *top*.

All other photographs were specially taken for this book by Roger Phillips.

**Artists**
Norman Barber and Ian Garrard/Linden Artists produced the majority of drawings in the Catalogue of Plants. Others were drawn by Leonora Box/Saxon Artists and Vana Haggerty.
Ray Burrows and Corinne Clarke **24–25**, **150** *bottom*, **151**, **163** *bottom*, **170**, **172–173**, **190–191**; Chris Forsey **172** *bottom*; Kevin Maddison **20–21**, **155**, **164–165**; Norma Martyn **160–161**, **174–175**; Peter Morter **156–157**, **168–169**, **180–181**, **184–185**; Valerie Sangster **149** *bottom*; Michael Saunders **180**, **181** *bottom*; Rodney Shackell/Anglo Continental Agency **194–197**; Alan Suttie **146–147**, **148**, **150** *top*, **181** *top*, **186**; David Watson **149** *top*, **153** *top left*, **171**; Sidney Woods **152–153**, **158–159**, **166–167**, **188–189**, **192–193**; Paul Wrigley **28–29**, **162**, **163** *top*, **187**.

The publishers also thank the following architects and individuals for allowing photographs to be taken in their homes and offices.
Mr & Mrs J. Bigg; Annie and Dave Druiff; Miss N. Foy; Mr & Mrs A. Hale; Ms Sue Hertzog-Grant; Mr & Mrs I. Kennedy Martin; Tom Rand and Ian Wilson; Richard and Su Rogers, Architects; Dr & Mrs W.N. Rogers; Mr B. Sheer; David Thurlow of Cambridge Design; Mr & Mrs J. Tressider; Peter & Juliet Glynn Smith.